URBAN APARTMENT BLOCKS

LINKS

URBAN APARTMENT BLOCKS

Edition 2008

Author: Carles Broto

Graphic designer & production: Raquel Castro

Collaborator: Oriol Vallés

Text: Contributed by the architects, edited by William George and Marta Rojals

© Carles Broto i Comerma

Jonqueres, 10, 1-5

08003 Barcelona, Spain

Tel.: +34-93-301-21-99

Fax: +34-93-301-00-21

E-mail: info@linksbooks.net

www.linksbooks.net

URBAN APARTMENT BLOCKS

LINKS

index

introduction

The typology of collective housing has undergone major transformations in the course of the 20th century. The postulates of the Modern Movement, which involved a radical change in the conception of the habits of life and in the organisation of residential architecture during the first half of the 20th century, led to the development of new proposals for collective housing. The ideal pursued was that of a healthy dwelling in a happy world, a scenario for life and for new forms of coexistence that reinforced the community feeling among its inhabitants without forcing them to give up their independence. Though we are now on the threshold of the 21st century, it cannot be said that the objectives of this ambitious enterprise have been achieved. The economic growth that took place in a large part of the world after the Second World War led to the creation of mass housing programmes governed by the laws of speculation and lacking planning, which not only made our cities ugly but also contributed greatly to the degradation of the life of their inhabitants. Furthermore, the avant-garde experiments that pursued a scientific reformulation of society and the city through architecture have in most of the cases proven to be failures. It is therefore not surprising that though architects feel an understandable disenchantment with the knowledge of how much remains to be done, there is a favourable climate for reflection and invention. Numerous conditions affect the residential typology and raise challenges that are often difficult to solve. Factors such as scale, services, local regulations, budget cuts or typological and formal demands of clients are only a few of the limitations that force architects to work in a very narrow margin of action and make it difficult to offer audacious solutions to the changing needs that have arisen in the last few years. The standards that govern housing are out of date, far from the real demands of their residents. Nevertheless, architects still find the dwelling a fascinating subject. The possibility of designing an inhabitable space, of creating an environment in which a group of people live and interact, is a challenge that few professionals can resist. Whether it is a residential complex or a vertical dwelling, a public or a private initiative, a building aimed at a heterogeneous public or at a community with special needs (students, workers, the elderly, etc.), each scheme must ensure that its inhabitants can create their own safe and comfortable space: a home. The projects in this volume illustrate the latest tendencies in collective housing. They include both large and small-scale residential projects that share a common spirit: they are rigorous and imaginative proposals that give priority to the inhabitants and use the environment in which they are located as a framework for defining them and giving them meaning; attractive and functional solutions conceived by architects who are highly committed to current trends. Under the apparent diversity of these proposals there is an underlying desire to give the housing space dynamism and personality, to make each housing unit mould itself to its occupants so that they can transform it at will. Another characteristic common to most projects is the use of simple materials -often those found in the architectural tradition of the area- and pragmatic and economic construction solutions. In the works of architects such as Herzog & De Meuron, Marc Mimram and Alexandra Czerner, to name just a few of the famous and emerging architects included in this book, we can find stimulating answers, ingenious solutions, unexpected points of view and proposals that will without doubt influence the conception of residential architecture in the century to come.

Philippe Guyard

Apartments & Commerce

Paris, France

Photographs:
Michel Denance

Architect:
Philippe Guyard Architect

This volume houses 21 apartments that reinterpret the characteristic residential buildings of the historic centre of Paris. The location of this volume, designed by the French architect Philippe Guyard, deals with two different urban situations, resulting in a project that provides a dual response to the design of the facade.

On one side, facing Place de Stalingrad and Quai de Seine, the building shows an orderly composition based on a screen wall of light-coloured stone panels that partially conceals an interior wall of large glazed planes. On this side of the building, Guyard sought to provide the apartments with panoramic views, taking advantage of an exceptional urban situation facing Place de Stalingrad, La Villete lake and the rooftops of Belleville. This landscape is enjoyed through the long and clearly horizontal windows, which are partially covered by the vertical stone panels that filter the sunlight very efficiently in summer. The apartment interiors are very well illuminated in this side of the building. The bedrooms and a large living room are situated along the facade and the kitchens and bathrooms perpendicular to it.

The Rue de Flandre facade is narrower and looks onto an area which is far noisier than Quai de Seine: fourteen hours of very heavy traffic pass by here each day.

In response to these conditions, the architects used a facade model with a regular composition, determined by a peculiar version of the curtain wall and the orthogonal layout of the hermetically closing frames that protect the dwellings from the bustle. These openings are marked formally at the sides by two narrow strips of quadrangular stone scales that give identity to this side of the building.

On this side the greatest expressive effort is concentrated at the top, with large windows and a zinc plate cladding. Unlike the La Villete side, here the internal layout of the apartments places the living room and bedrooms crossways toward Rue de Flandre. The living room is a very bright space with views in two directions: toward the street and toward the square.

Careful attention was paid to the architectural language of the buildings of the environment, which Guyard sought to reinterpret in this scheme, which expresses his will "to recompose the conventional window and to approach it as a screen in powerful connection with urban life".

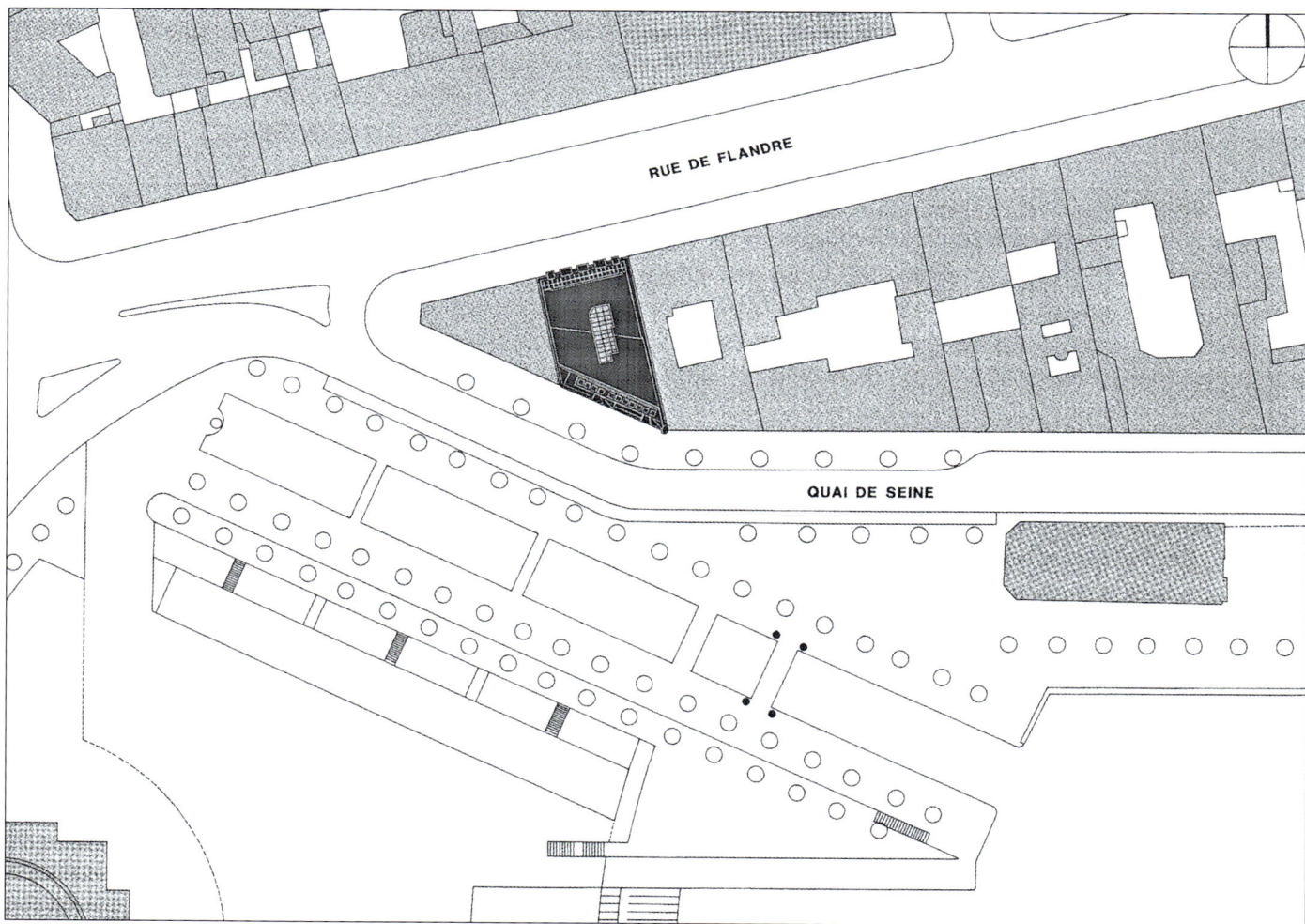

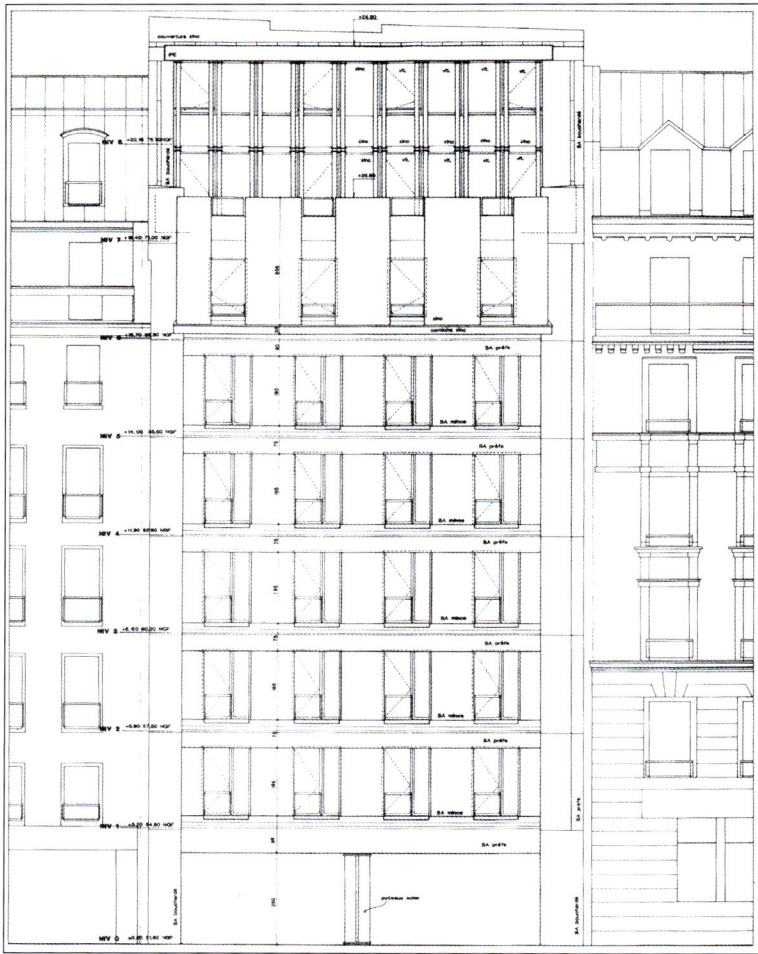

Facade to Flandre street

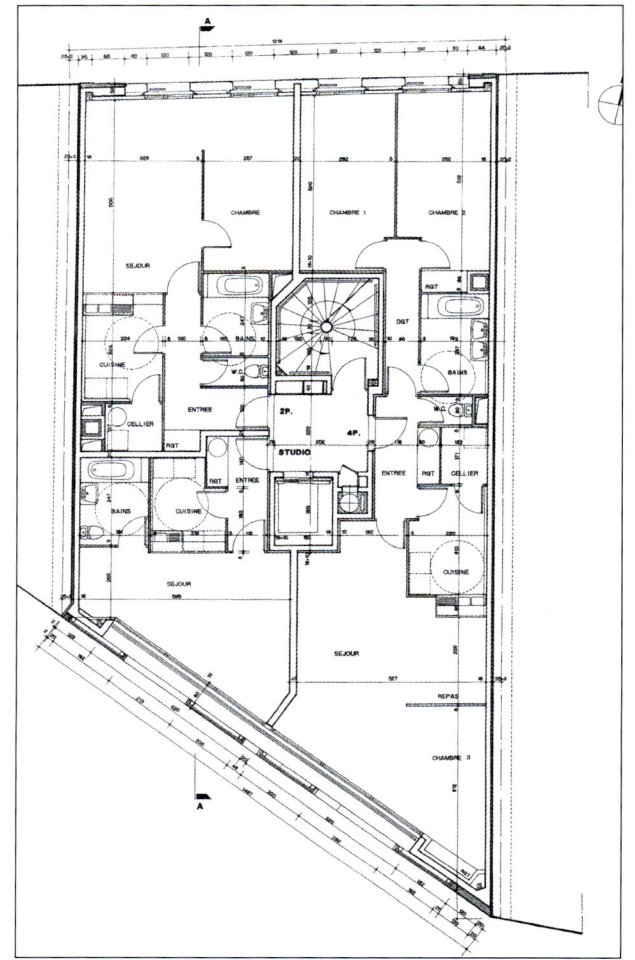

First, second and fifth floor plan

In the project of this building there are two very different urban situations, which leads to a double proposal for the facade.

The side facing Place de Stalingrad and Quai de Seine –which can be seen in the photographs on this double page– are characterised by an ordered composition based on stone panels superimposed on a glass facade. The side facing Rue de Flandre is a peculiar version of the curtain wall, with a certain amount of adornment. Its most striking feature is the zinc cladding at the top.

Seventh floor plan

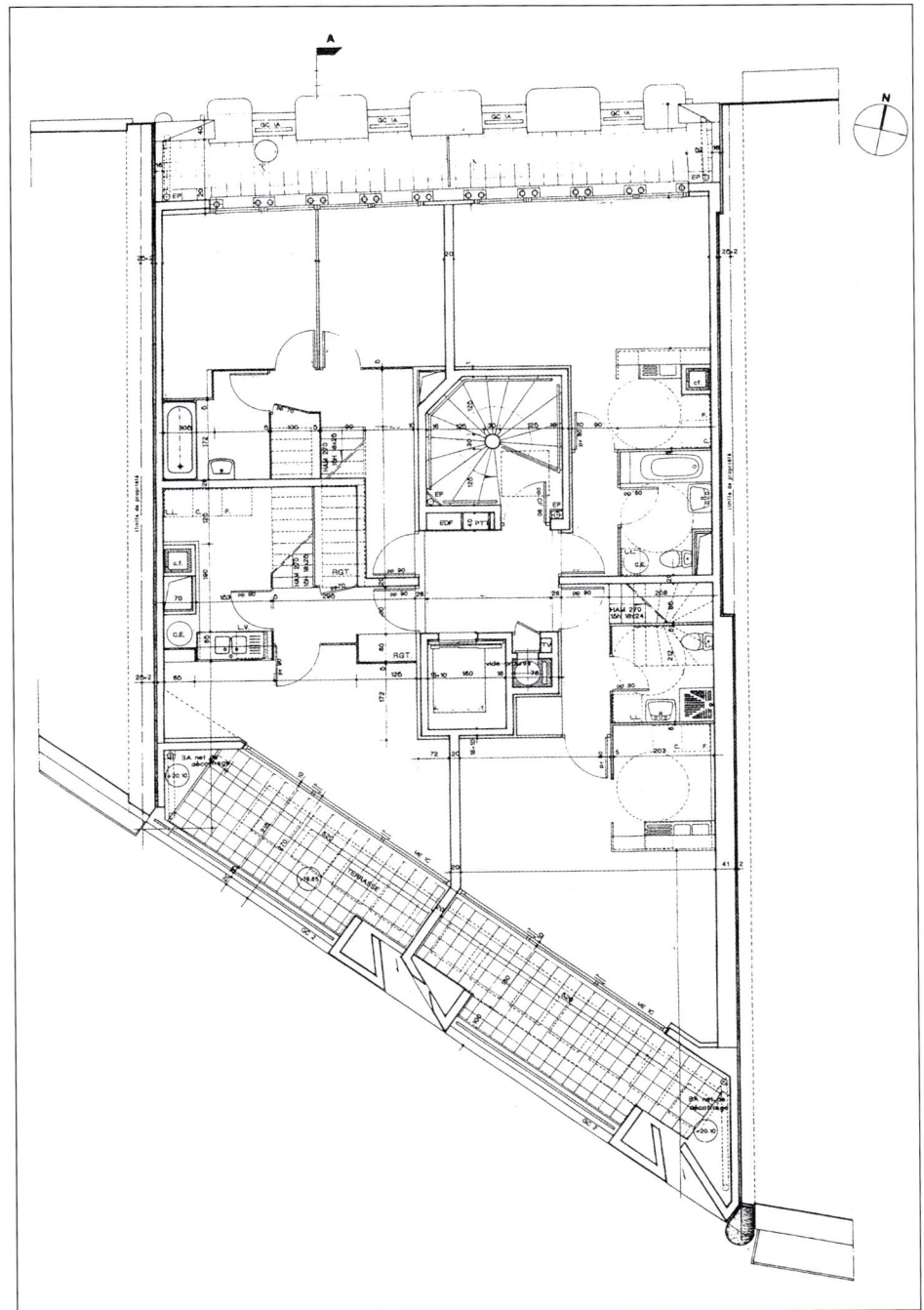

Detail of the façade to Quai de Seine

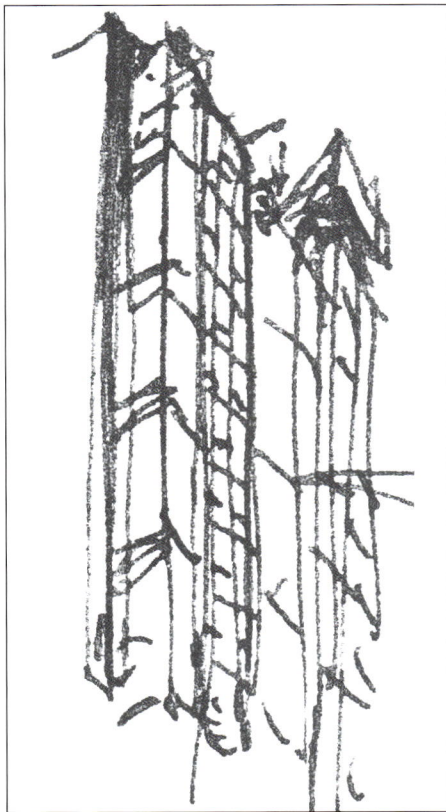

The pictures on this double page show some detailed views of the windows and concrete structure seen from the interior. Left: sketches by Philippe Guyard and, on the following page, detailed sections of the screen wall of the facade to the quai de Seine.

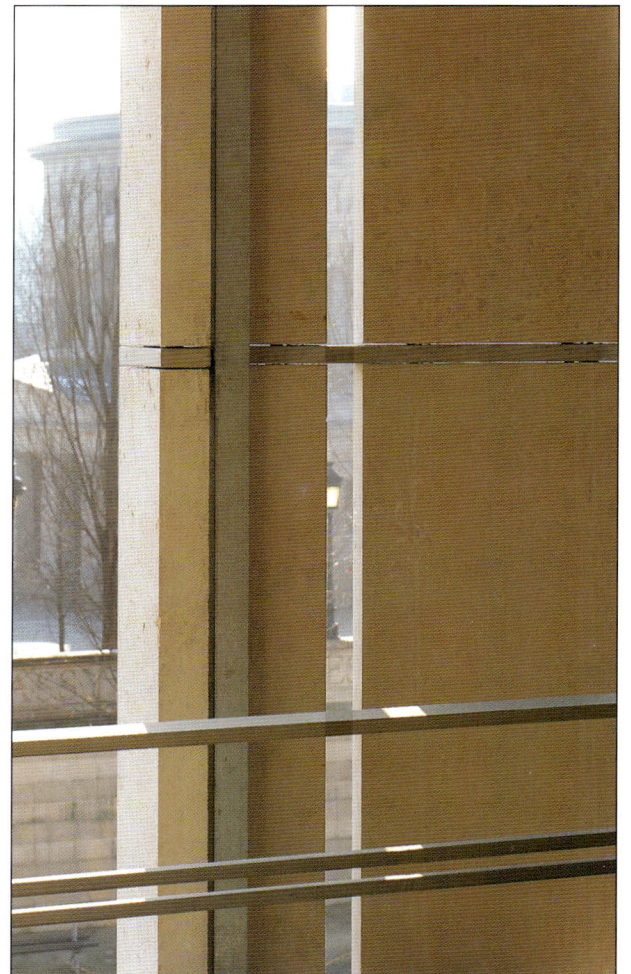

Horizontal section of the facade to the rue Bassin de la Villette

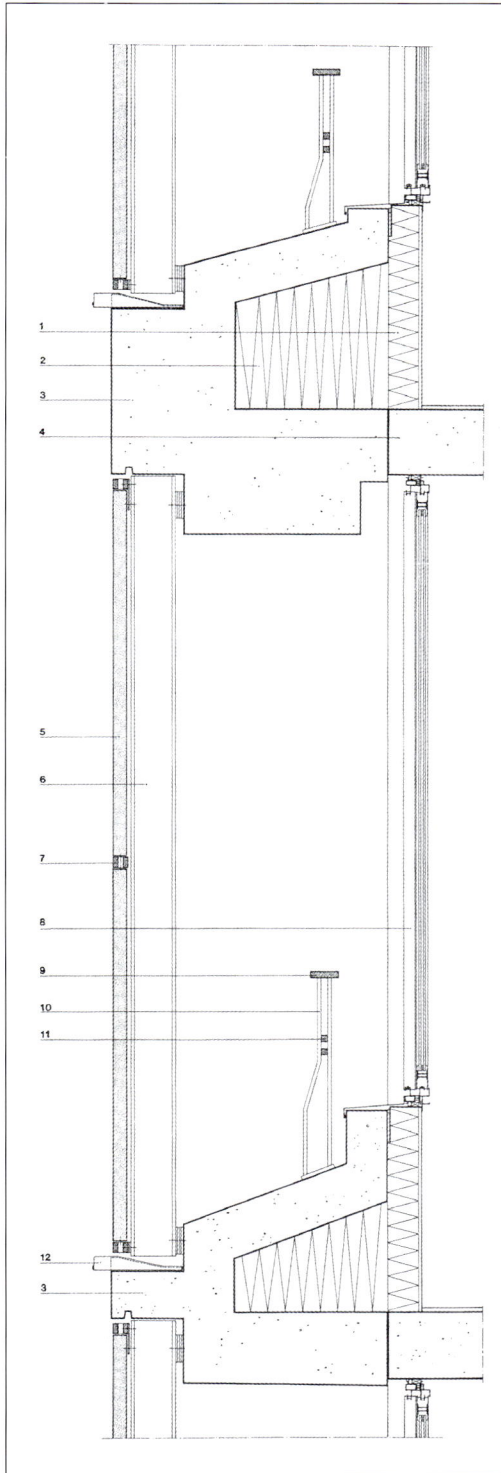

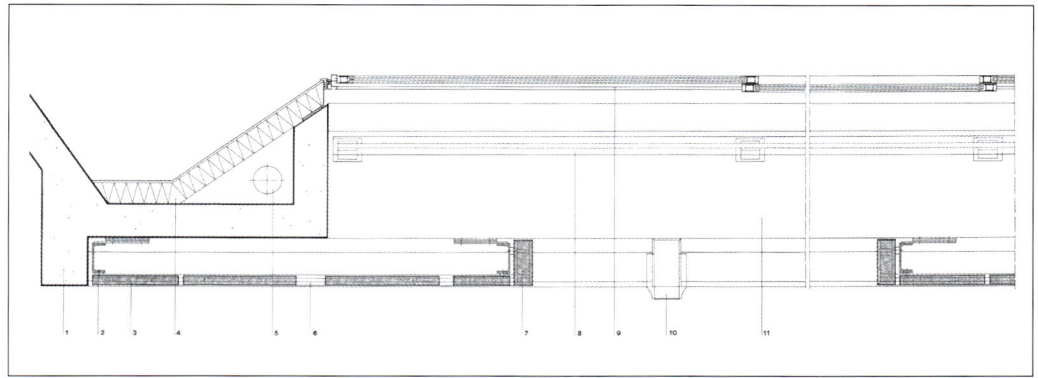

Vertical section of the facade to the rue Bassin de la Villette

1. insulating membrane
2. insulating material
3. precast concrete
4. concrete slab
5. stone panel
6. galvanised steel section
7. stainless steel trim and gudgeons for fastening stone tiles

8. aluminium sliding window
9. galvanised steel guardrail
10. zinc lip
11. reinforced concrete wall
12. galvanised steel fasteners
13. rainwarter pipe
14. stainless trim

Dick Van Gameren & Bjarne Mastenbroek

Housing with rooftop parking

Nijmegen, The Netherlands

Photographs:
Christian Richters

Architect:
Dick Van Gameren &
Bjarne Mastenbroek

In the Nijmegen project the programme was chopped into three unequal pieces which were more or less lined up along the slight curve of the road, thereby forming a transition between an unbroken street facade and a more detached arrangement of buildings.

The three were made more individual by alternating the access from front to back and by differentiation in the material used. This bricolage is held together by a rooftop car park which works as a cornice in delimiting and unifying the composition.

Height differences and transparency have been used to make the project work as a whole while nonetheless enabling a differentiated experience within the narrow site. At the same time this approach has resulted in a park like widening of the road at the point of trasition to the Hunnerparl and the river. The complexity of the articulations in the plan at the staircases has been tackled in a controlled way.

The project neither marks a sharp polemic position nor illustrates a strong theoretical standpoint. Its merit lies not in invention but in the virtuoso use of known elements.

The fifties aesthetics, the taste for ostensibly untreated materials, the galleries projecting from the facade, the seemingly chance encounter of 'quality' and 'cheap' materials and the simple bolting together of programme components, are revised here from a serious and coherent point of view.

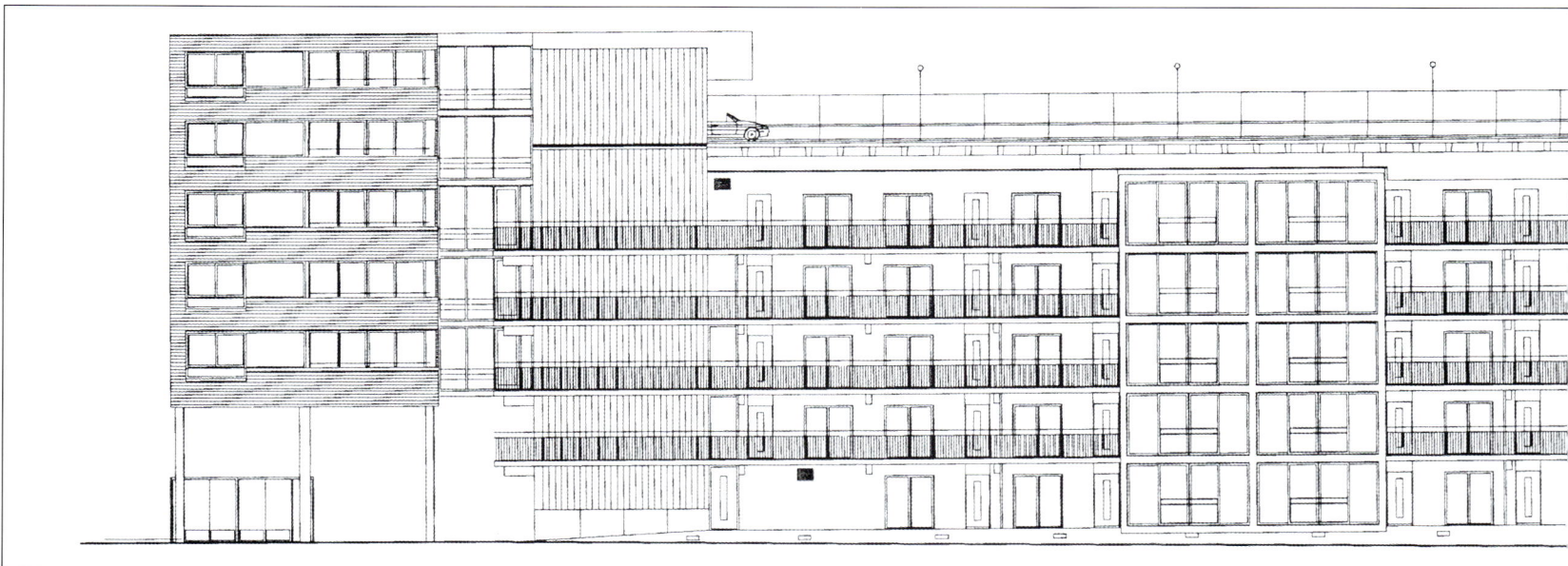

Street facade

With overhanging galleries, the main facade has been treated so that it forms a unity through the interplay of transparencies used.

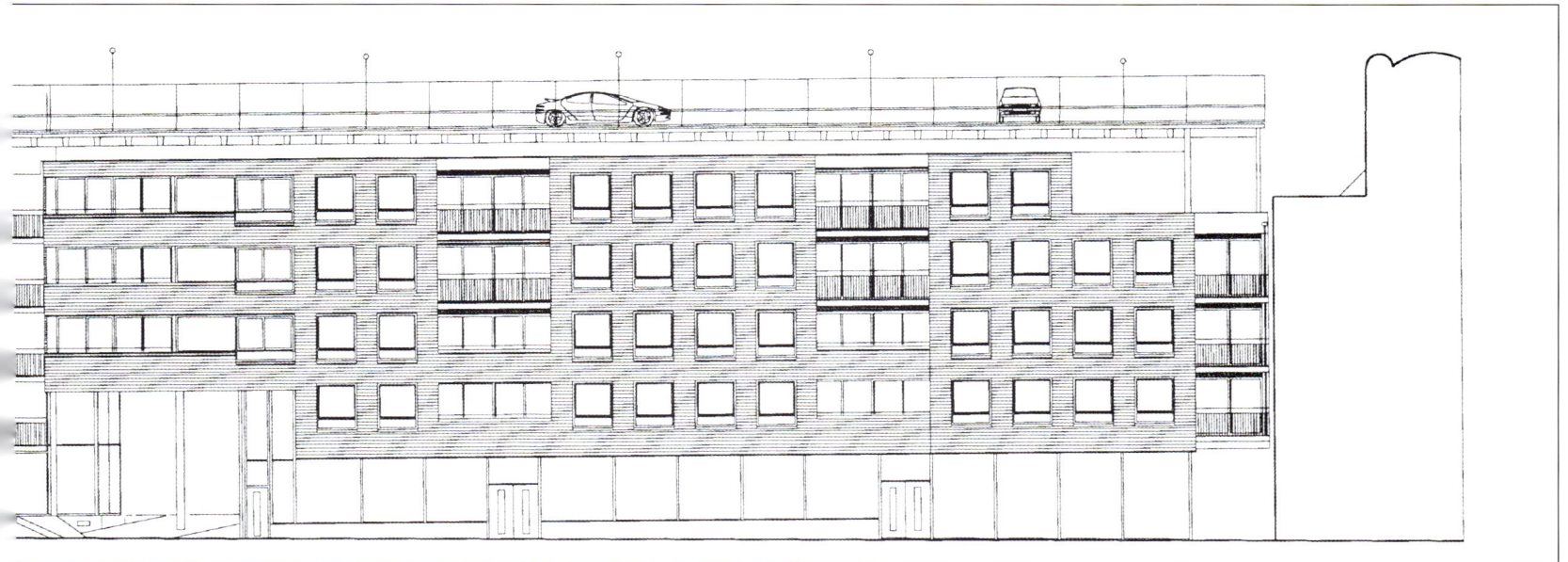

The residential complex is developed in three volumes aligned with the curve of the street. The three bodies are individualised thanks to the use of different materials and to the rupture caused by the access areas.

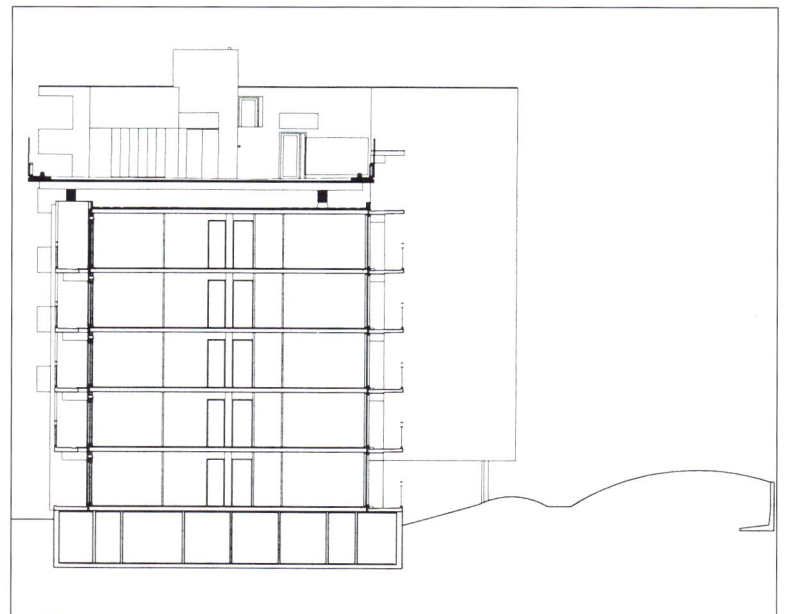

Cross section

Cross section

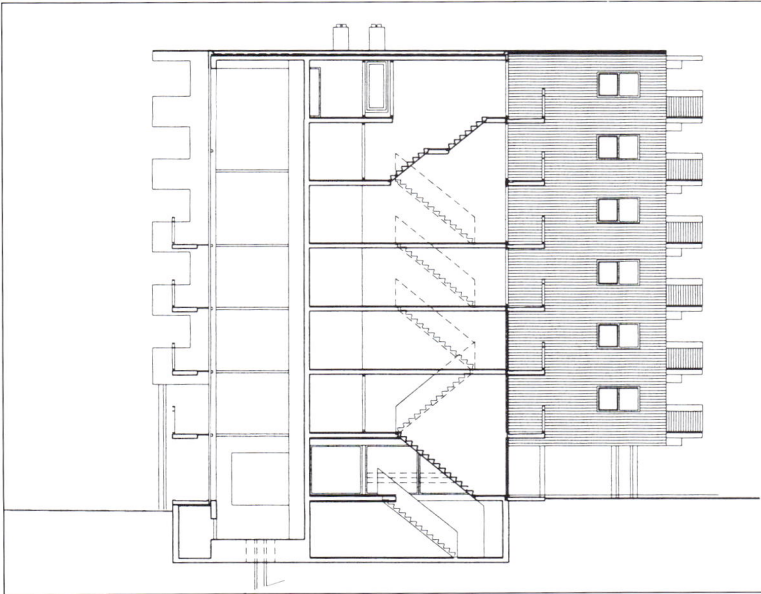

The roof floor houses a large parking area. This acts as a cornice, defining and unifying the composition of the facade plane.

Cross sections

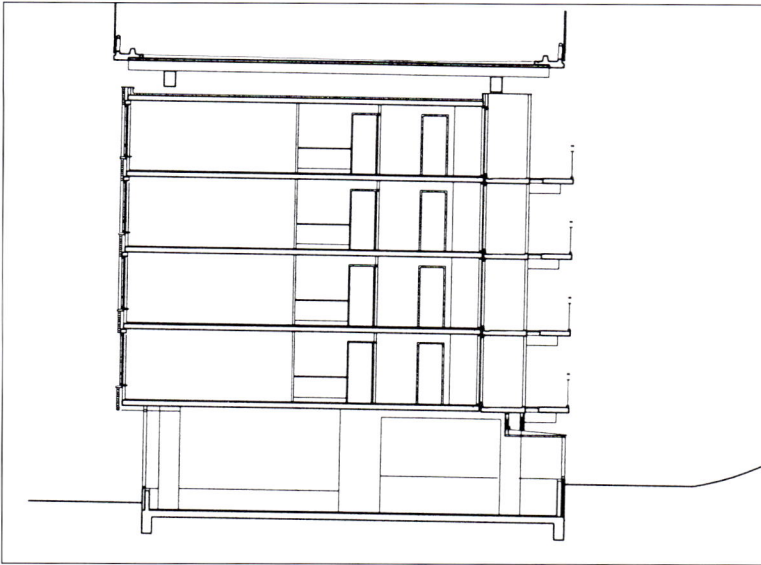

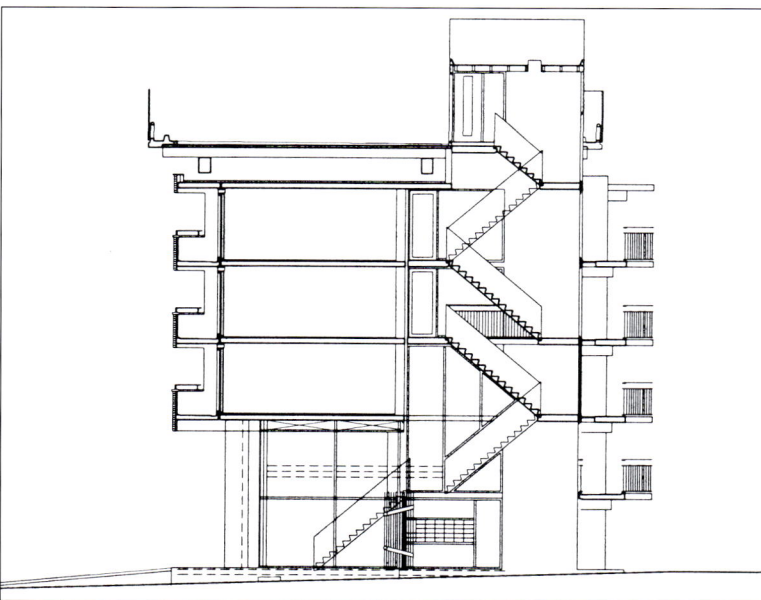

Fifth floor plan and parkingroof

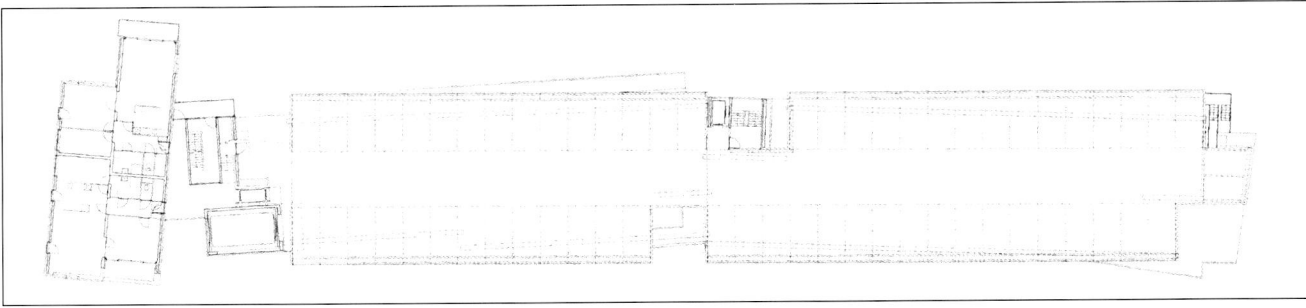

Second floor plan

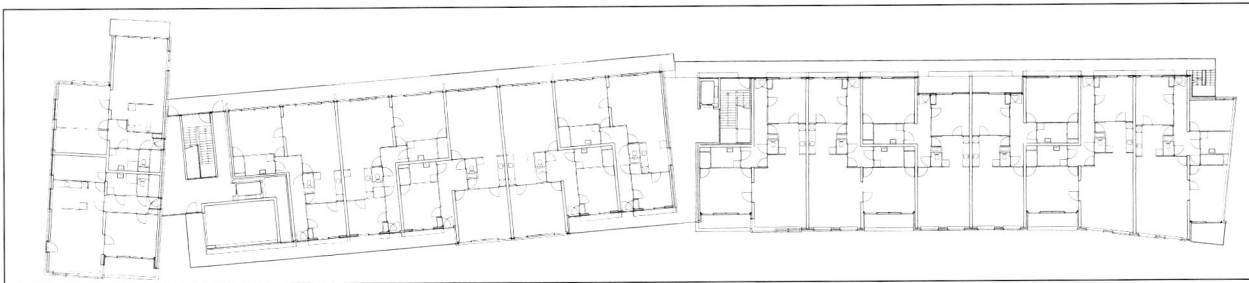

First floor plan

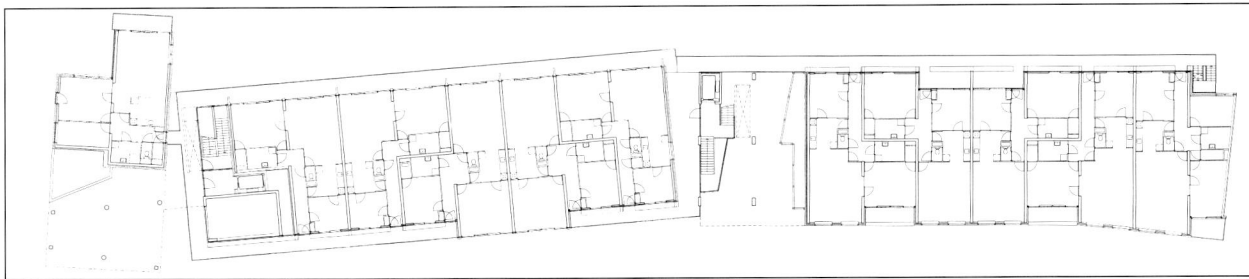

Ground floor plan

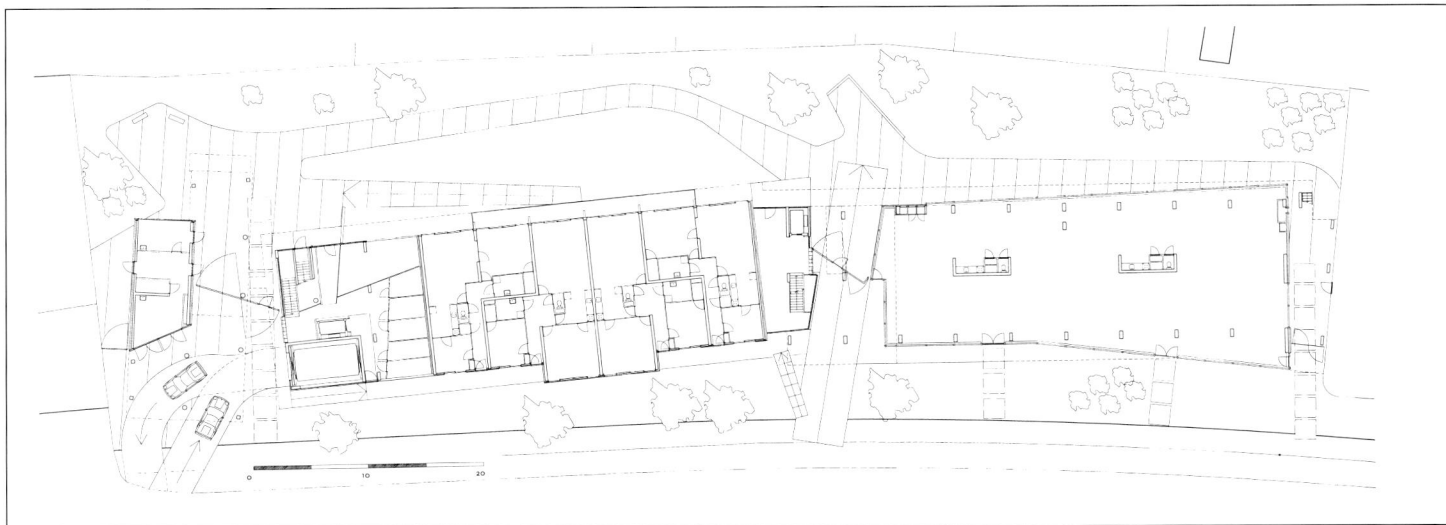

The central access area on the ground floor leads from the street to the interior green area and to the blocks of dwellings.

Gabetti & Isola, Fusari

Restoration of the Former" Ceramiche Titano" Building

San Marino, Republic of San Marino

Photographs:
Vaclav Sedy

Architect:
Gabetti & Isola, Fusari

The scheme for this apartment building completes a site in transformation. Originally designed as a china factory, the existing building was constructed in various stages. Modifications were made some years ago when it was transformed into a Ferrari museum. The new brief called for a building with services on the lower floors, residential units on the upper floors and an underground garage.

The existing exterior walls of ashlar stones were restored, while additional floors, conceived with a prevalence of sections, wooden boarding and curtain walls were added.

Galleries for offices and shops were created behind the facade on the lower floors, with direct access from the road on the front and back facades. The shop-side face of these internal galleries is a continuous partition of floor-to-ceiling glass which traces a curving path alongside the existing wall. The resulting corridor forms an open, outward-looking loggia.

Single-story and duplex flats, with long, uninterrupted loggias and deep balconies were inserted into the residential areas on the top floors. Like the shops below, these loggias were created inside the existing facade and are defined on the inner side, which gives onto the flats, by a sinuous glass wall. The loggias on the upper floors jut out over the facade, creating deep balconies, cutting into the stone facade below and stretching upwards to form lofty attics. The support beams of these sharply projecting balconies are connected vertically by tie beam struts.

Wooden planks set on a metal framework comprise the flooring of the loggias and balconies, which are enclosed by sheets of glass with wooden handrails and electrically-operated awnings. The new roof cladding consists of earthen tiles over a base of wooden boards.

Second floor plan

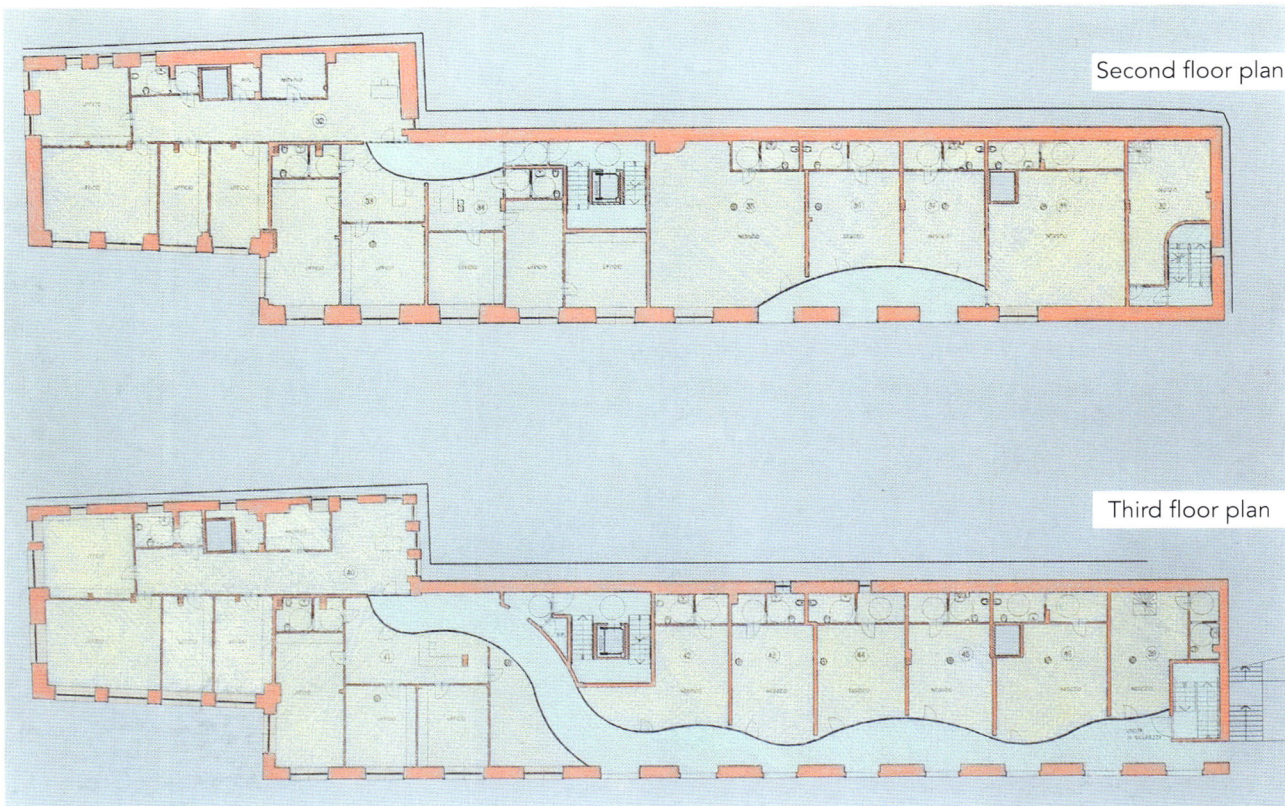

Third floor plan

Fifth floor plan

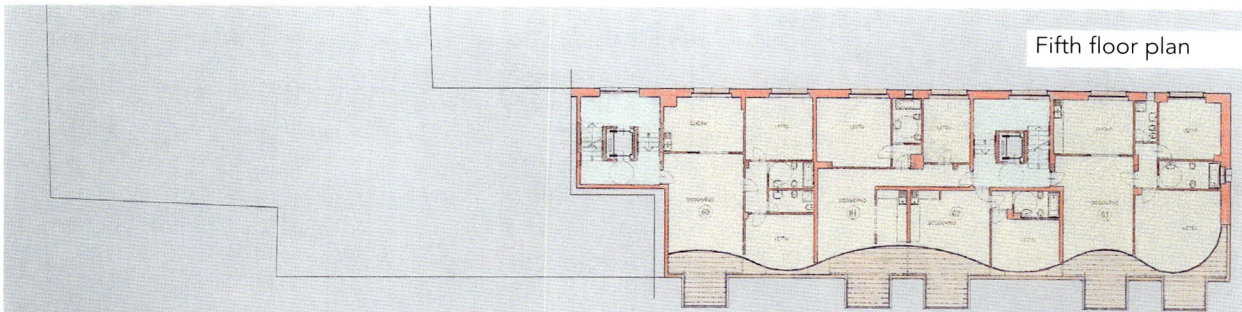

Sixth floor plan

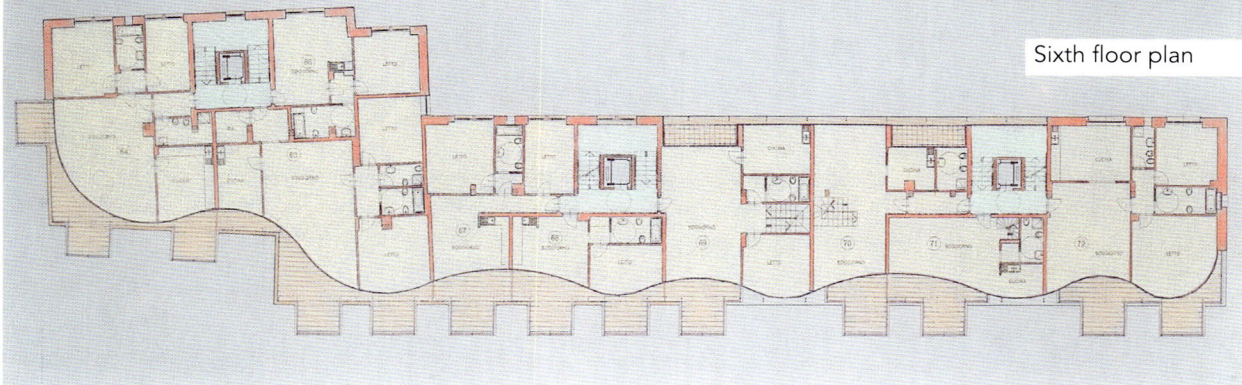

Seventh floor plan

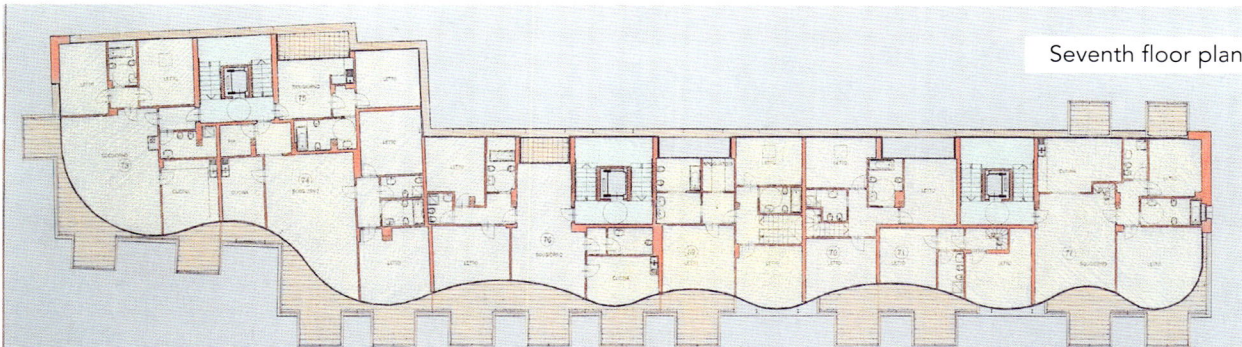

Roof floor plan

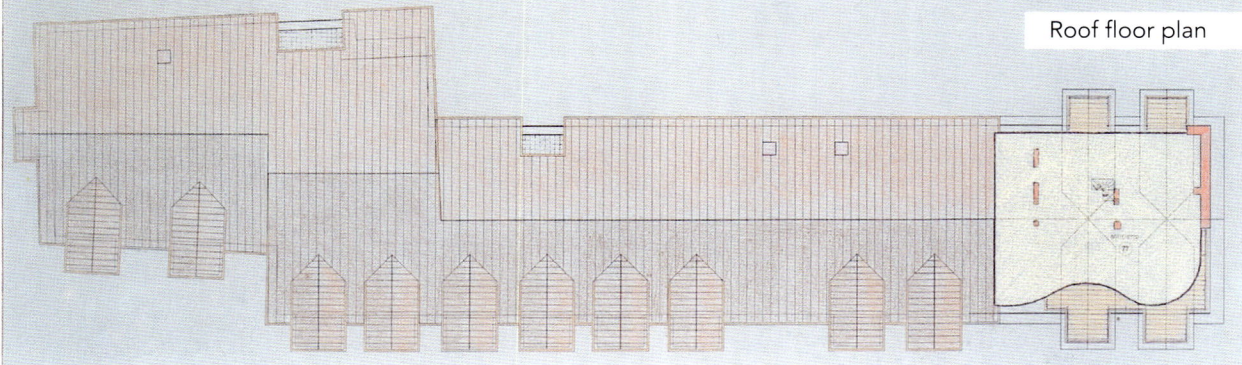

South-east elevation

The existing walls of ashlar stone were restored; sections, wooden planking and curtain walls predominate in the new upper floors. The awnings along the balconies are electrically operated and regulated by anemoscope for safety reasons. The new roof cladding consists of earthen tiles lying on a base of wooden boards.

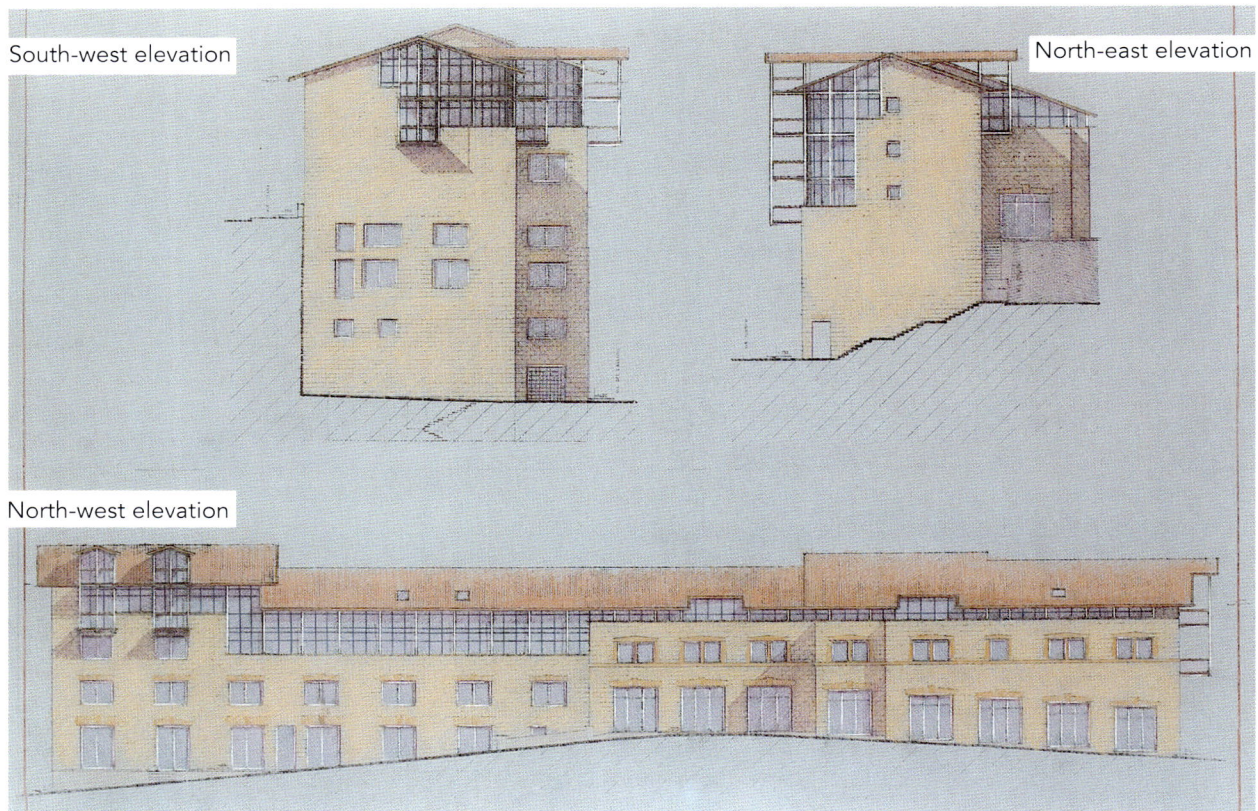

South-west elevation

North-east elevation

North-west elevation

Section A-A'   Section B-B'   Section E-E'

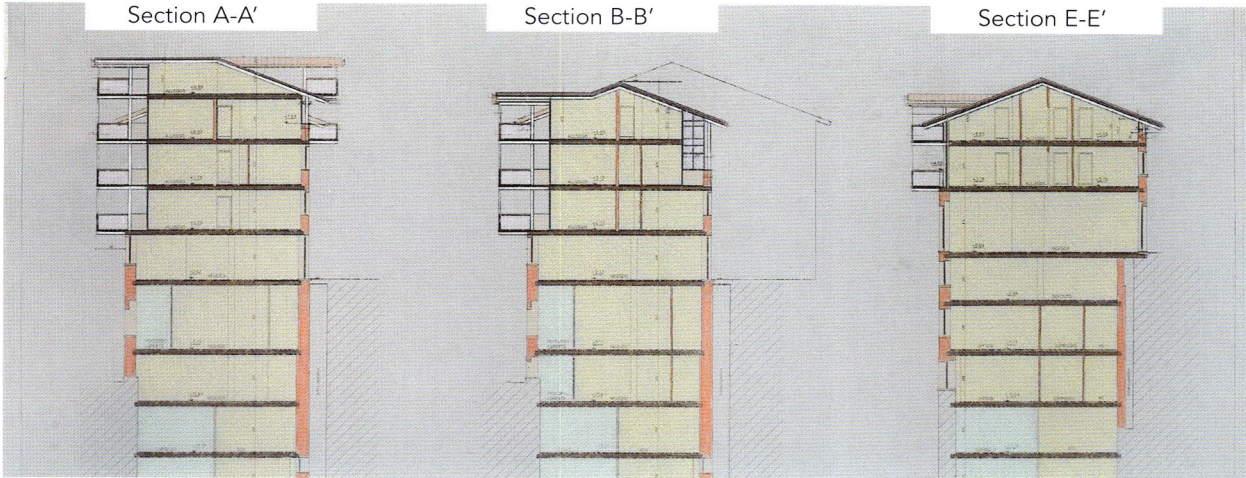

Flats with long uninterrupted loggias and deep balconies were inserted into the top floors. The loggias were created inside the outer edge of the existing facade and are defined on the inner face by a long, sinuous glass wall. On the top floors, the loggias jut out over the facade, creating deep balconies whose support beams are connected vertically by tie beam struts.

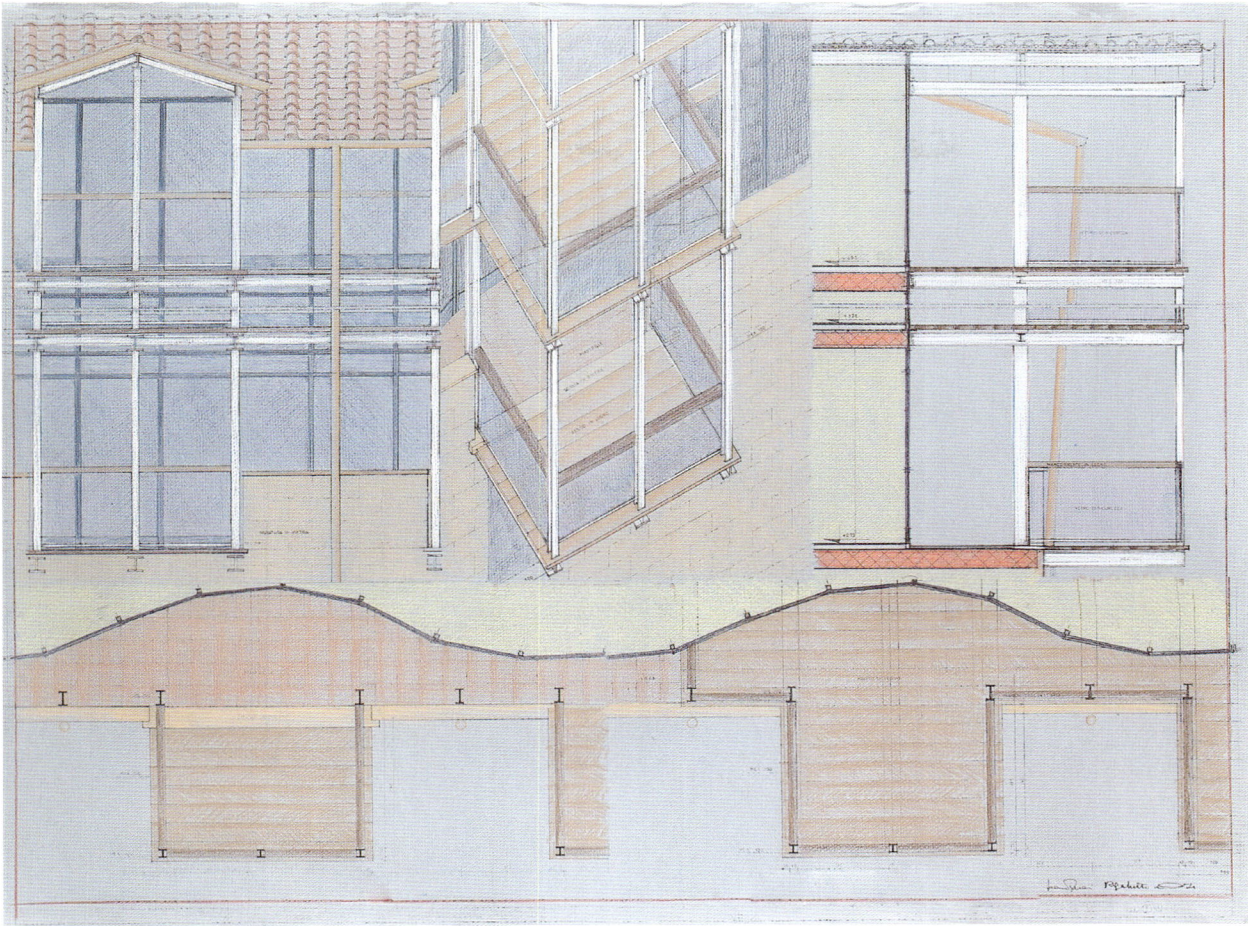

Mann + Schneberger Architekten BDA

Building Complexin Mainz

Mainz, Germany

Photographs:
Werner Huthmacher/ Artur

Architect:
 Mann + Schneberger Architekten BDA

This building complex, occupying almost an entire city block in the old quarter of Mainz, partially consisted of single houses dating from around the Middle Ages to the 1970s. The program required the reorganization and partial remodeling of an existing senior and nursing home, to be carried out over a series of construction phases.

The primary purpose of the remodeling work was to improve accessibility for the disabled by installing ramps connecting all levels. Another consideration was the wish to bring the facilities up to date and create a more modern environment. The rooms, mostly single occupancy, have been furnished with integrated sanitary installations for the elderly as well as the latest advances in nursing and care facilities.

Preliminary examination of the site indicated that the larger part of the building was the most suited for remodeling. The only exception was the building located on the Schlossergasse side, which was completely replaced.

The facades have been intentionally designed to harmonize with the characteristics of the neighboring constructions and are composed of four-story cubes with set back attics and plaster finishes.

The ground floor, where the entrance, an extended foyer and the administration area are located, constitutes the new center of the complex. An elliptical volume defines the foyer, the largest portion of which juts out into the courtyard to greet visitors. Foldable sliding panels strung from guide rails along the curve of the interior portion of the ellipse can be left open for everyday use or closed for events and presentations.

The upper floors contain the nursing and care facilities as well as the individual rooms, each of which enjoys a private loggia.

In accordance with the clients' wishes, the design of the private dwellings incorporates sophisticated visual relations to the exterior space. The overall goal, aesthetically speaking, was to execute a complex project, while at the same time using a direct, uncomplicated architectural style.

Over half of the elliptical foyer juts out into the court-yard to greet visitors. Foldable sliding panels strung from guide rails along the curve of the interior portion of the ellipse (as shown on the following pages) can be left open for everyday use or closed for events and presentations.

1. Hall   3. Reception
2. Foyer   4. Offices

Ground floor plan

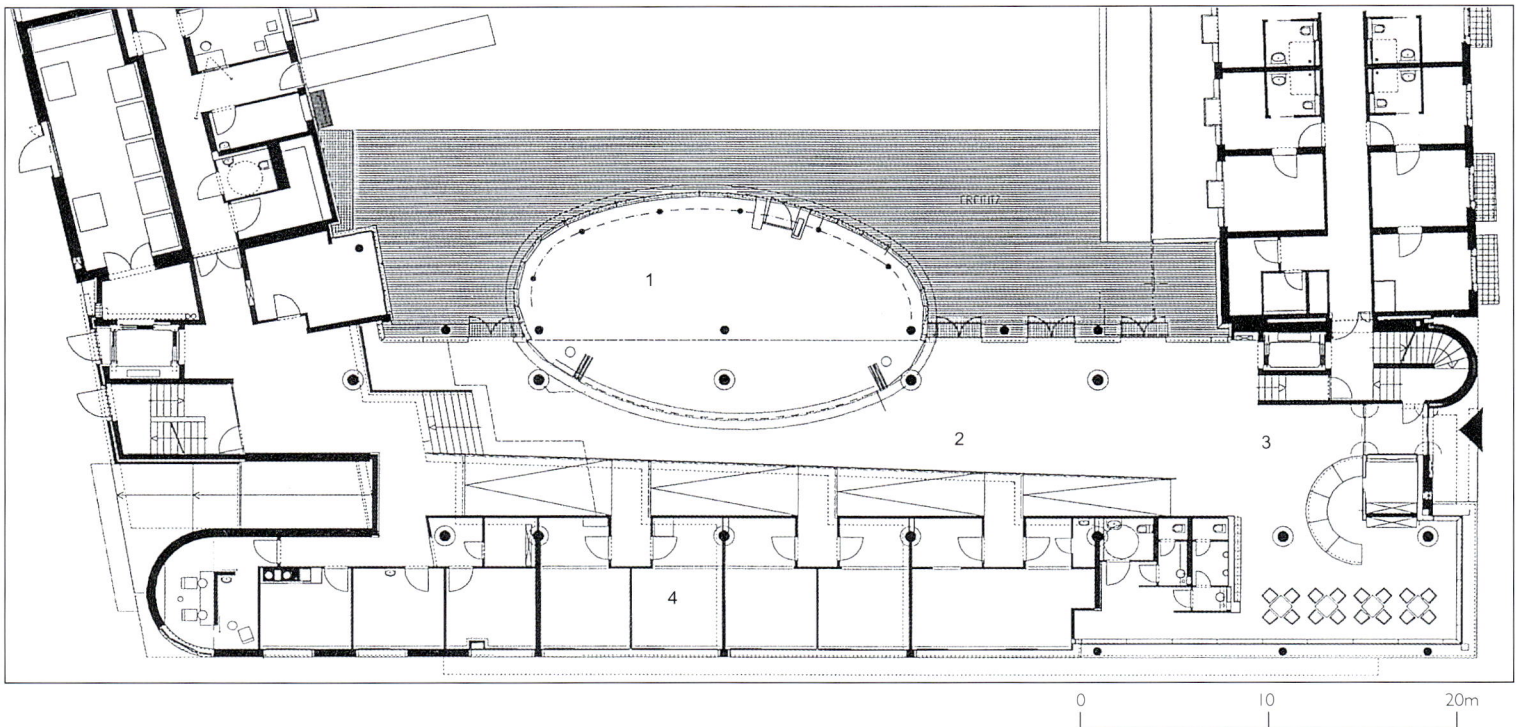

0   10   20m

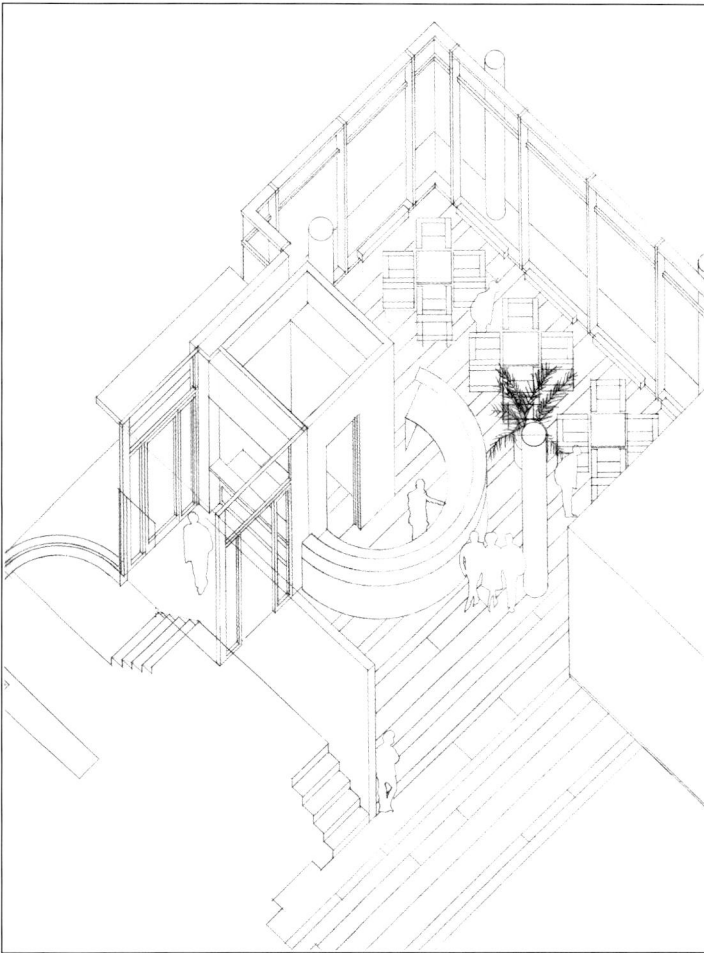
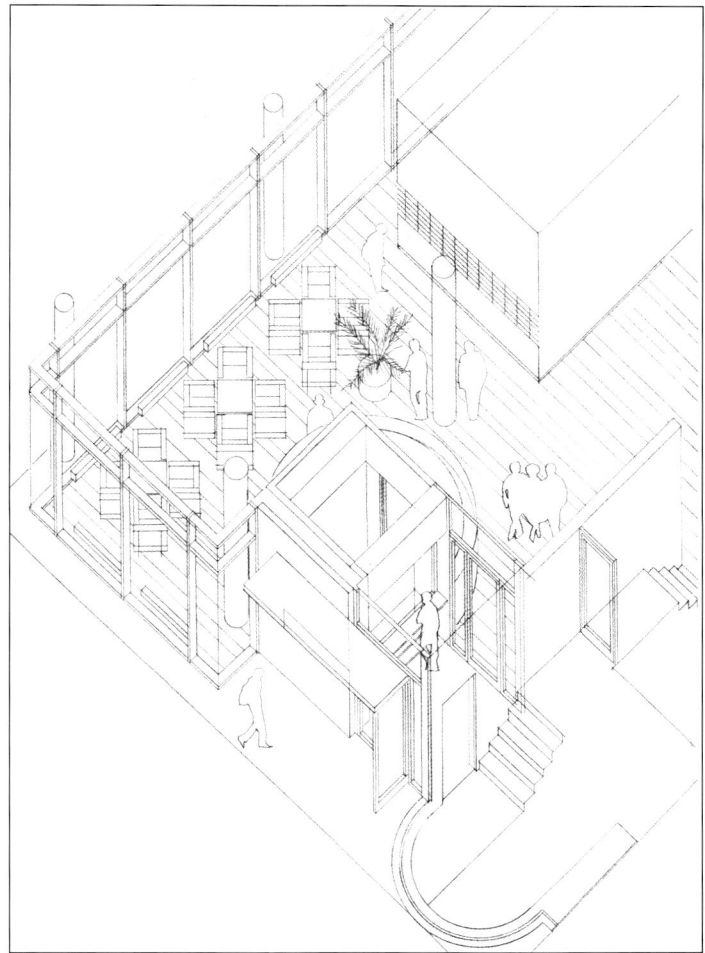

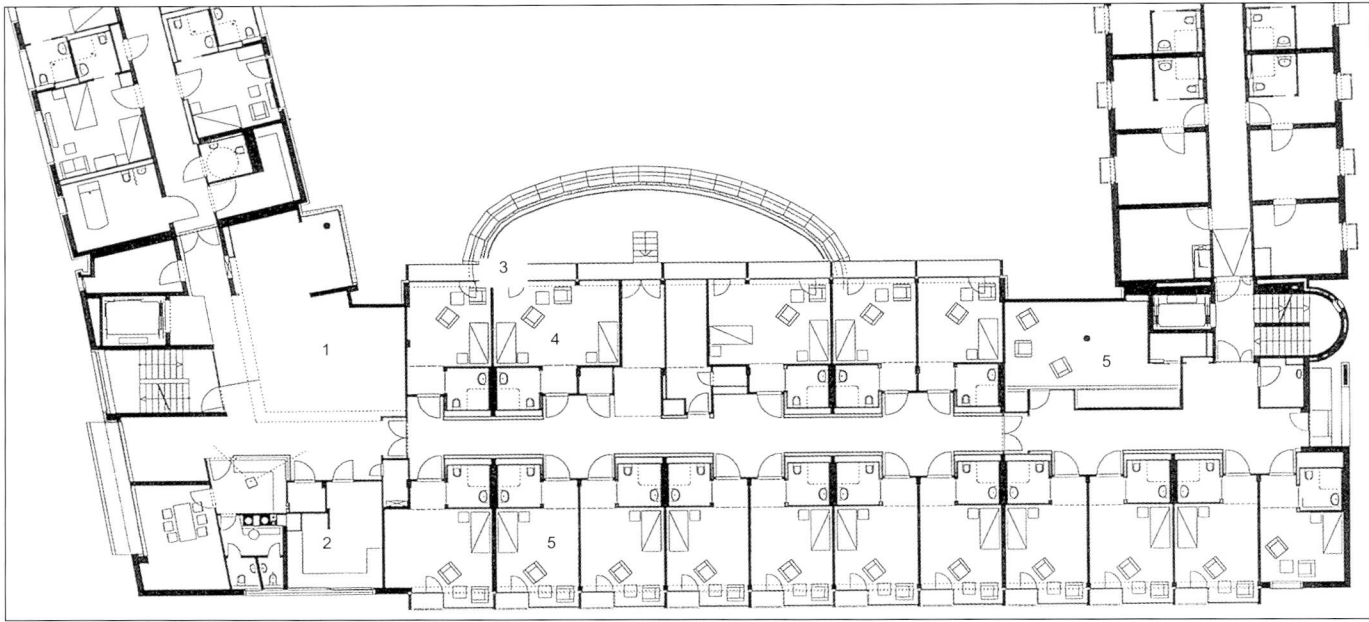

1. Dining room   4. Bedroom
2. Kitchen   5. Living room
3. Terrace

First floor plan

1. Dining room   3. Bedroom
2. Kitchen   4. Living room

Penthouse floor plan

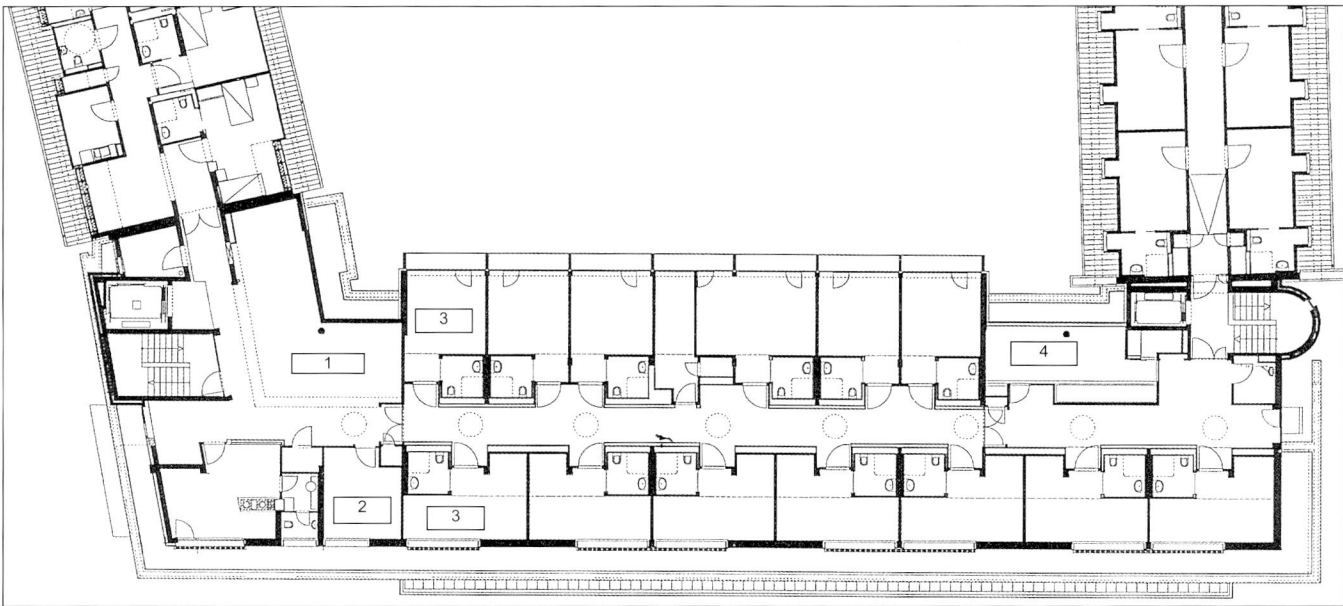

The primary purpose of the remodeling work was to improve accessibility for the disabled by installing ramps connecting all levels.

The facades have been intentionally designed to harmonize with the characteristics of the neighboring constructions and are composed of four-story cubes with set back attics and plaster finishes.

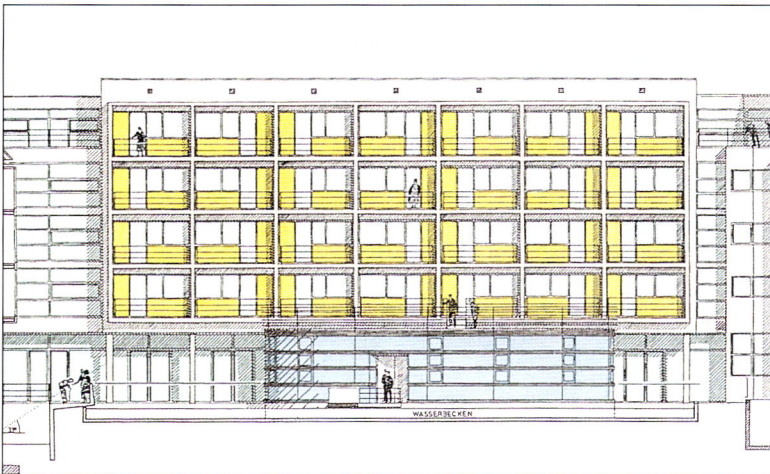

Interior elevation

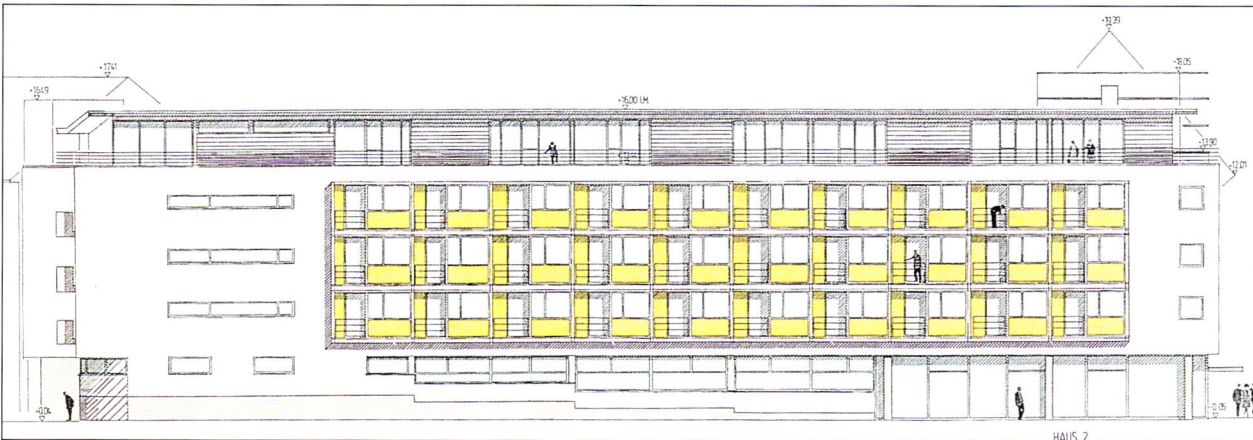

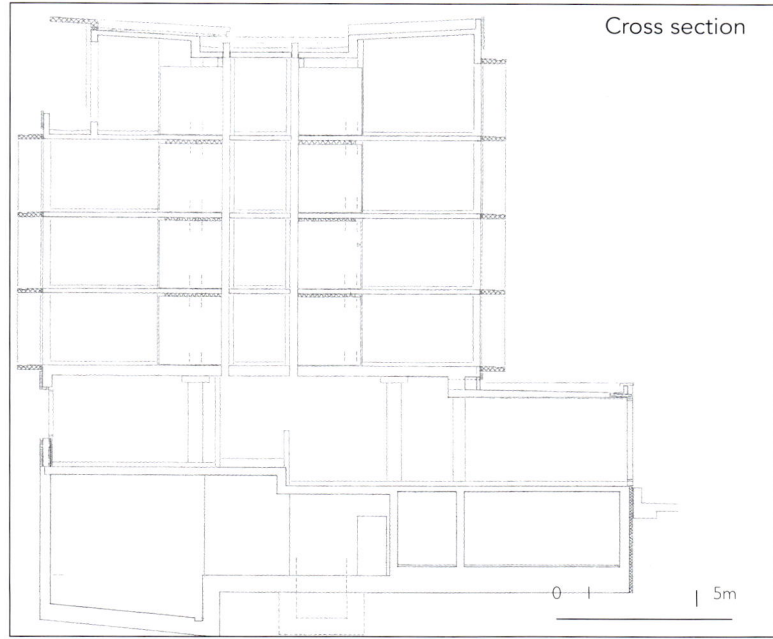

Cross section

0 5m

Valérie Vaudou & Laurence Allégret

Housing in Paris

Paris, France

Photographs:
Hervé Abbadie

Architect:
Valérie Vaudou & Laurence Allégret

La Villette, located in the northeast of Paris, once hosted a great number of slaughterhouses. The area has since been totally transformed due to the construction of an urban park and a museum. The buildings used for the slaughtering process were progressively demolished and replaced by housing and public facilities for the neighborhood. One of these interventions is located between the Saint Martin canal and the Rue de Thionville, shaping a double building with certain unusual aspects for a social housing development. The big openings on the front and the aluminum facades give the eight story building on the canal's shore an image that looks more like an office building than a housing complex. This ambiguous identification is due to the fact that this type of building rarely has large openings and they usually cannot enjoy too much natural light. On top of that, the gray Alucobond panel skin has nothing to do with glass, tile, and concrete, or the rest of the mineral finishing of the architecture found between La Rotonde de Ledoux and La Villette. 42 Quai de la Marne injects some character and restraint into this architectural maelstrom.

According to the architects' wishes, the building should subtly adapt to the local vocabulary: the aluminum wrapping recalls the metallic exterior skin of a neighboring thermal power plant and the powerful structure of Eiffel's railway bridge crossing the canal. The division of the higher floors through dark gray lacquered aluminum sections underlines a certain refinement of the metallic skin.

The same skin covers the elevation towards the interior courtyard. While the large openings facing the canal have a constant image, open to the sky and the urban landscape, the sliding panels of the rooms facing the courtyard provide this façade with a random image. Toward the Rue de Thionville, the five-bedroom duplex has a hybrid façade. Unfortunately the fourth elevation does not get the same finishing since a great amount of the budget was destined to the deposit on the canal's shore.

The architects have not centered the budget on the exterior only; the dwellings are spacious, comfortable, and abundant in light and good views. The bedrooms get direct and indirect natural light, and the daytime areas have big openings and introduce a certain modulation of space.

This architecture demonstrates how the combination of compromised architects and clients can, for everybody's benefit and particularly the users', open options where they seemed closed.

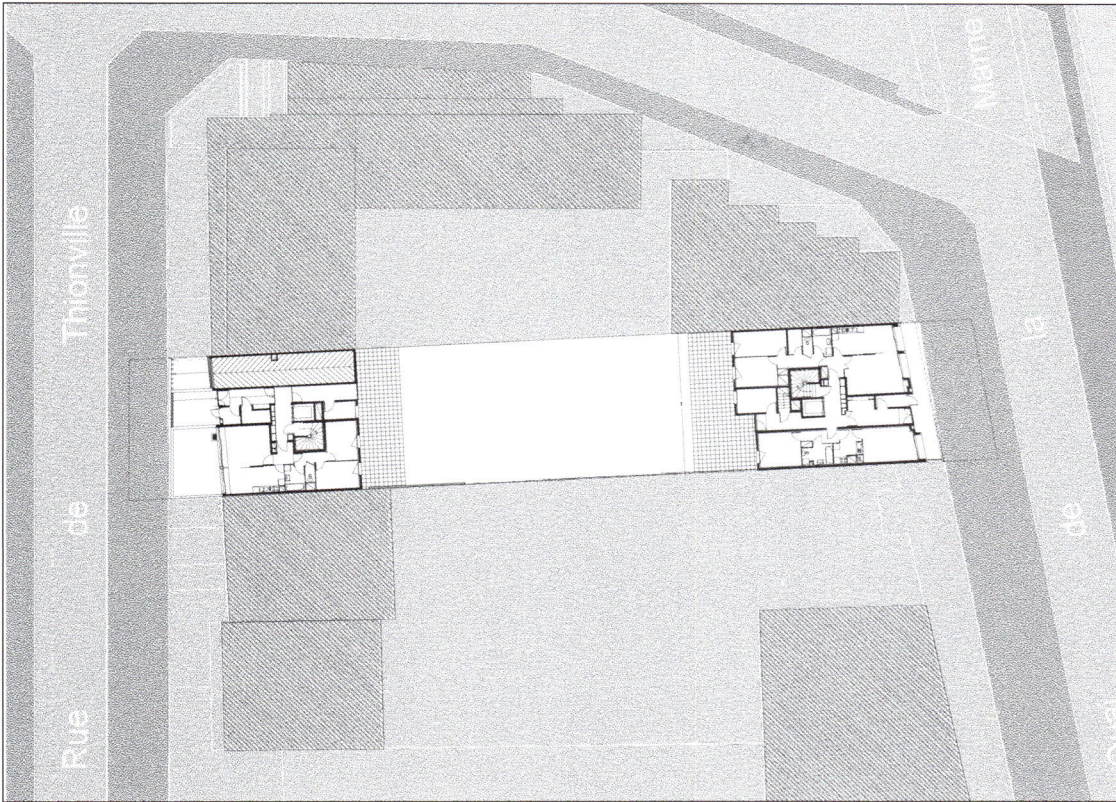

The narrow lot, measuring 13 by 68 meters, inspired the arrangement of two blocks and a spacious central garden courtyard. The double block visually distances itself from the traditional social housing image via large openings facing the canal.

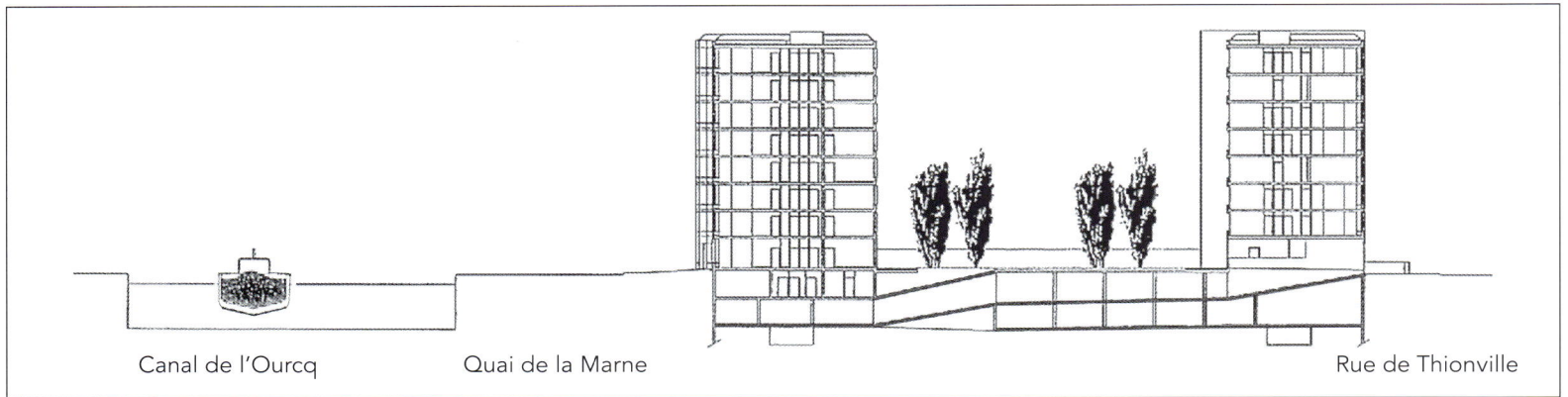

Canal de l'Ourcq   Quai de la Marne   Rue de Thionville

The elevation facing Rue de Thionville is a combination of large windows and Alucobond sliding panels. The facade receives an ever-changing random image thanks to the sliding panels.

The height of the parapet places the windows at the eye level of a sitting person and contributes to the quality of the home's lighting. The daytime area can be transformed through the movement of the sliding partition between the kitchen and the living room.

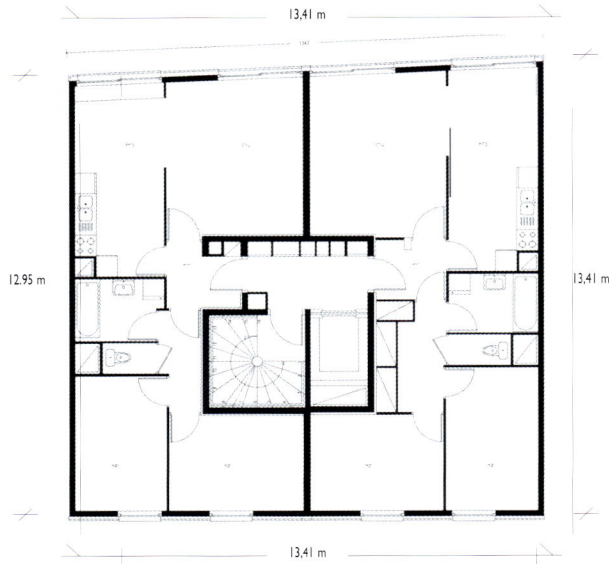

Standard floor plan for the building on Rue de Thionville

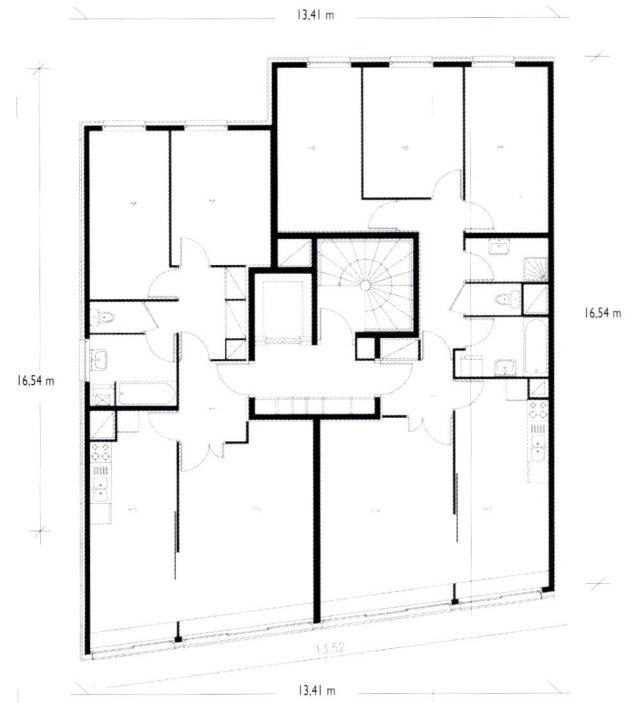

Standard floor plan of the building on Quai de la Marne

Emmanuel Combarel & Dominique Marrec

Social Housing for Students in Argenteuil

Argenteuil, France

Photographs:
Philippe Ruault

Architect:
Emmanuel Combarel &
Dominique Marrec

These 64 housing units for students are designed specifically for residents of a similar age and education level.

The façade displays monolithic shapes: facing north, the common structure is a standard module of 320 x 275mm repeated in every apartment, distributing the surface in a perfectly symmetrical manner. Overall harmony is the key to this project. Rhythmic changes, sequences strictly repeated or accelerated. There are several ways to create variations and break down monotony: the façade alternates blind walls and openings in a checkerboard pattern. All the apartments have half of their external façade exposed to natural daylight. Each opening can be closed with an internal shutter. The shutters, which are antique red, with pixilated images of the façade design, can be used as magnetic billboards onto which to attach memoranda or memorabilia.

From the street, the building presents a rather complex design.

Two long horizontal walkways, which cut the building longitudinally, give access to the apartments and create the dividing line between North and South, the transition between the wing on Careme Street and the western side with the hall and garden. The west façade, above the hall modules, has hybrid geometry, seeking a sense of urbanity in its heterogeneous environment.

On the south side, the balconies extend the dwellings between 8 and 15 sqmt more. The façade pattern of full and empty spaces, gray and neutral, is outlined by colorful separations. The sky's reflection in the windows blends with the colored shutters. At ground level, the garden is a Tetris pattern of concrete paving slabs and squares of thick carpet moss.

Street, access and garden intersect in the lobby, where the mailboxes, on the right, look like a colorful maze; there is also a bar, which extends into the garden.

The laundry is a comfortable living space, a place to meet people and chat, but elsewhere in the building the amount of space dedicated to public areas or corridors is reduced to the minimum required.

Paradoxically, a consistent framework and the façade's strict composition allow flexible living-space combinations, with more than 113 different types out of the 164 dwellings contained in the building. The surface area of the simplex or duplex type apartments varies between 17 and 40 sqm.

Ground floor plan

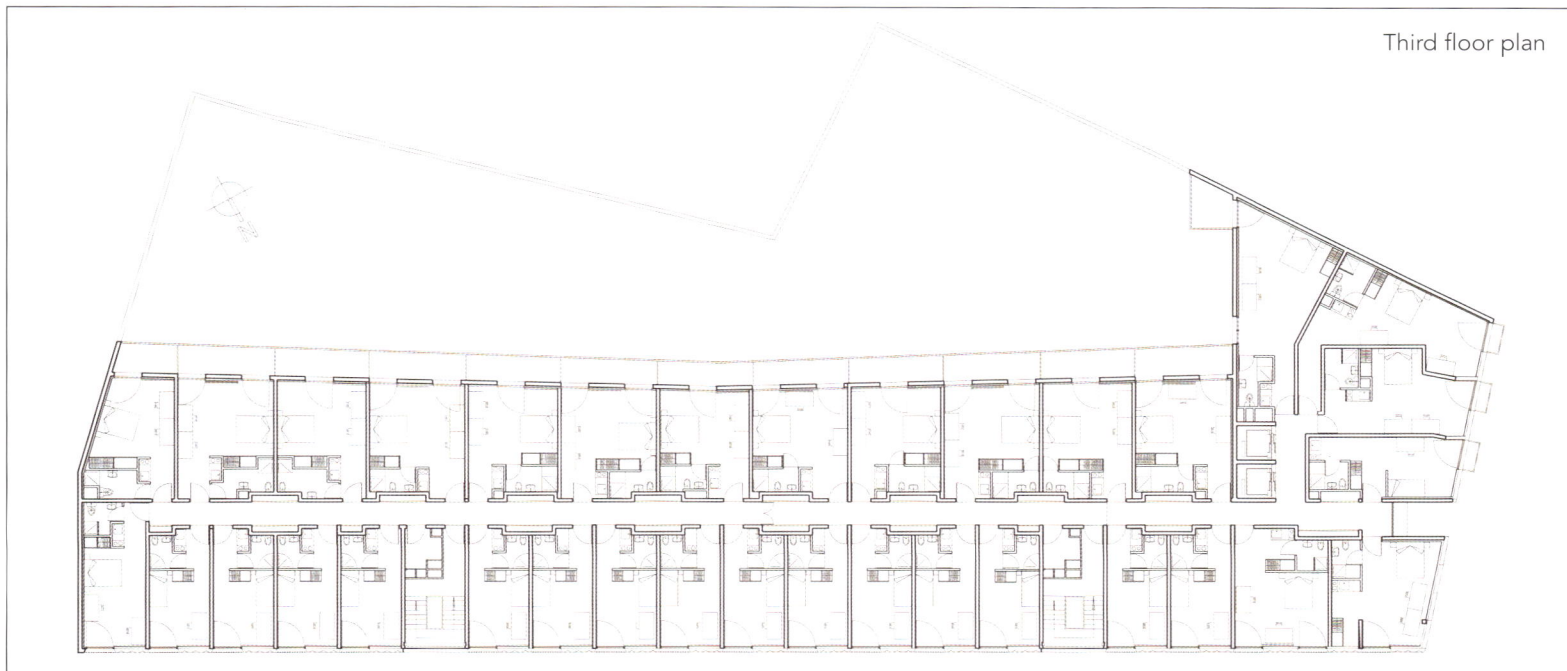

West elevation

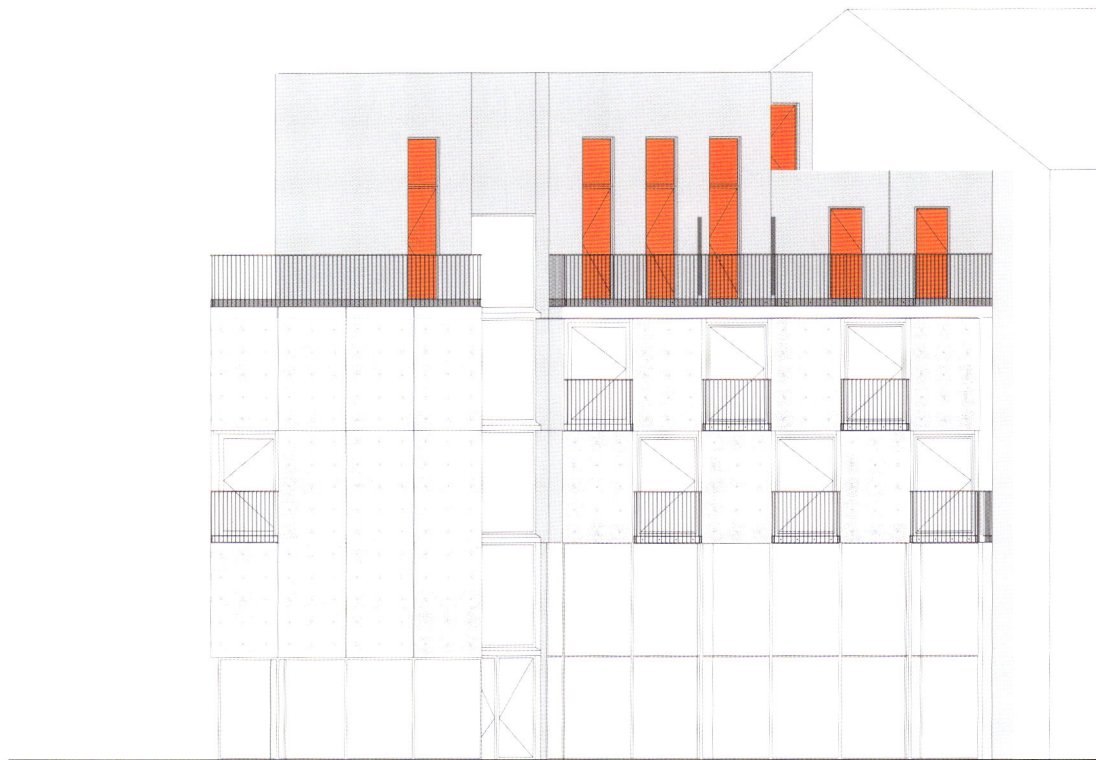

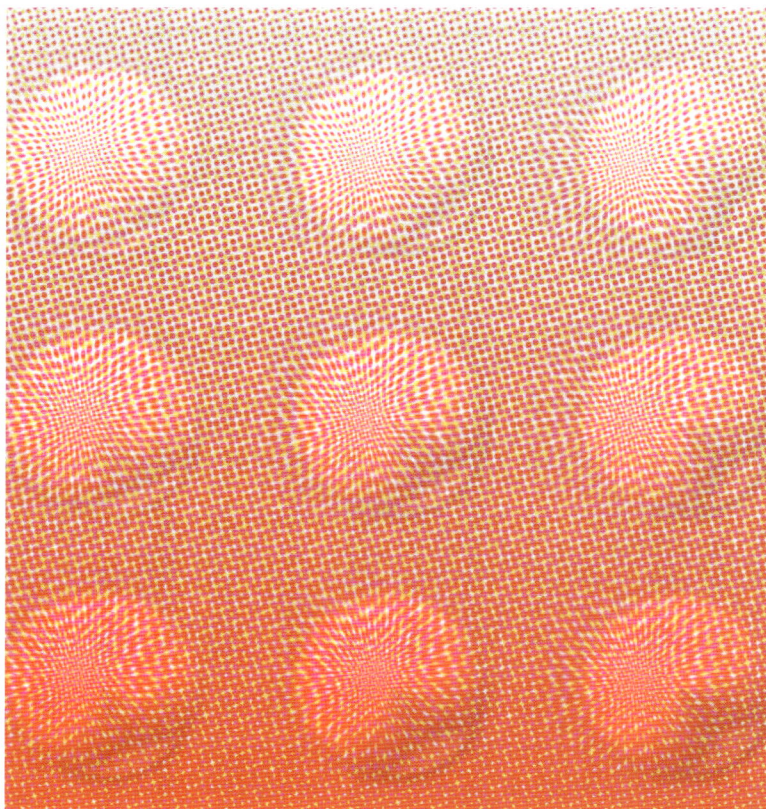

South elevation

Dekleva Gregoric Architekti

Housing L

Sezana, Slovenia

Photographs:
Matevz Patemoster

Architect:
Dekleva Gregoric Architekti

The new apartment building considers and upgrades the spatial distribution and formal characteristics of two existing blocks of apartments at the edge of a housing neighborhood facing the
shopping and industrial part of the small town of Sezana. The total usable surface area of the
building is 2370 sqmt, shared out on 6 floors. The concept of '3 for 1' (3 buildings instead of
1) enables the new addition to become an essential part of the whole and not merely an extension of it. `3 for 1` is a systematic volumetric structure with a distinctively vertical compositional
line. The formal approach emphasizes the already present structural appearance of the existing
buildings and redefines the sloped roof in order to restore the individual identity of each vertical element. The front elevation bends inward at the base, to accentuate the street side of the
building and its entrance area.

The selection of the façade materials corresponds to the nature of the building material under-
neath: concrete structural walls become side elevations, rendered and painted red; the brick
front walls are clad in fibrous cement panels, installed in a vertical layout to enhance the façades
verticality. Light plays differently on the two finishes and accentuates the building's volume. The
formal strategy is to use a variety of resources to stress the individual nature of every element
of the project. This sharp definition effect spills over onto the neighboring buildings, thereby
enhancing them also.

The apartments are compact, opening onto a small introverted loggia with an integrated stor-
age space. The two alternating positions of the loggia on the elevation result in two options of
interior distribution; in one of these the outdoor space is entered one way only - from the living
room; in the other the loggia is accessed from the living room and from the bedroom as well.

The building sets up a new formal repertory for future housing developments in the area, cur-
rently under construction. The insertion of this new element in the surrounding context intro-
duces an element of definition into the urban landscape, a sharper focus on the otherwise bland
surroundings.

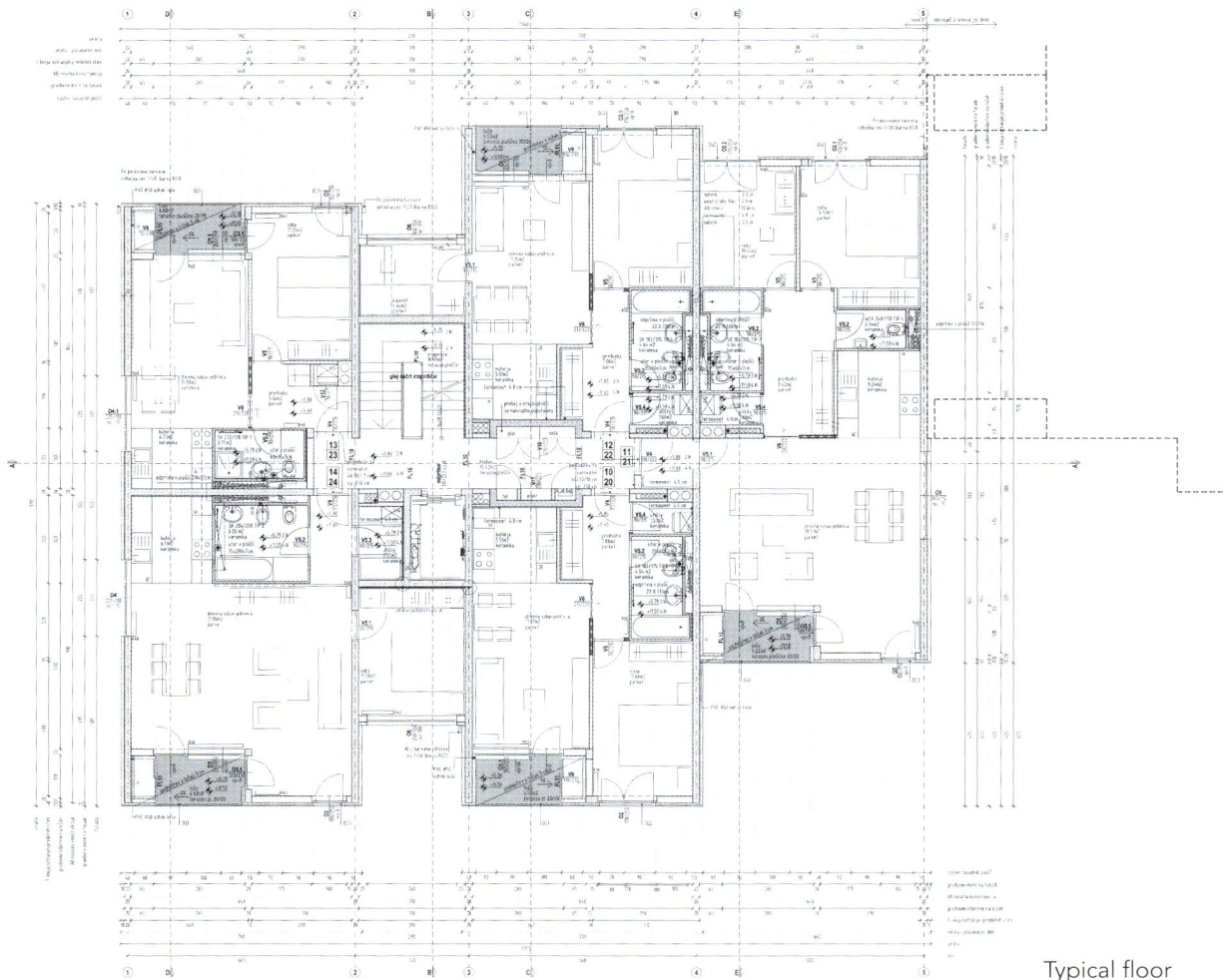

Typical floor

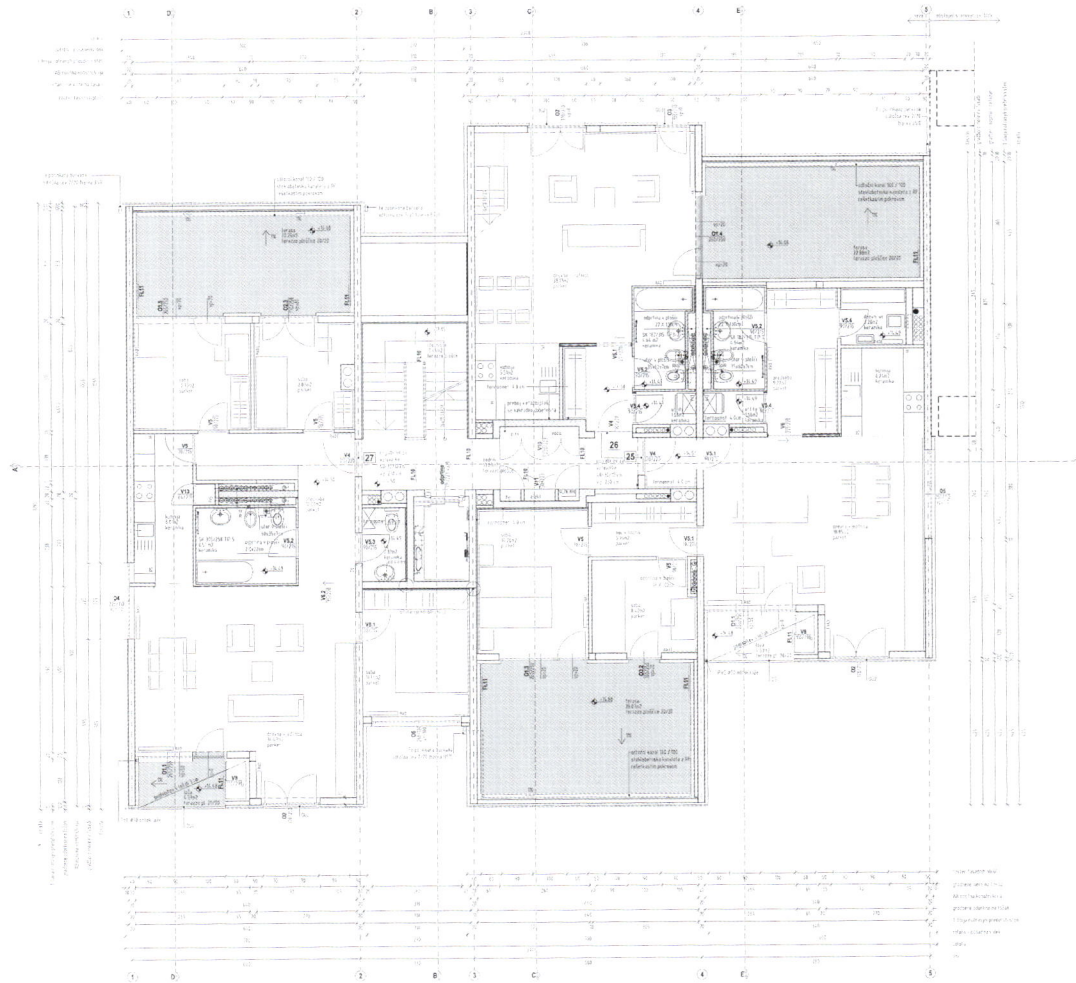

Top floor plan

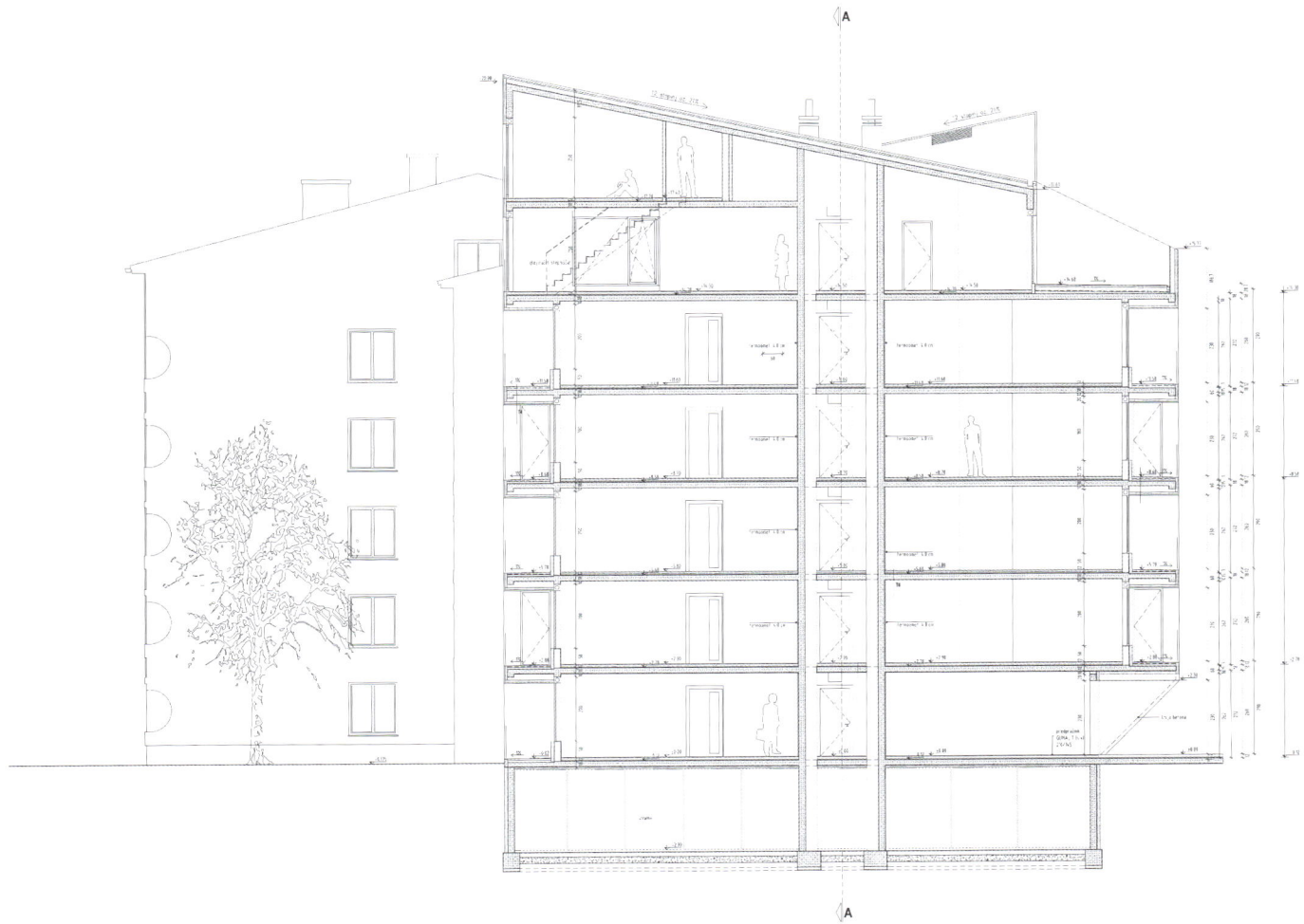

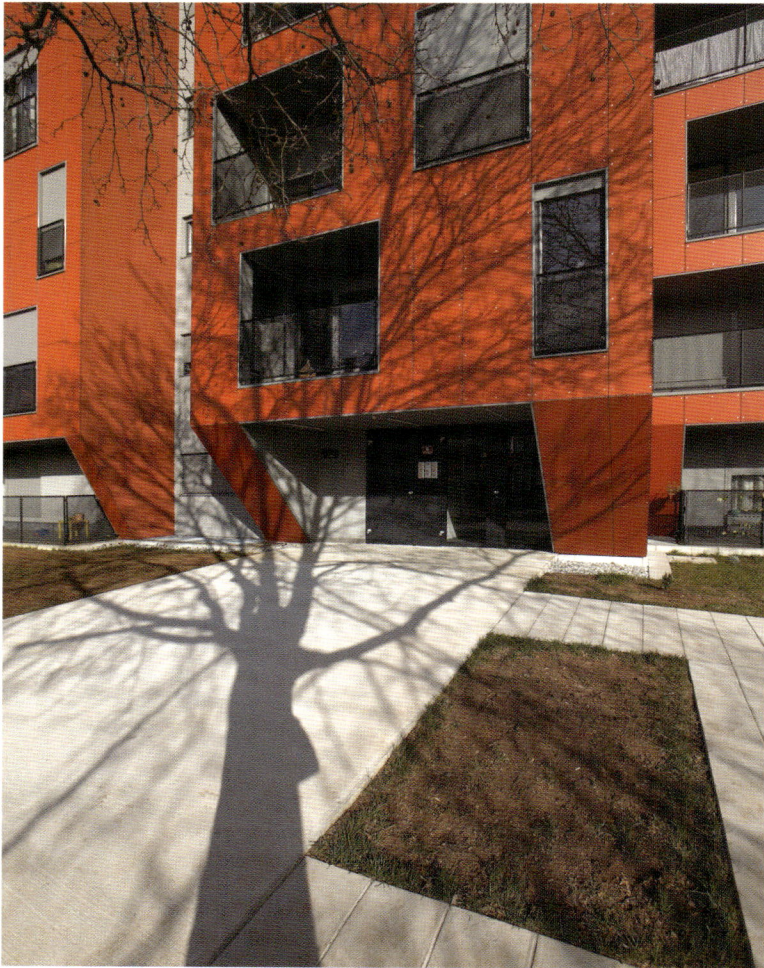
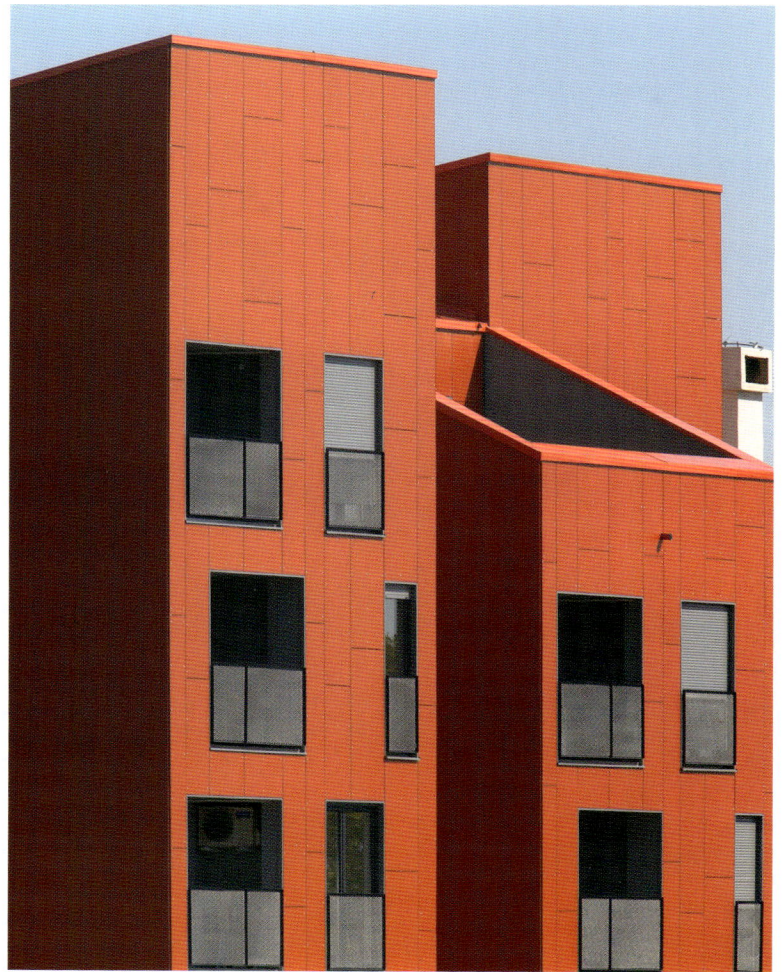
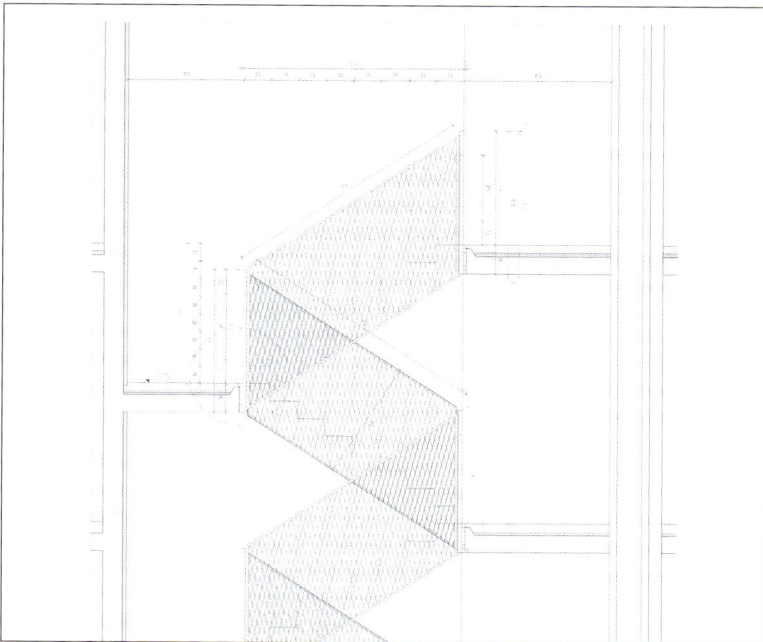
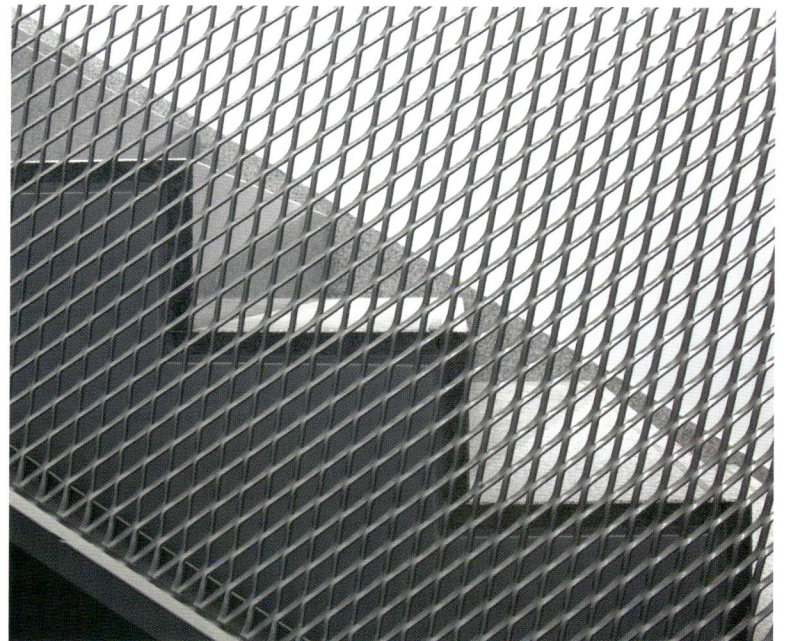

VMX Architects

Apartment Block at Sarphatistraat

Amsterdam, The Netherlands

Photographs:
Contributed by the architects

Architect:
VMX Architects

The University of Amsterdam commissioned the re-development of their property on Sarphatistraat in the centre of Amsterdam. The site is on a sensitive, historical street. The master plan proposed three new buildings: an ofice building, an apartment block and student housing. VMX Architects were commissioned to design the apartment block. All three buildings have been constructed with rental space and mixed functions on the ground level. The building's depths and heights conform to the original building lines of the Sarphatistraat. The student housing was financed from the revenue created by the apartments, the office block and the commercial ground floor space.

Given the fact that the apartments where suppose to be rented to visiting scholars, VMX designed them as in-between space: between hotel room and house.

The units are conceived as one large open space with an enclosed bathroom and open kitchen. The service ducts are the only fixed elements in this 100 sqm open space and allow for five possible configurations, giving the inhabitant maximum freedom in the arrangement of the space. The open character of the floor plan is translated in the façade by substituting the traditional arrangement of one window per function for one huge oval window.

Access to the apartments was restricted by the commercial space at ground floor and an existing single-storey building. Gallery access was the most suitable method. The gallery side is extensively glazed to allow as much light in as possible. Private balcony boxes off the gallery provide outdoor space. Steel sections, cables and transparent mesh give a lightweight functional appearance to this facade.

The street façade is made in dark basalt concrete

panels, making a link to the exiting facades. With this building, not only have the historical building lines been restored, also the character of the street with its many brick warehouses has been restored in an up to date manner.

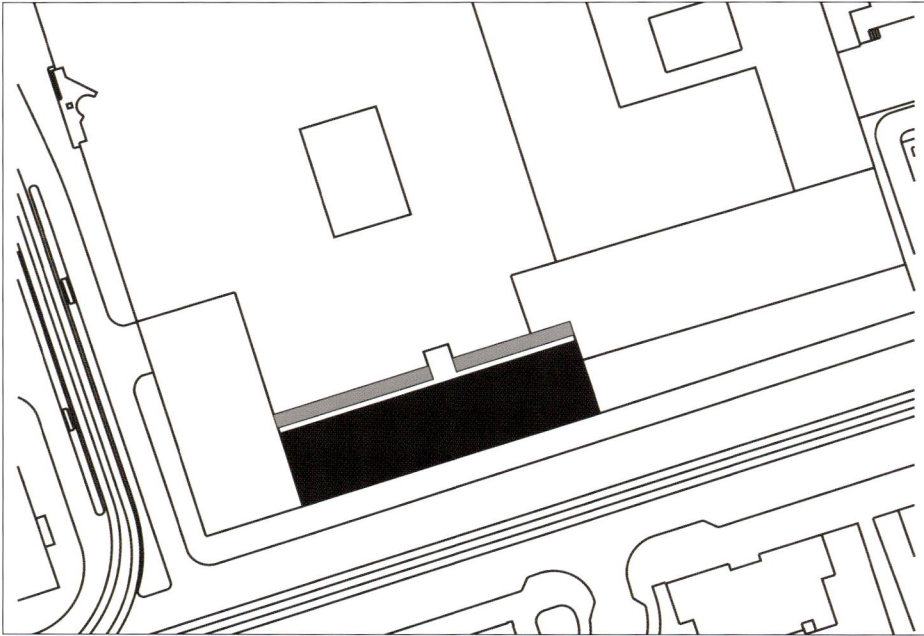

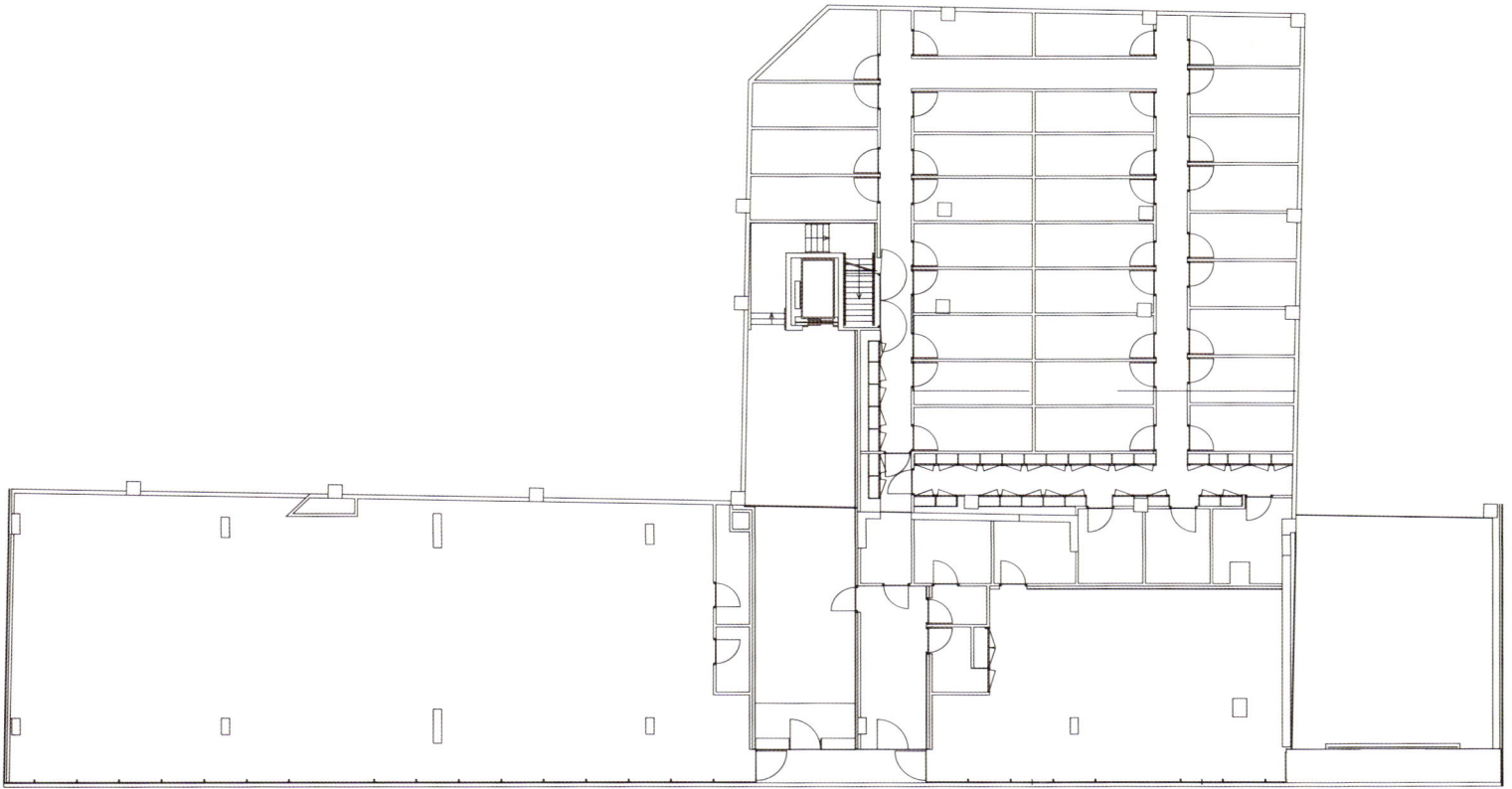

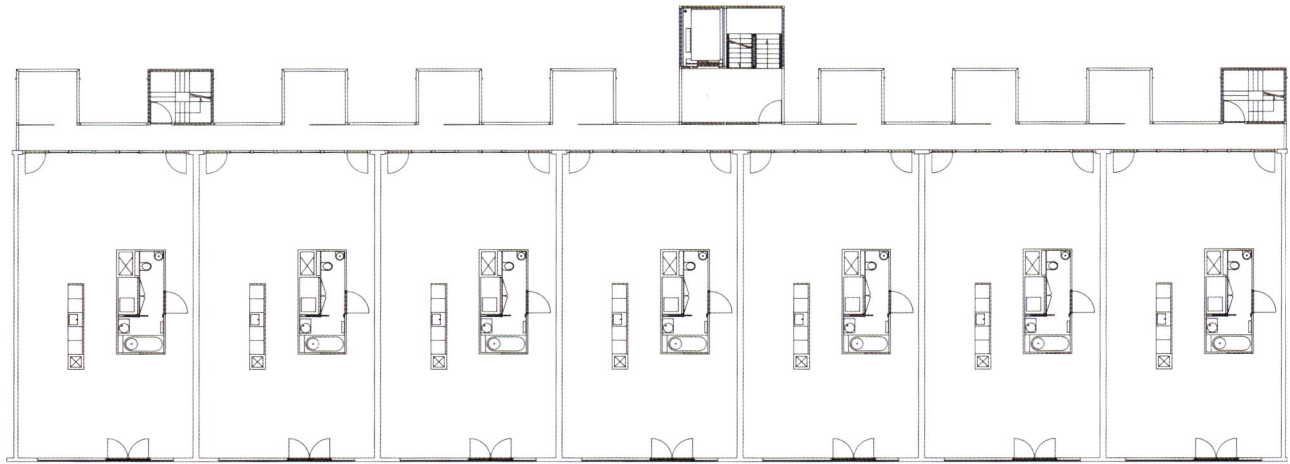

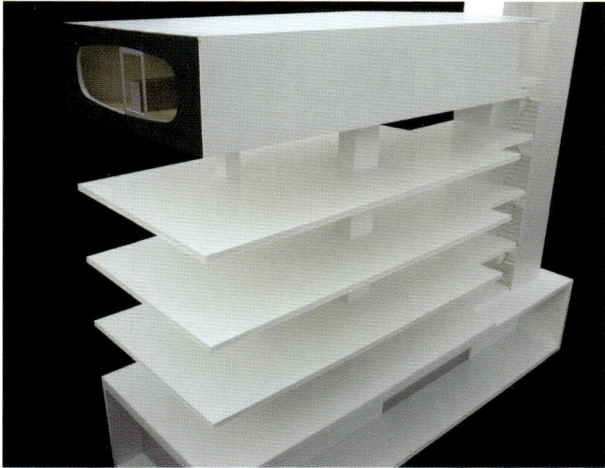

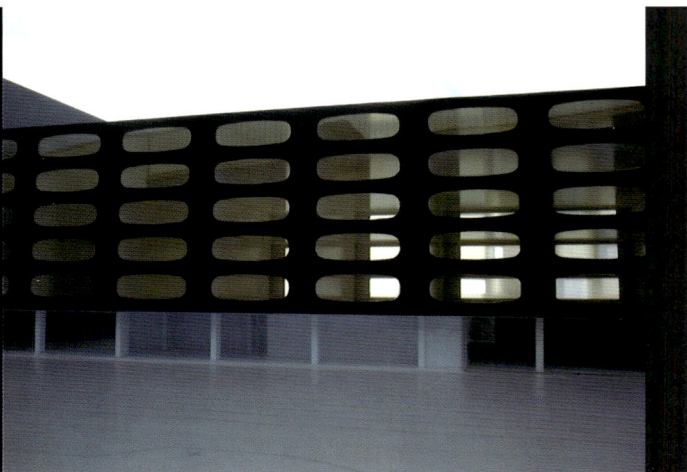

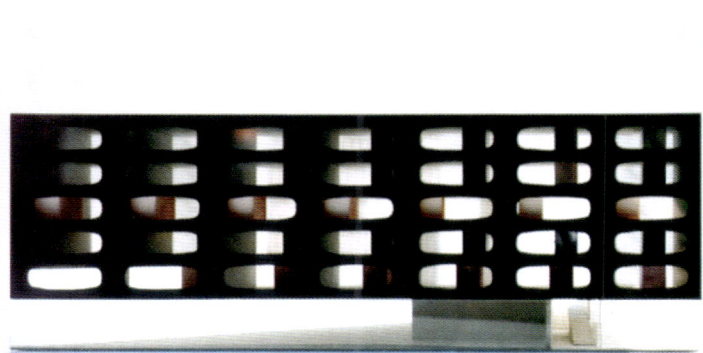

Jacques de Brouwer, Bedaux de Brouwer Architecten

Coba Ritsermastraat

Tilburg, The Netherlands

Photographs:
Ger van der Vlugt

Architect:
Jacques de Brouwer, Bedaux de
Brouwer Architecten

The site of a former barracks has been turned into a city park surrounded by buildings. Adjoining this park, Jacques de Brouwer designed the two brick faced apartment blocks intended to provide rental housing.

These two blocks form a new tree-lined street between them, Coba Ritsemastraat. This street links the busy Breadasweg with the park and also anticipates a similiar development on the other side of the Bredaseweg.

Behind the completely flat street elevation on the west side are 24 stacked maisonettes.

The living rooms of the upper maisonettes are located on the fourth level to take advantage of the view.

The row on the east side contains 25 apartments. The dwellings on the ground floor have a front door on the street side while the floors above are accessed from galleries at the rear.

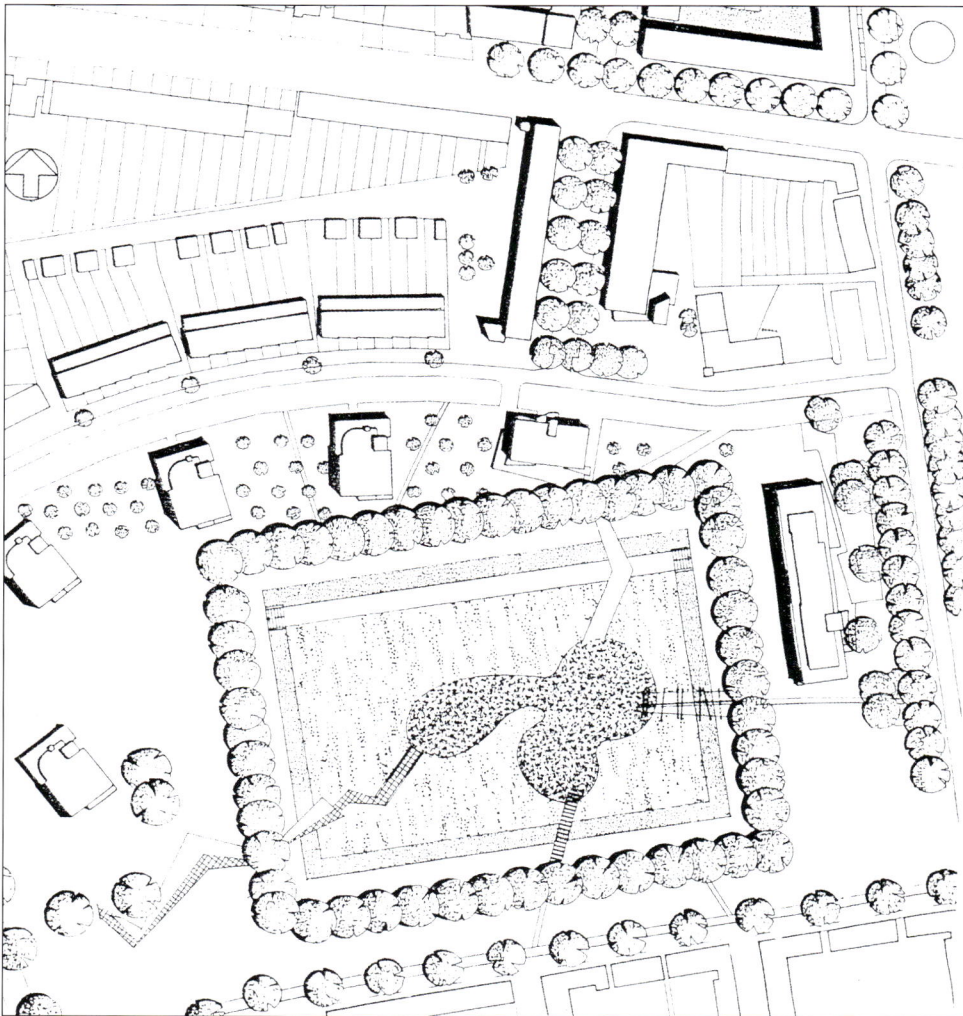

The residential complex forms part of a large and ambitious reconstruction project of the sector of the town of Tilburg near to the recently created Kromhout Park.

As seen on the site plan, the two buildings located on the site run along a new linear axis of circulation that communicates Bredaseweg with the nearby park.

With its simple structure and its exposed masonry facades featuring white window frames, the two blocks of dwellings clearly mark the limits of the new axis of circulation.

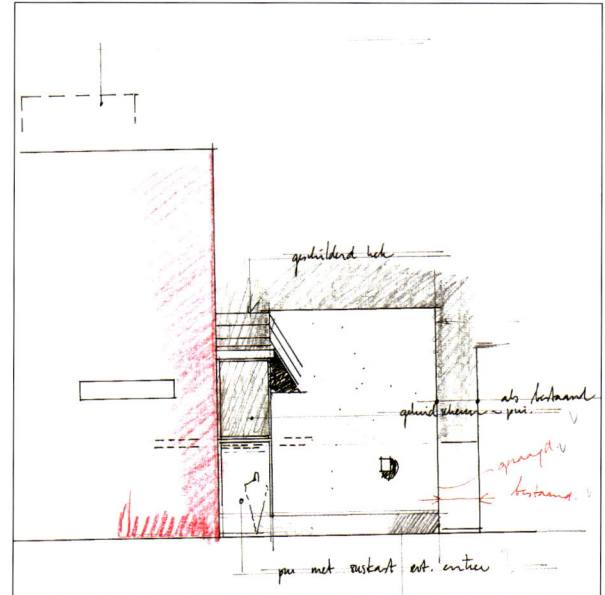

Ground floor plan

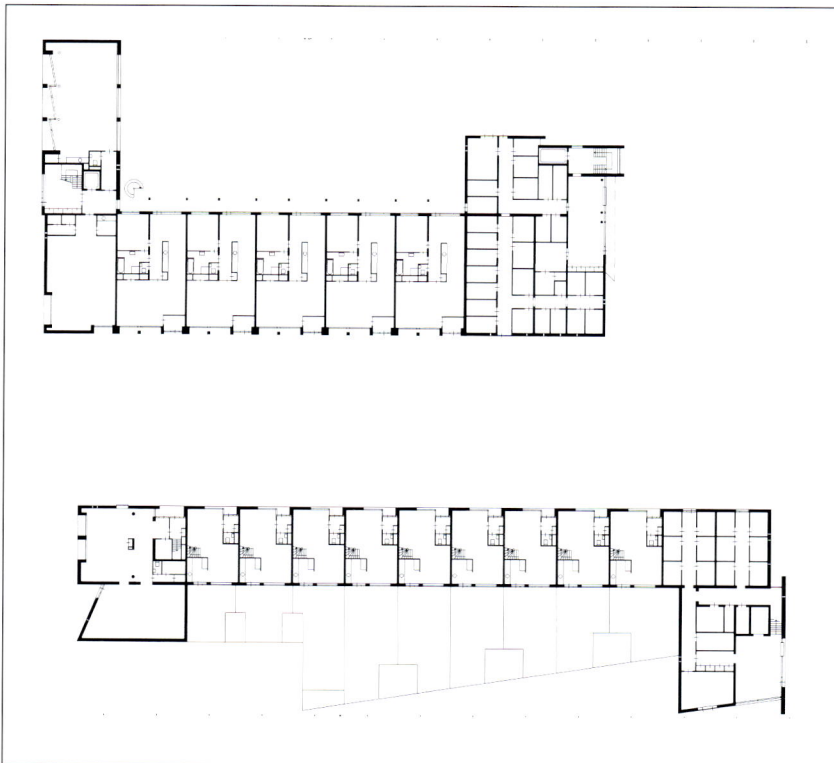

First floor plan

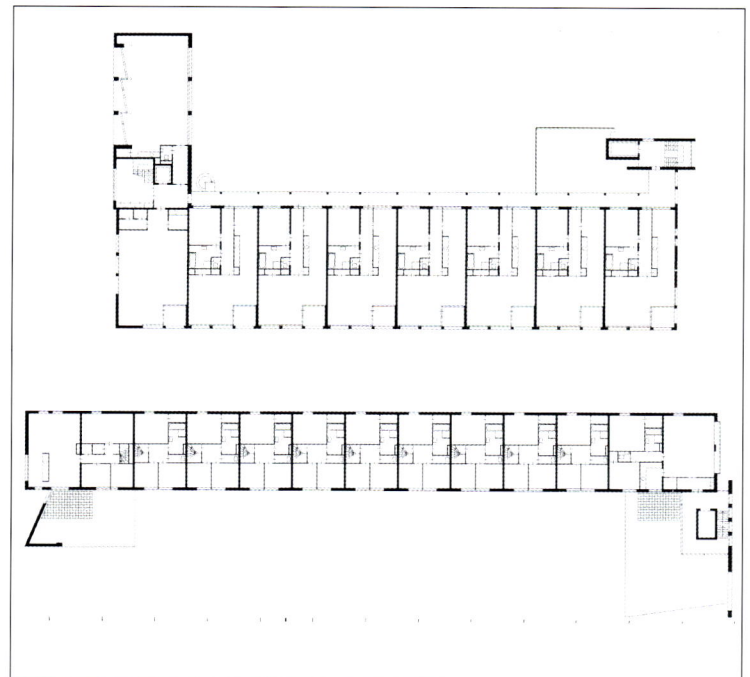

Second floor plan

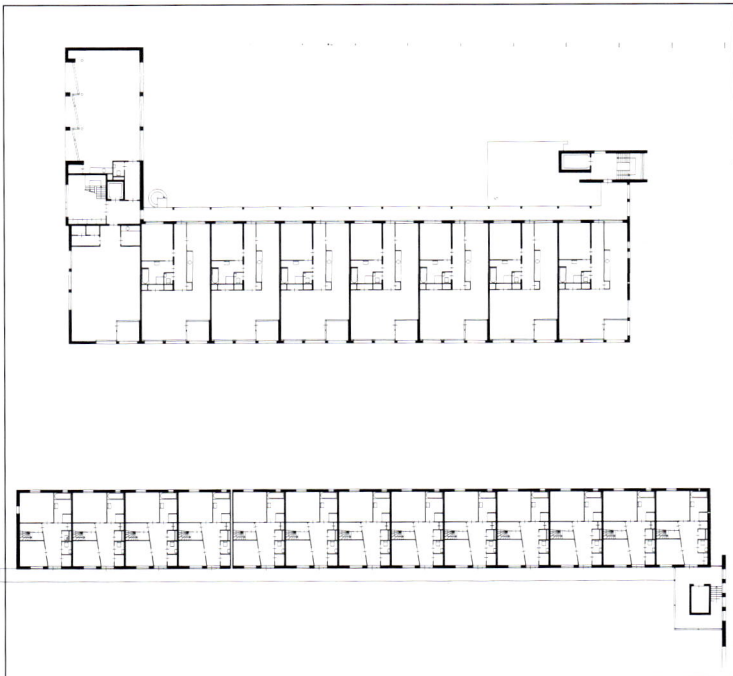

Third floor plan

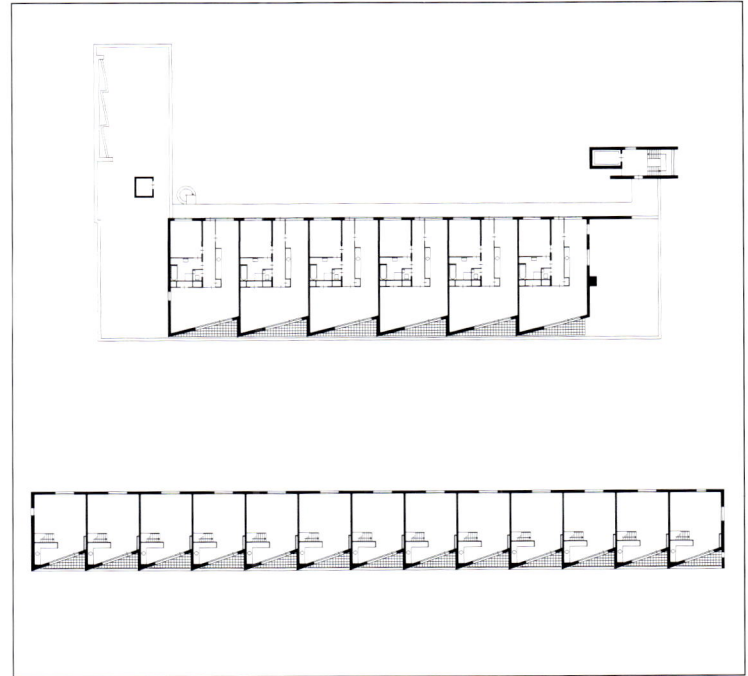

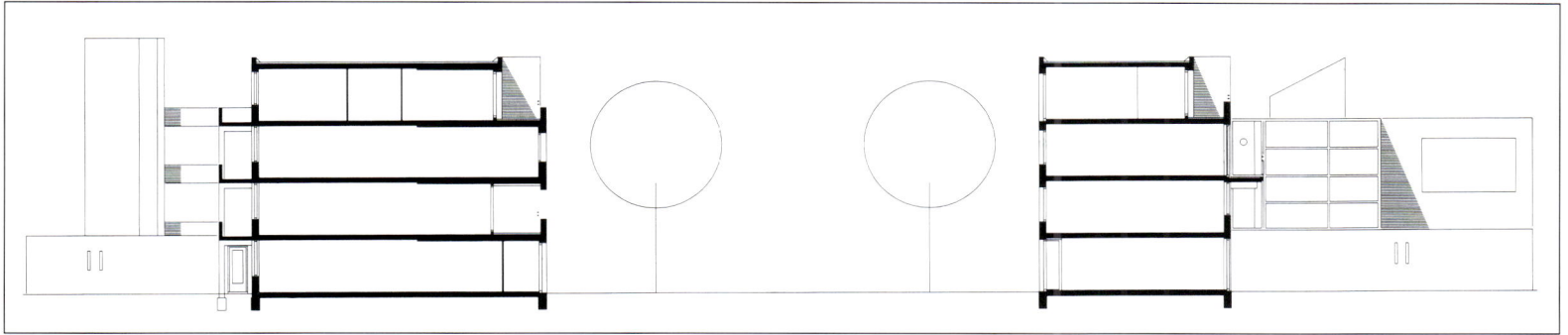

Cross section

The building located on the east part is lower and turns to adapt to the existing buildings in Bredaseweg.

Maki and Associates

Hillside West

Tokyo, Japan

Photographs:
Toshiharu Kitajima Shinkenchiku-sha

Architect:
Maki and Associates

Hillside Terrace is a complex composed mainly of apartments and shops. It is located in Dai-kanyama, not far from Shibuya Station, a major terminal in central Tokyo. The first phase of the project was initiated at the end of the 1960s and there have been several subsequent phases leading up to Hillside West, which was constructed in 1998.

Hillside Terrace was a creative experiment in urban design, aimed at constructing a townscape using the architectural language of modernism. The most recent scheme - Hillside West - follows this philosophy in its pursuit of the creation of an informal realm within an urban setting.

The Hillside West site lies between Kyu-Yamate Avenue to the front, and a quiet residential street at the back, with a 5,5 meter difference in level between the two streets. The complex is laid out in three main volumes, each with its own specific character and each adopting the height of the neighboring developments.

Different colors ranging from white to gray, and different materials such as aluminum, glass and Corona mosaic tile have been used on the building's surfaces. The rear space between the individual tracts has been laid out as a small garden, which forms a transition between the courtyard areas at the center of the complex and the residential street. There is a semi-public route threaded between the three buildings that enables pedestrians to cut through the site to the residential street at the rear.

In front of the living areas there is a louvered screen suspended at a distance of 75 cm from the facade. This screen enhances the private character of these areas by acting as a visual filter, and it also provides shading for the balconies on this face. The screen is made of aluminum tubes which not only allow the penetration of fifty per cent of the light, but which also seem to reflect the light into the depths of the rooms beyond, thereby creating a bright and airy interior atmosphere.

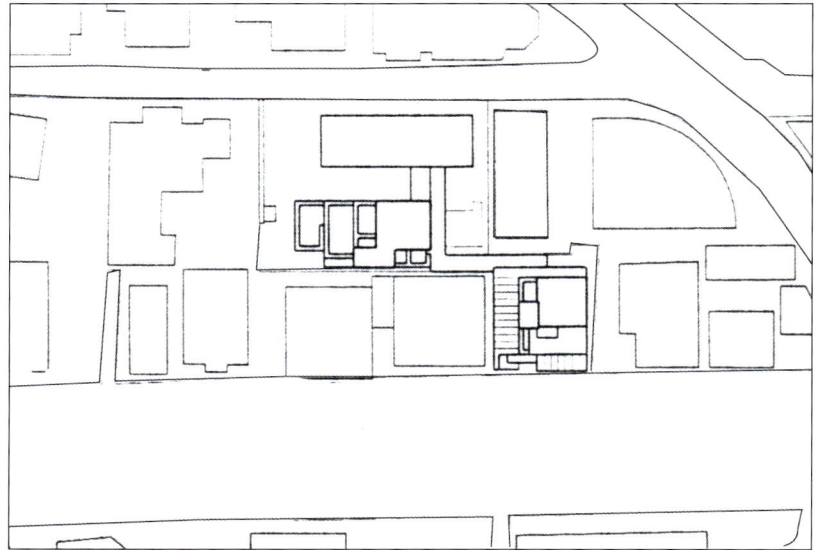

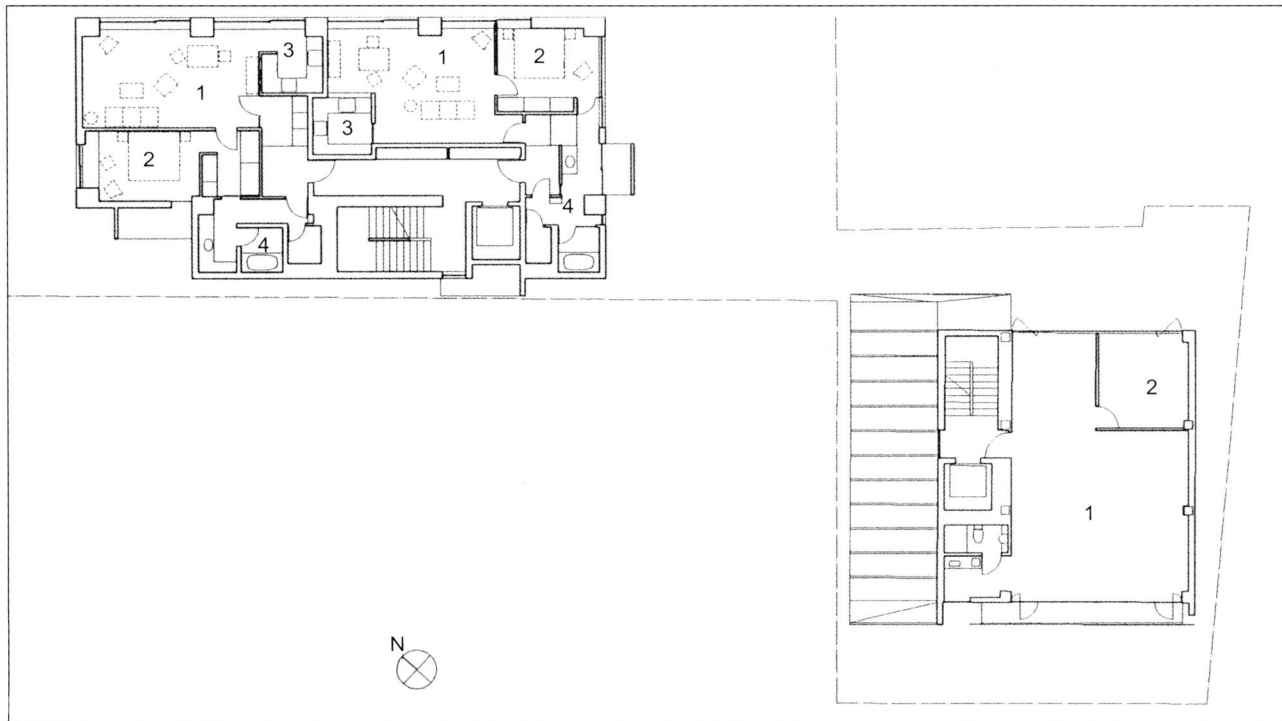

Third floor plan

1. Living Room
2. Bedroom
3. Kitchen
4. Bath

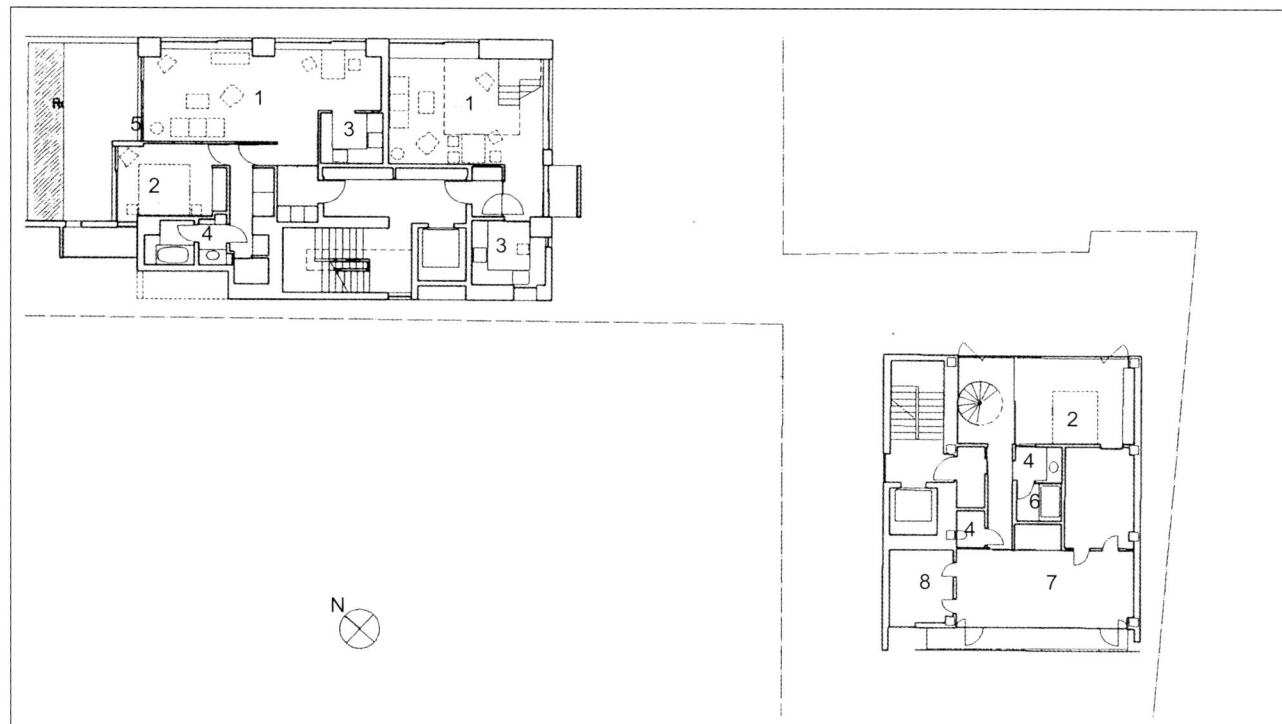

Fourth floor plan

1. Living Room
2. Bedroom
3. Kitchen
4. Bath
5. Roof Terrace
6. Closet
7. Living Room
8. Library

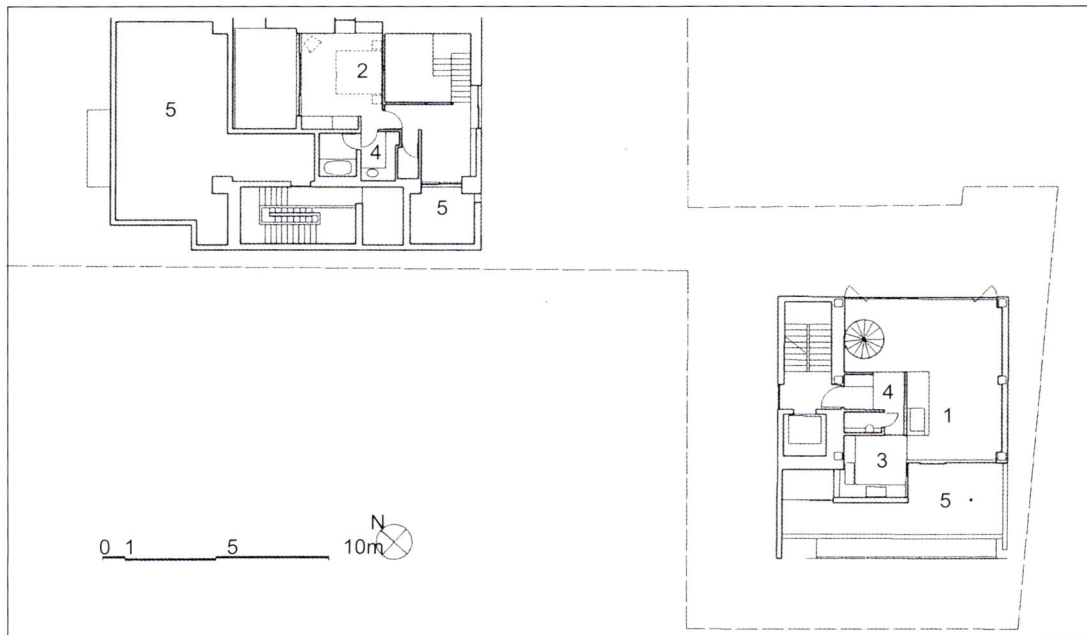

1. Living Room
2. Bedroom
3. Kitchen
4. Bath
5. Roof Terrace

Fith floor plan

The curtain facade construction consists of 15 mm diameter aluminum tubes at 30 mm centers. The aluminum tubes are riveted to a framework suspended from the steel load-bearing structure of the building. The true facade behind the screen consists of room-height aluminum casement elements.

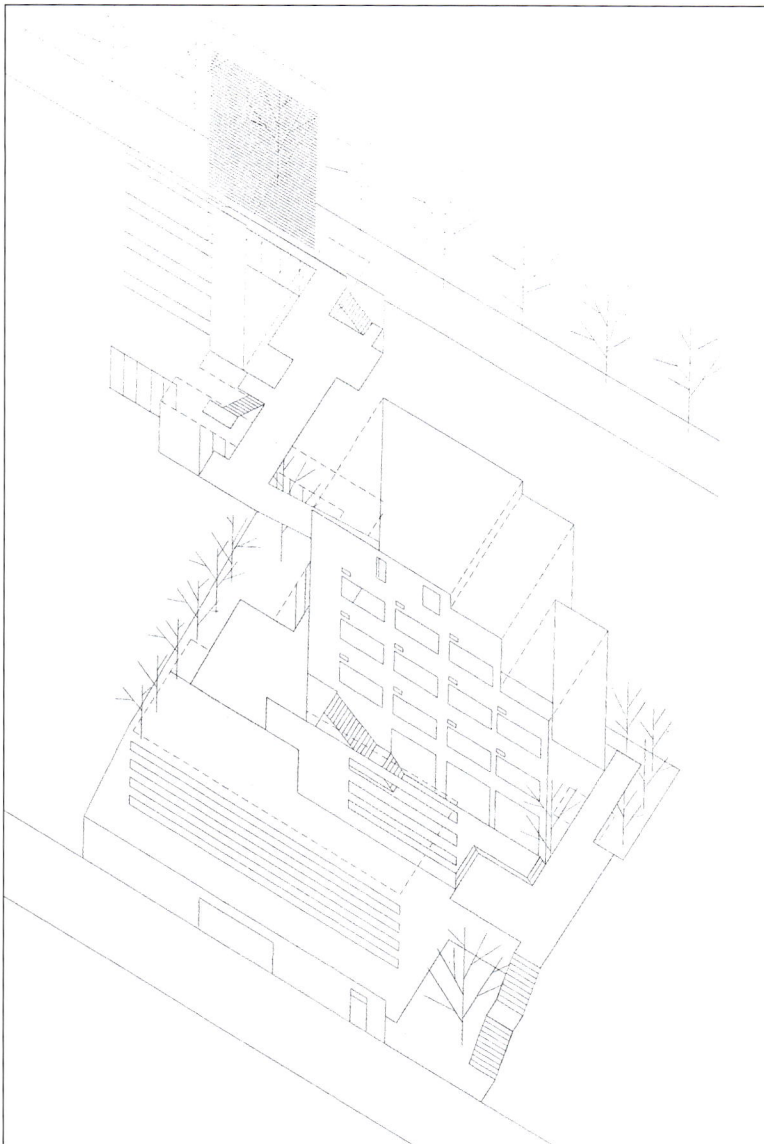

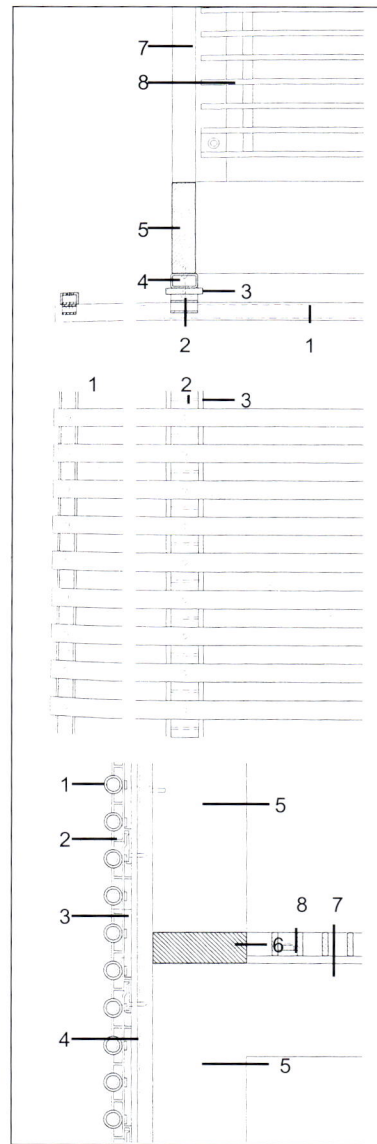

1. 15 mm dia. aluminum tube, riveted
2. Aluminum section
3. 5/30 mm aluminum flat
4. 22/12/1.5 mm stainless-steel RHS
5. Steel flats: 19/75 mm
6. 25/75 mm steel flat
7. 6/25 mm steel flat
8. 4.5/19 mm galvanized steel flat

Enclosure detail

Brullet, Frutos, de Luna y Sanmartín

129 Social Housing Apartments

El Prat de Llobregat, Spain

Photographs:
Lluís Casals

Architect:
Brullet, Frutos, de Luna y Sanmartín

This project was developed within a fairly unstructured urban development plan, where the housing block is a very isolated unit, surrounded by large plots with constructions whose volumes have not been designed with the urban fabric of the overall complex in mind. Thus, it was decided to accept the block's isolated situation, giving it an autonomous image with regards to the other constructions. The idea is that its considerable size will give it a passive role in the organization of the new pedestrian avenue and urban zone.

The block's isolation also led to the decision to route the apartments' pedestrian access through the large inner courtyard. The courtyard access enabled the correction of the one-meter difference in floor level to the ground-floor apartments on one side, also allowing access to the apartments facing the pedestrian avenue from a level above the ground floor shops.

Two slightly inclined planes, which thereby allow maximum visual control of the space, comprise the courtyard, which has been fitted with trees; the surface has been paved in order to prevent rapid deterioration and to avoid elevated maintenance costs.

Aside from the main courtyard access, there are also pedestrian access routes on the other three corners of the block.

For the actual construction of the apartments, an effort was made to optimize the established surfaces of 70 and 90 sqm for the 129 apartments by introducing the concept of adapting the dwelling to different uses. Each unit has a day and night zone, based on the meticulous study of the relation between spaces: for cooking and eating, the location of the toilets, and the laundry area. The most important aspect is being able to integrate these spaces in diverse ways.

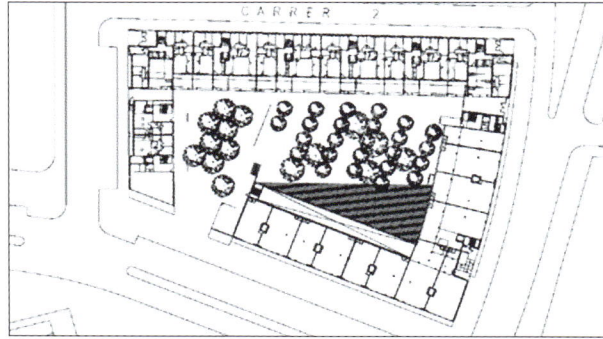

Site plan

Due to the block's isolation, access to the homes from the inner courtyard was established. Making use of the block's trapezoidal shape, a portion of the narrowest end of the courtyard was left unbuilt in order to create a large entrance, light penetration and openness toward the exterior.

Type floor plan

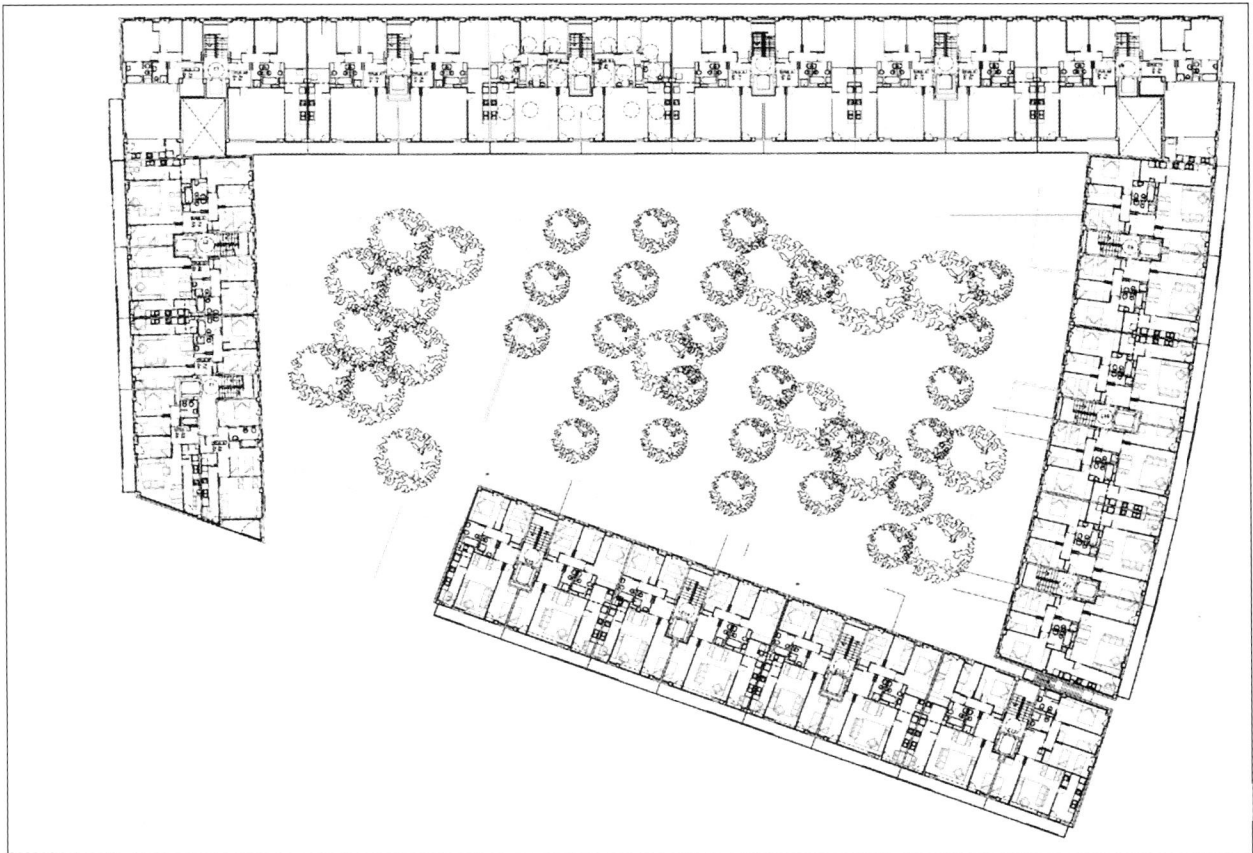

Ground floor plan

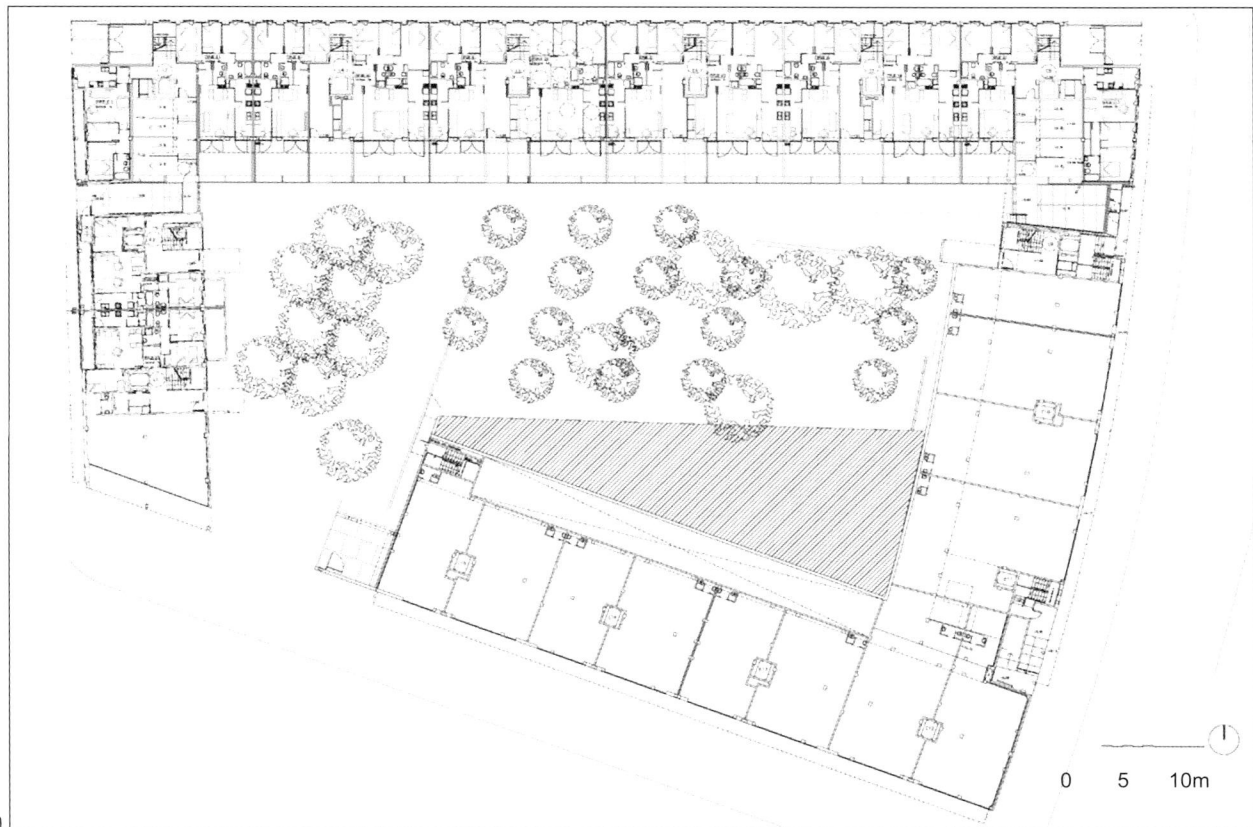

0   5   10m

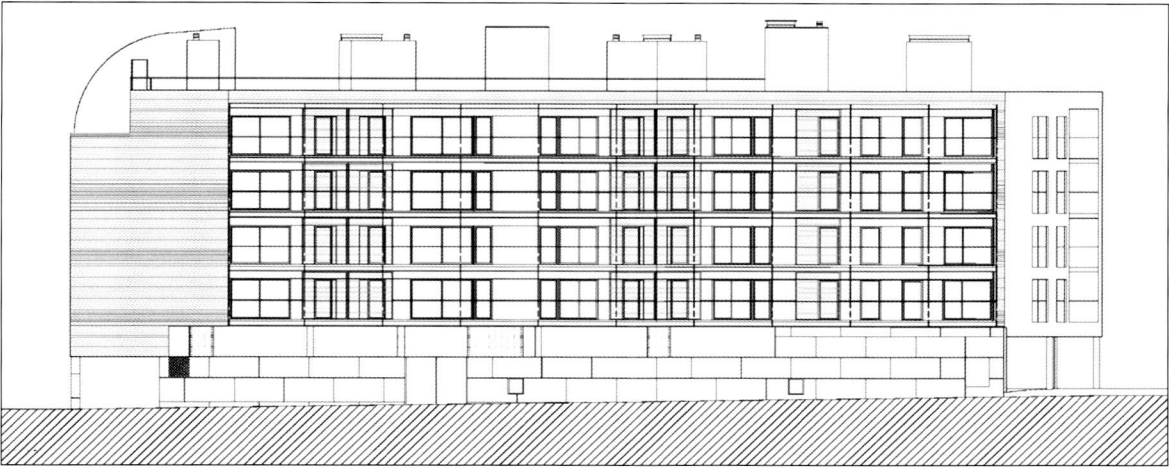

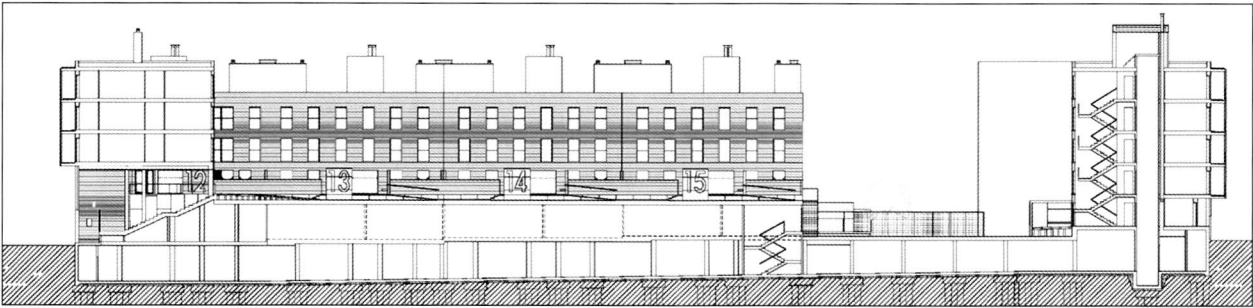

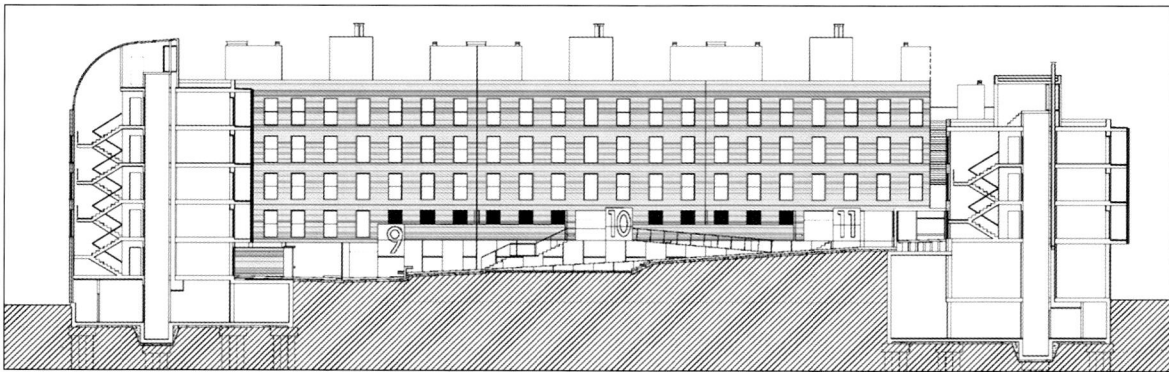

Sections

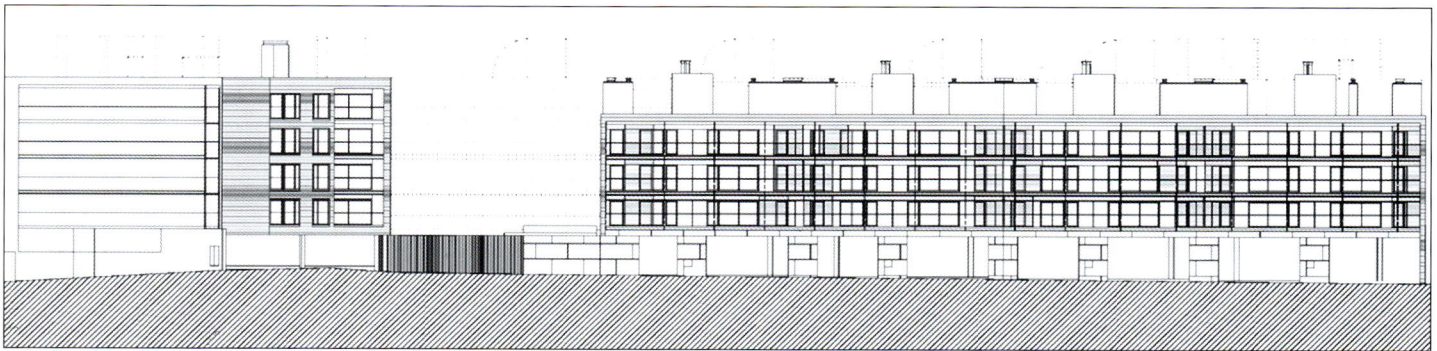

Elevations

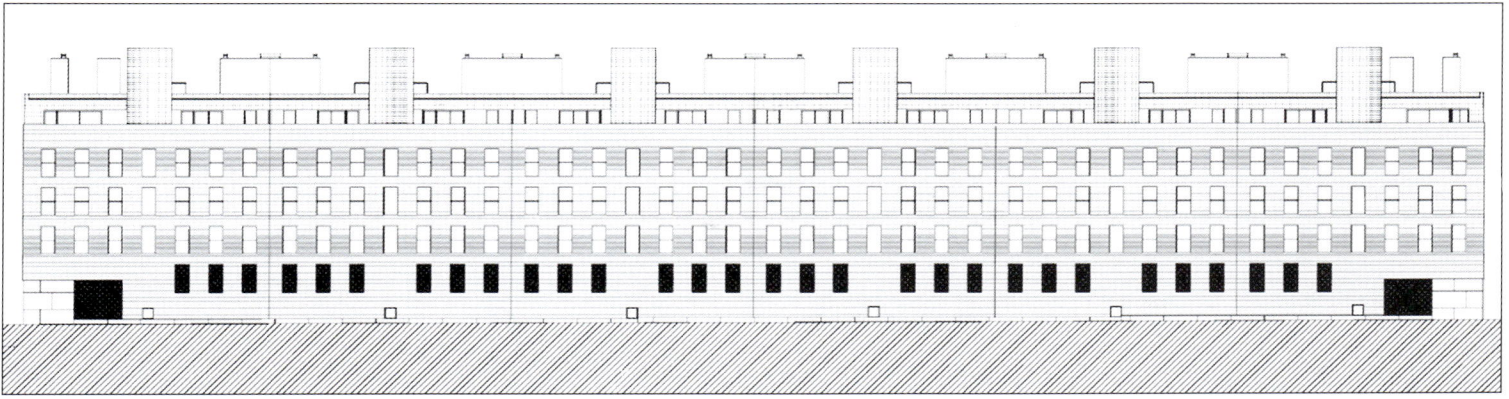

The block's courtyard is seen as a large space for recreation and relaxation, where the height of the buildings has been strategically designed to allow the maximum sunlight and to reduce shadows at certain times of the day.

Maurer & Orsi architectes

Nursing Home for the Elderly "Raymond Thomas"

Rennes, France

Photographs:
Michel Denance / Archipress

Architect:
Maurer & Orsi architectes

Here, the underlying premise behind the design is that any good project must be based on a study of the neighborhood and the way people live in the area. This process is in turn based on two ideas: the duty to preserve connections between streets, existing buildings and public space, which represents the heart of housing blocks; and the incorporation of human dimensions - that is, small scale for the occupants.

This two-story building is composed of a compact base, which contains services and four wings of private rooms, with east- and west-facing windows (as is the case with the surrounding buildings), arranged around a nucleus of communal spaces. An entirely glazed volume containing the reception hall, dining room and restrooms, which all face the public garden, makes up a portion of the base. The resulting transparency is particularly important as it visually connects the public spaces with the garden.

The administration spaces, laundry and storerooms are organized around a central patio, a spatial distribution which restricts the comings and goings of employees and rationally organizes vertical circulation.

Half perched on concrete legs and half laying on the base, the building shelters the parking lot from rain and creates a public space beyond the main entrance.

Different facilities, such as a library, tea-room and hairdressing salon, are dispersed throughout the various levels of the four wings. A sitting room is located at the intersection of the wings and provides an area where residents can meet.

All corridors are naturally lit and accented by the rhythm of the outer curves of the individual bathrooms.

Each individual resident's room constitutes the most intimate and personalized space of the nursing home, with each occupant furnishing it as desired. A balcony can be used nearly year-round, having a rolling shutter that lies flush with the exterior walls, enabling residents to adjust the level of light entering their rooms. The slope of the metal guard rail has been designed to allow wheelchair users to lean on it. All these advantages (furniture, natural light, outside views) let them choose their lifestyle and create their own world.

The primary construction materials used -zinc, steel and concrete- reveal an economy of means in promoting large rooms (an average of 25 sqm instead of the 20 initially stipulated in the program).

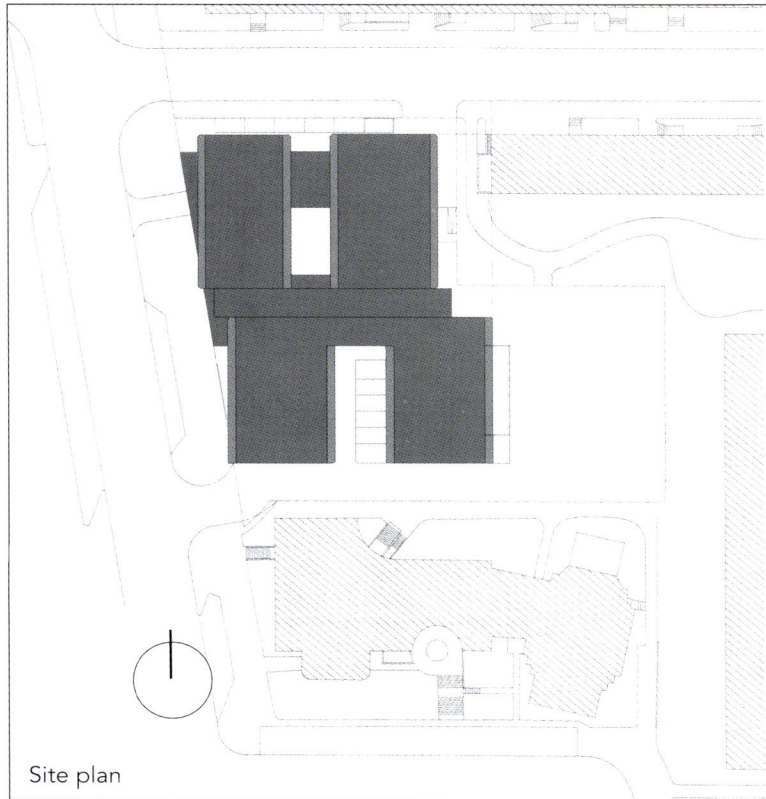

Site plan

This process is based on two ideas: the duty to preserve connections between streets, existing buildings and public space, which represents the heart of housing blocks; and the incorporation of human dimensions - that is, small scale for the occupants.

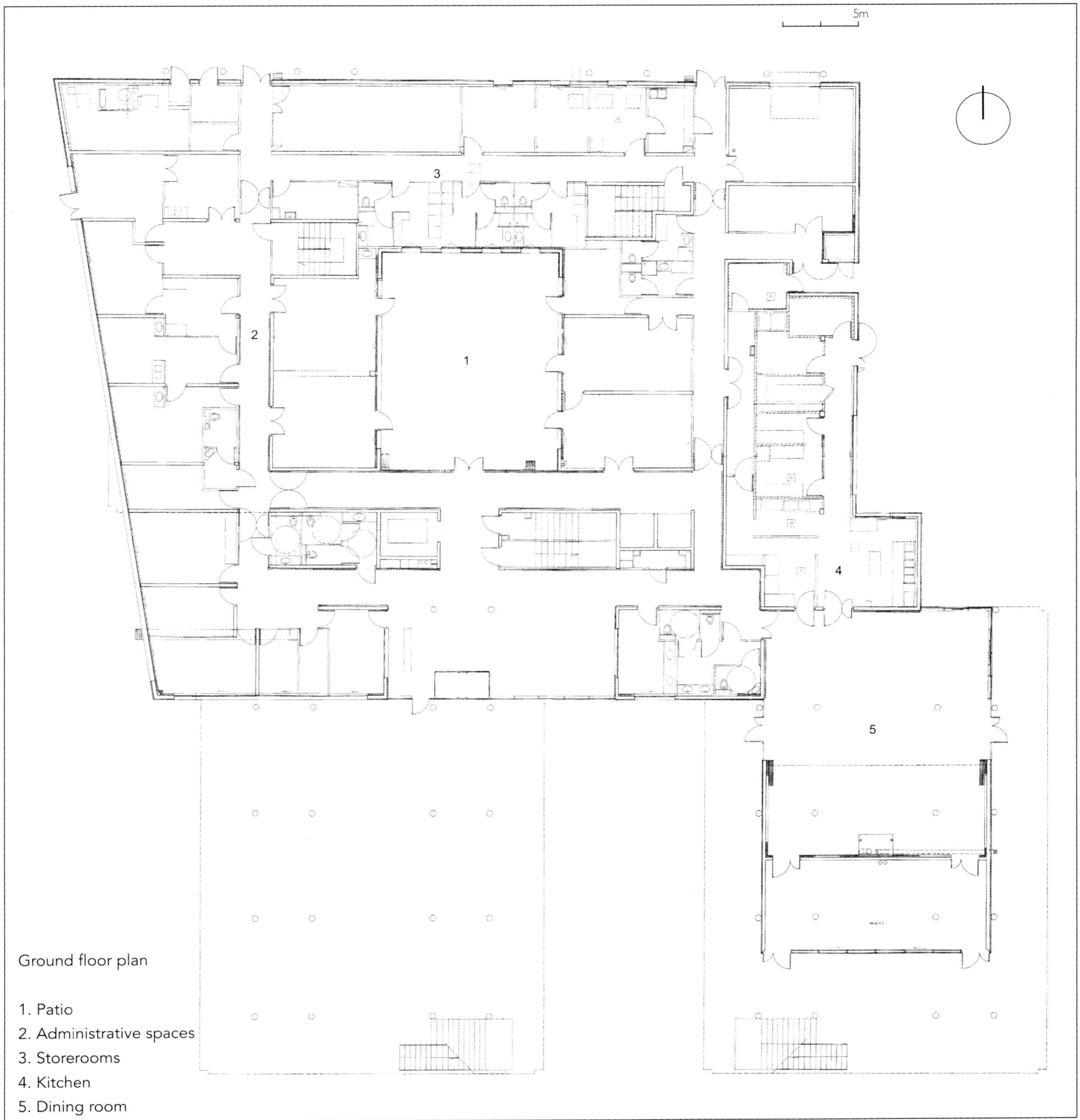

Ground floor plan

1. Patio
2. Administrative spaces
3. Storerooms
4. Kitchen
5. Dining room

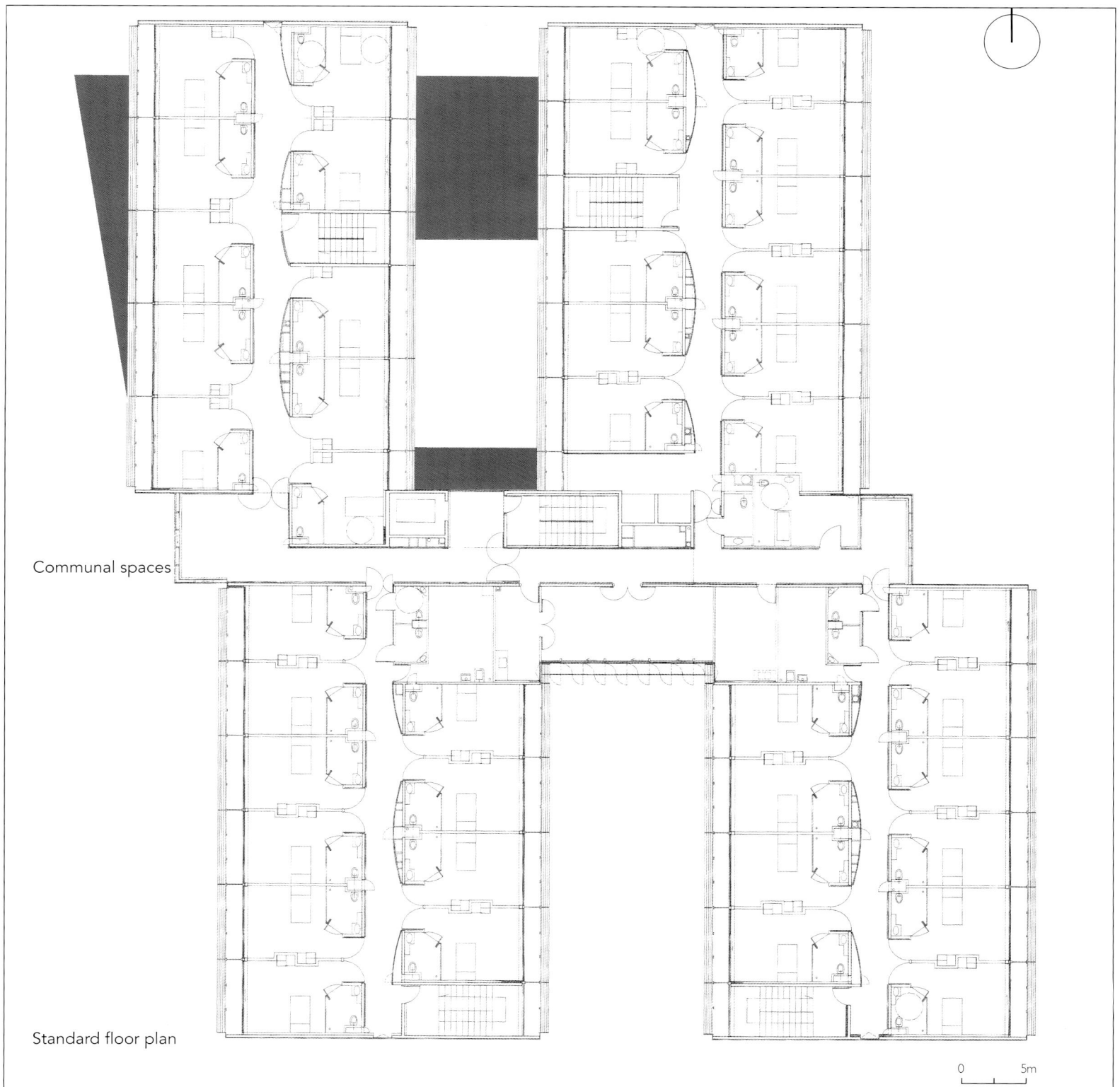

Communal spaces

Standard floor plan

0   5m

This building is composed of a compact base, which contains services
and four wings of private rooms, with east- and west-facing windows,
arranged around a nucleus of communal spaces.

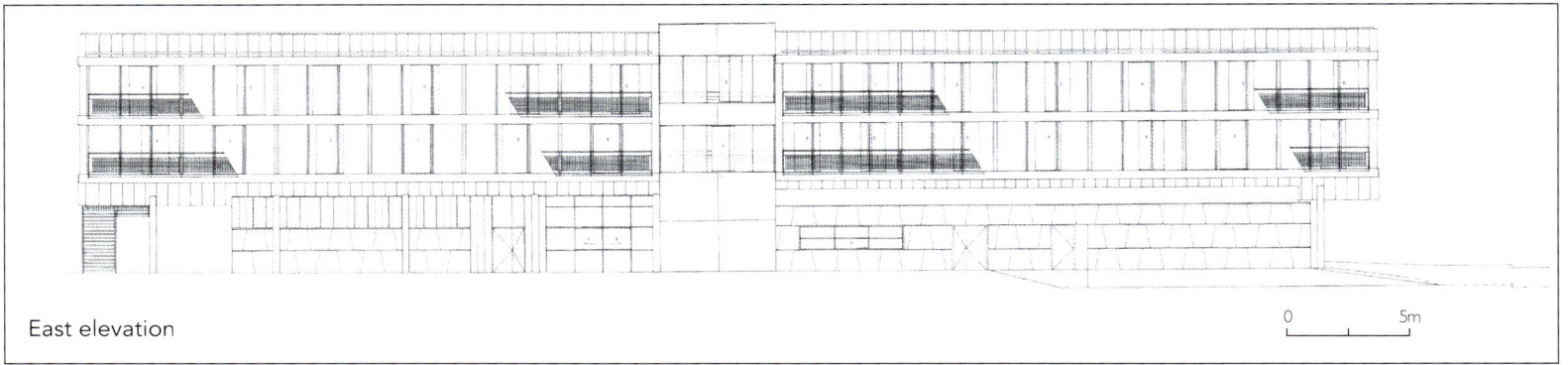

East elevation

0   5m

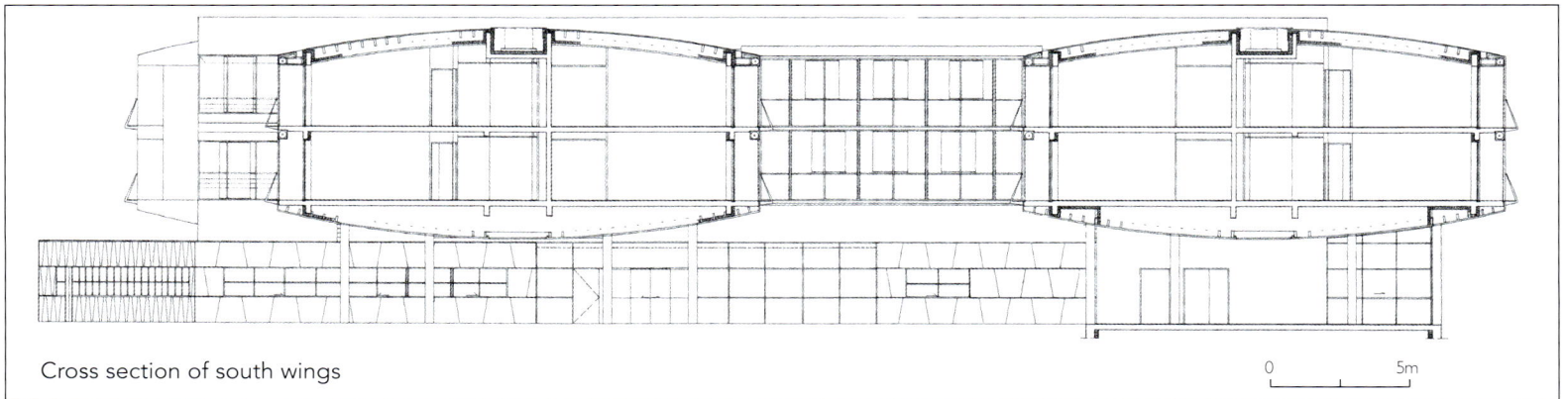

Cross section of south wings

0   5m

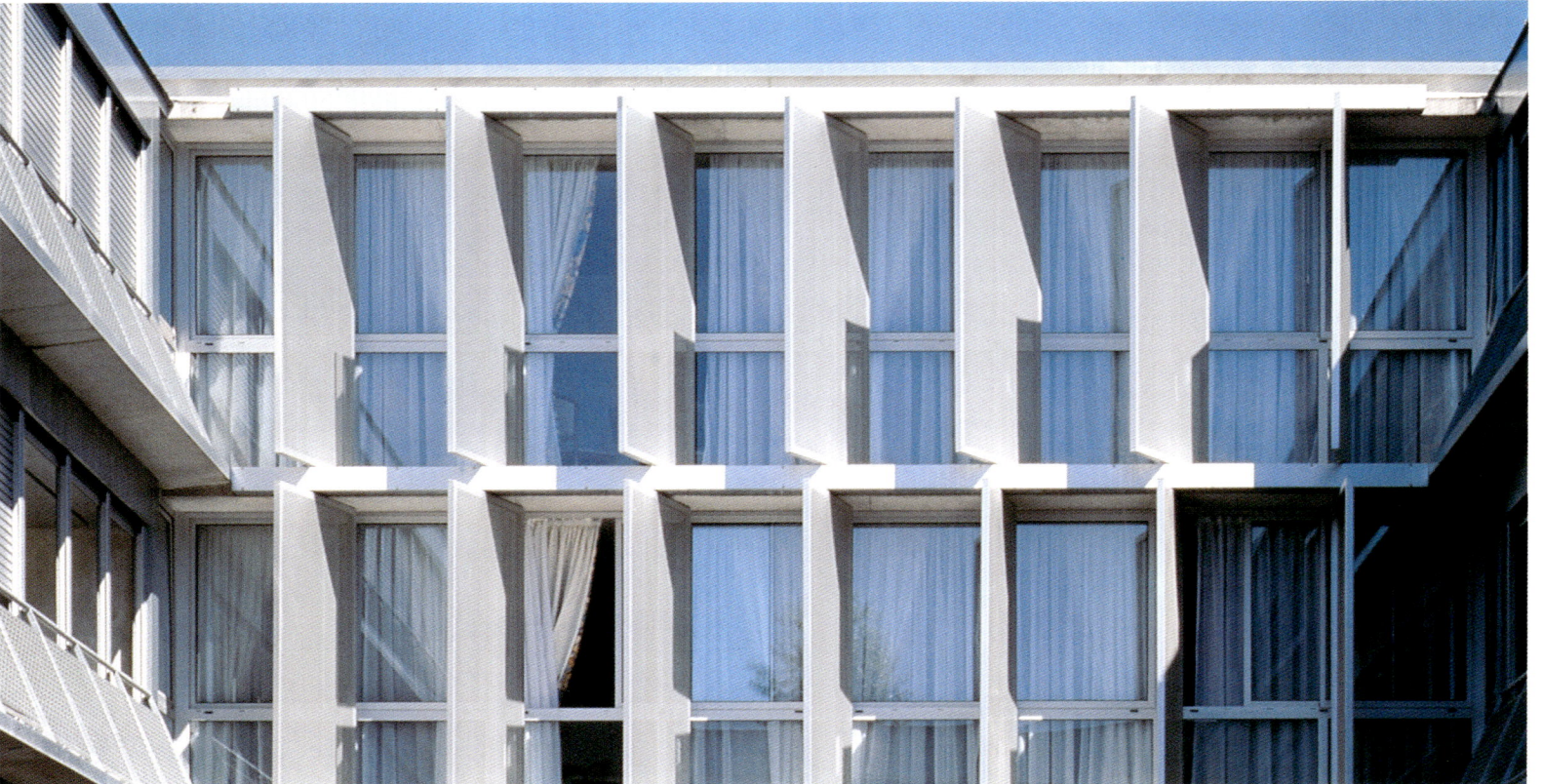

Floor plan of apartment type 1

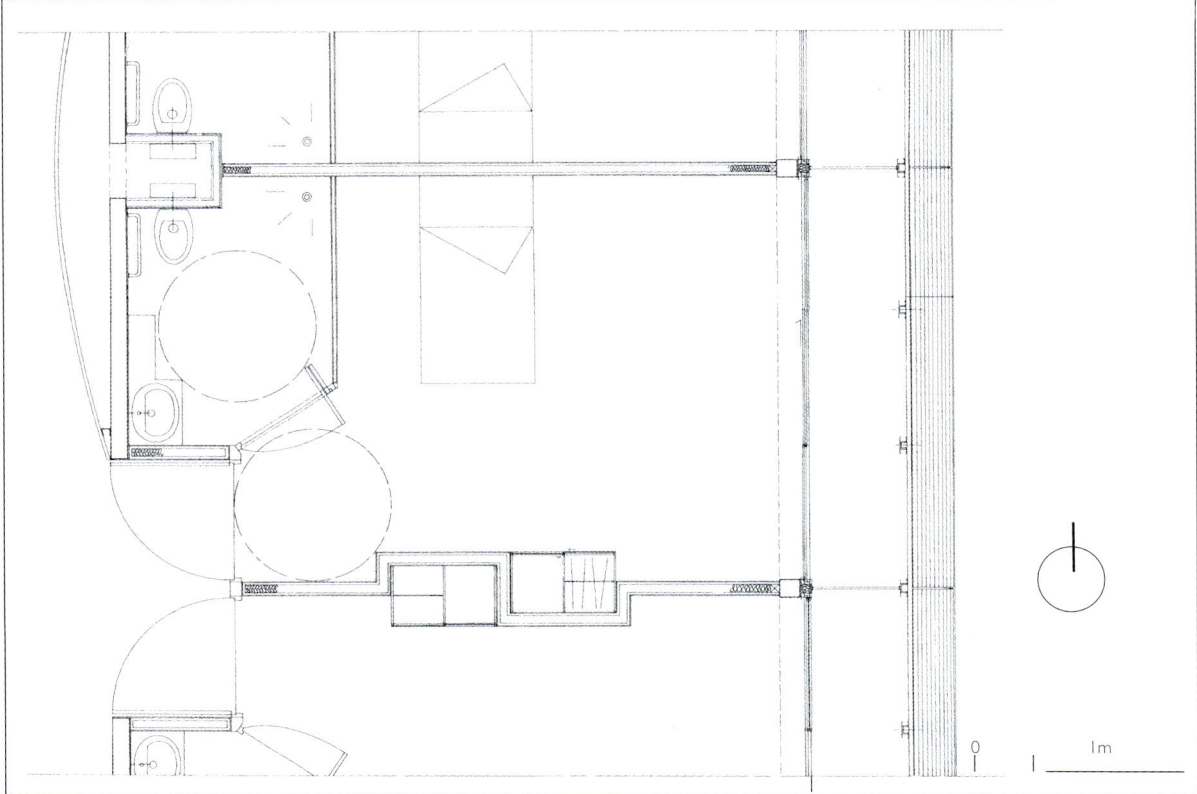

0   1m

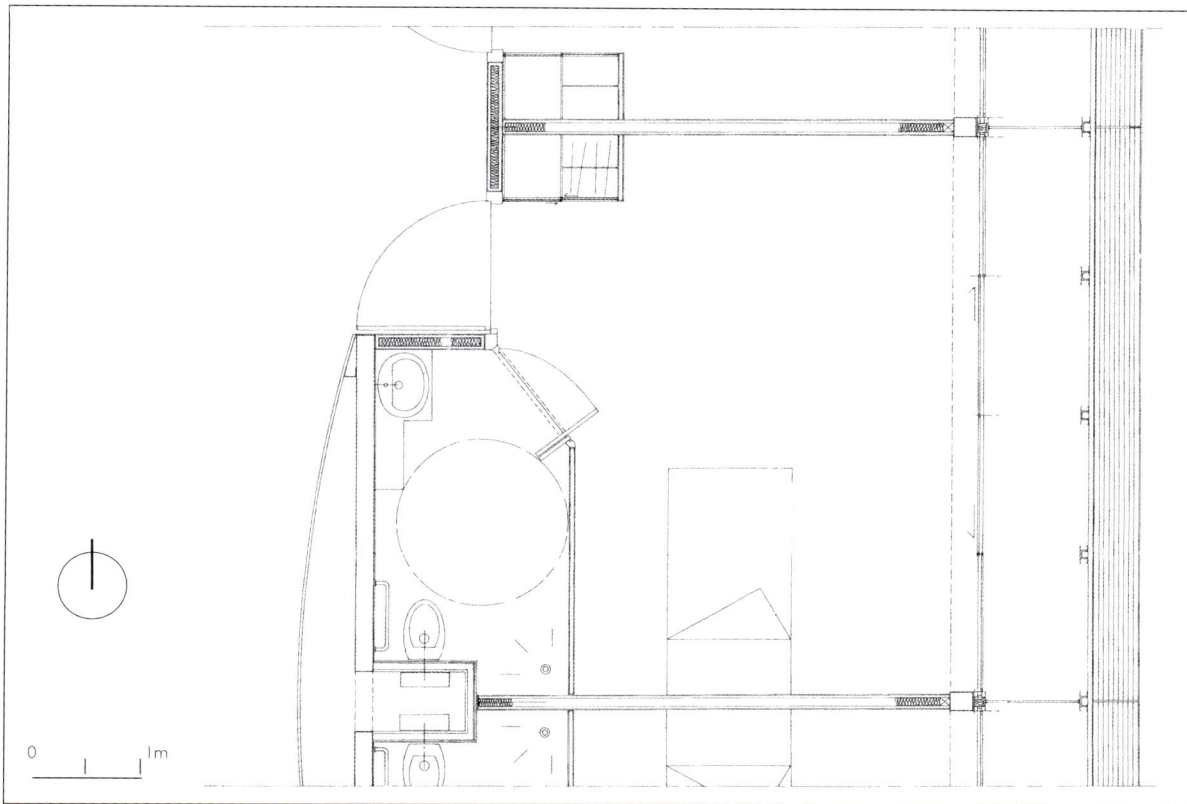

Floor plan of apartment type 2

Alberto de Pineda

Residence in Puigcerdà

Puigcerdà, Spain

Photographs:
Johvan Hovart

Architect:
Alberto de Pineda

To address the shortage of accommodation for the elderly in the region of La Cerdanya, the town council of Puigcerdà undertook the creation of a complex with 103 rooms, 91 of which are equipped for either single or double occupany, and 12 of which are single occupancy nursing units.

Set 1200 meters above sea level, the building is nestled into a wide, open valley, thereby allowing for the optimization of natural lighting conditions, in spite of its Pyrenean climate with extreme winter and summer temperatures.

Measuring 270x170x250 meters, the plot lies on an east-west slope with a four meter change in level. The coefficient between the building's floor space (which would be 5000 sqm) and the site's available surface area of 9280 sqm, was deemed highly advantageous and enabled a great deal of the surroundings to be lanscaped.

Since the city council required that the residence should display high environmental quality and that it should not be treated as a large receptacle for dwellings, a series of single-galleried pavilions, with south-facing rooms and north-facing walkways, were proposed. This layout creates sequences of building and patios, avoiding excessive densification within the complex and tending toward a more extensive -as opposed to compact- building. Thus, a series of small neighborhoods with a succession of streets and spaces arise.

Natural materials, such as stone, slate and wood, were used.

112 sqm of solar panels, covering 62% of the heating and cooling needs of part of the residence, were installed on the roof of the services module. These panels, lying along the slope of the roof on the same plane as the slate finish, have been entirely integrated into the structure. Together, these elements form a black gable roof, thereby achieving visual integration. The technical installations, including boilers and high-efficiency solar heating and cooling units, are on the ground floor.

This installation reaps an annual reduction of 12,701 m^3 of gas and 24 tons of CO2 emissions, thereby adhering to European standards on energy savings, use of renewable energy sources and emissions reductions.

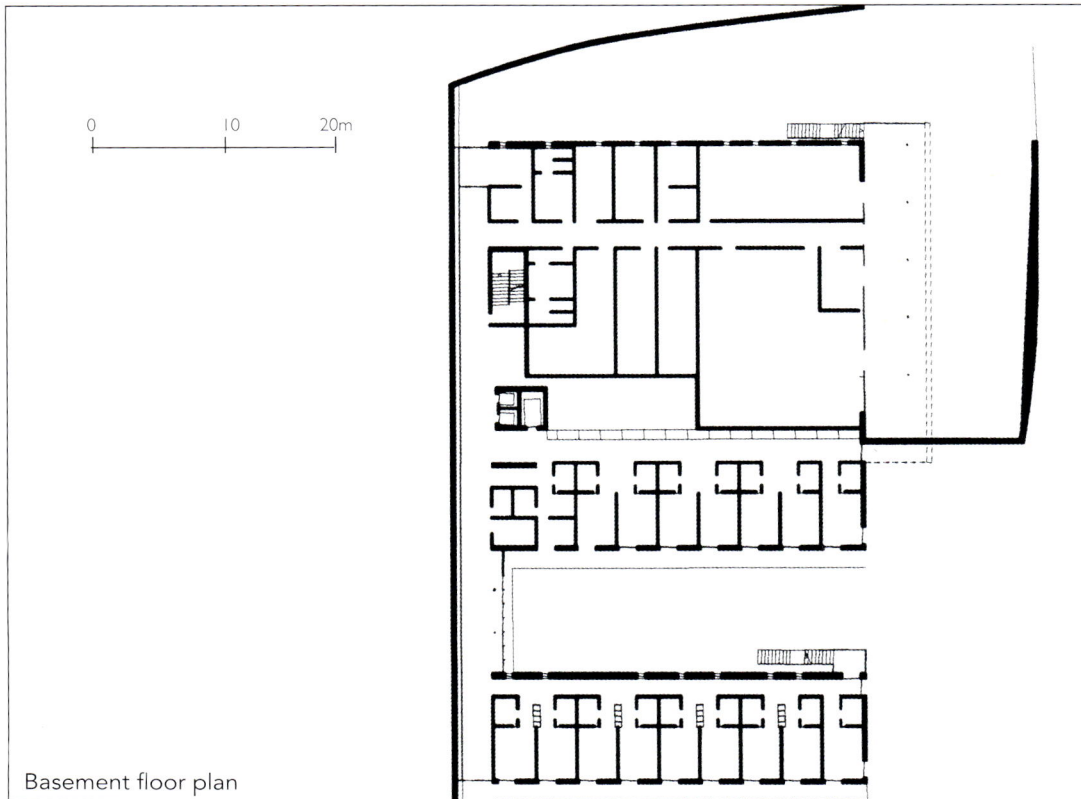

Basement floor plan

The building is shielded against the wind and the cold to the north via nearly blind stone walls with minimal openings. Conversely, it opens out toward the south, with a lighter facade and large window openings for the rooms. This means that the communal sitting rooms make full use of the sun's heat and also enjoy significant savings on energy.

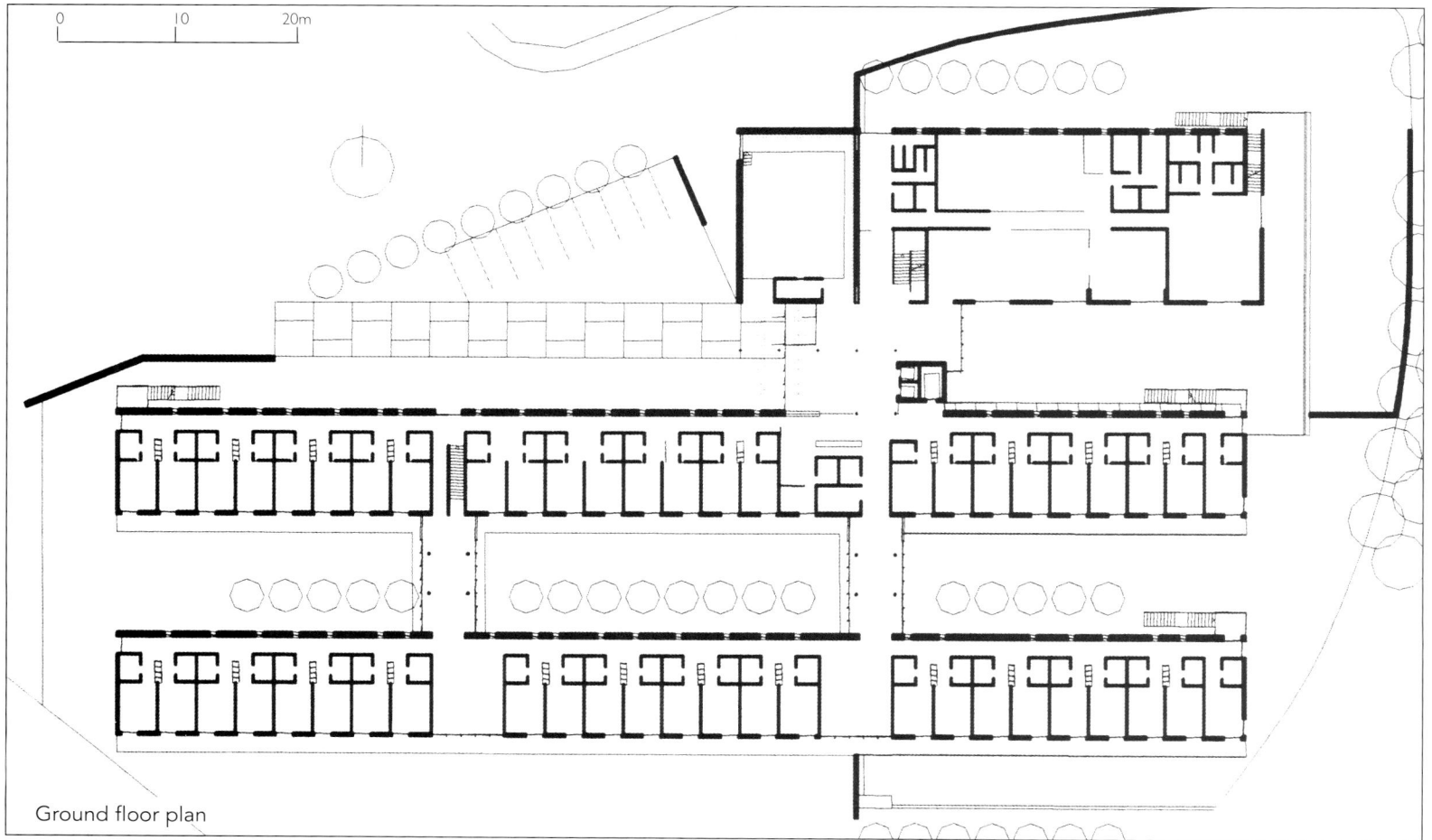

Ground floor plan

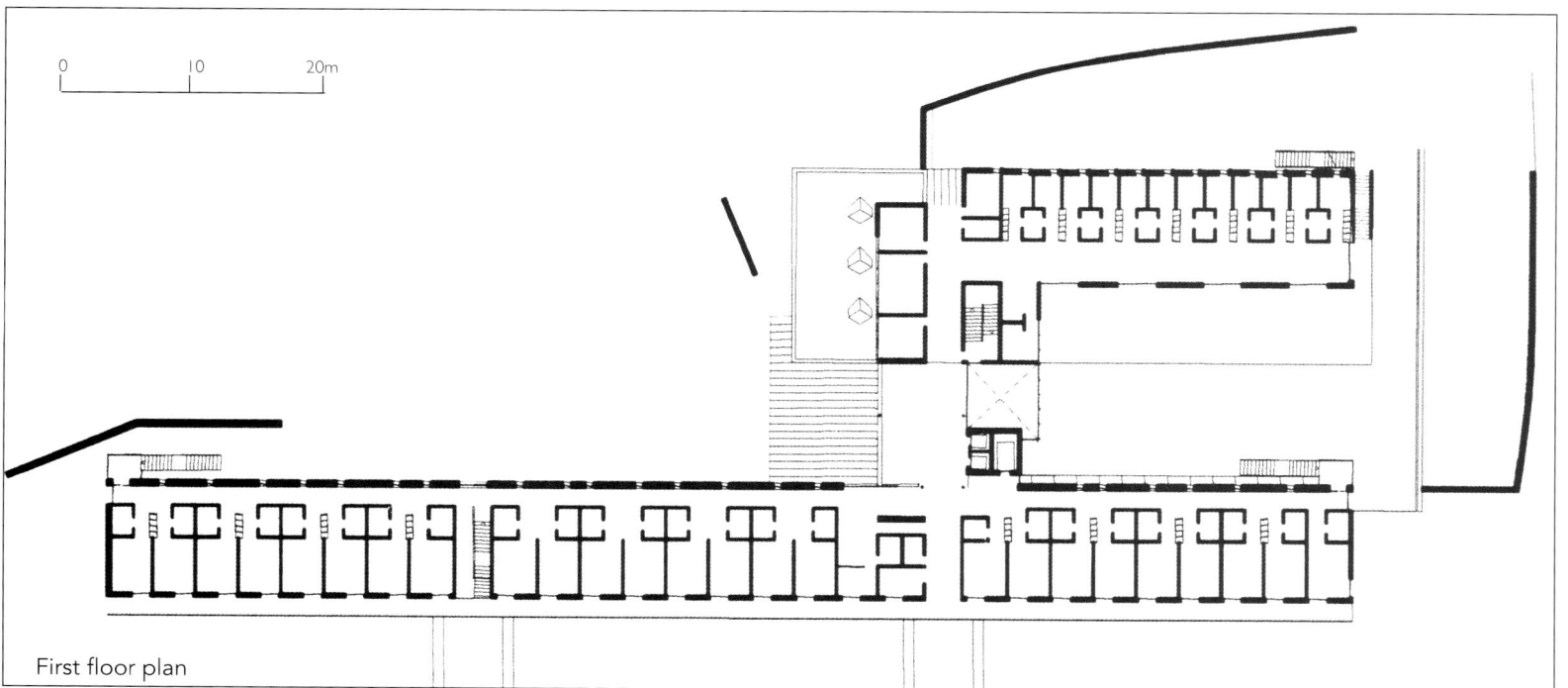

First floor plan

130

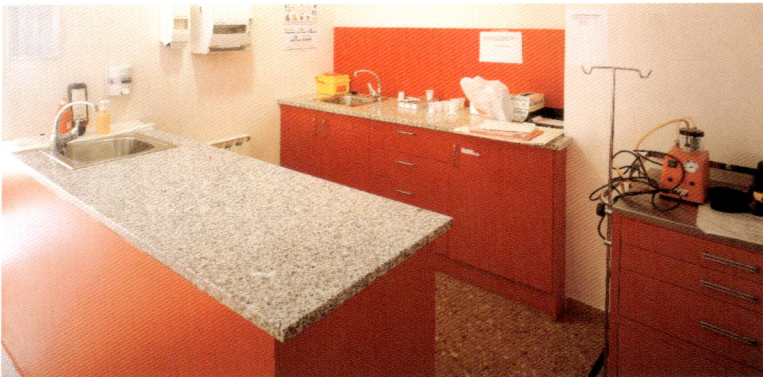

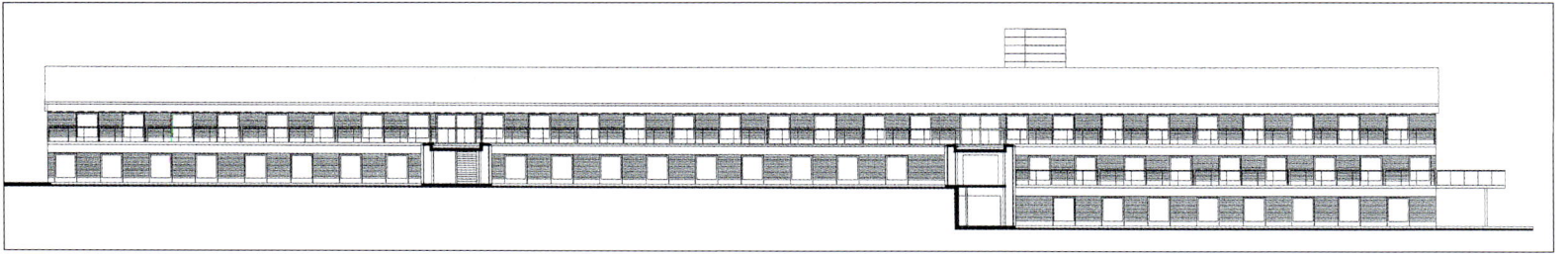

South elevation

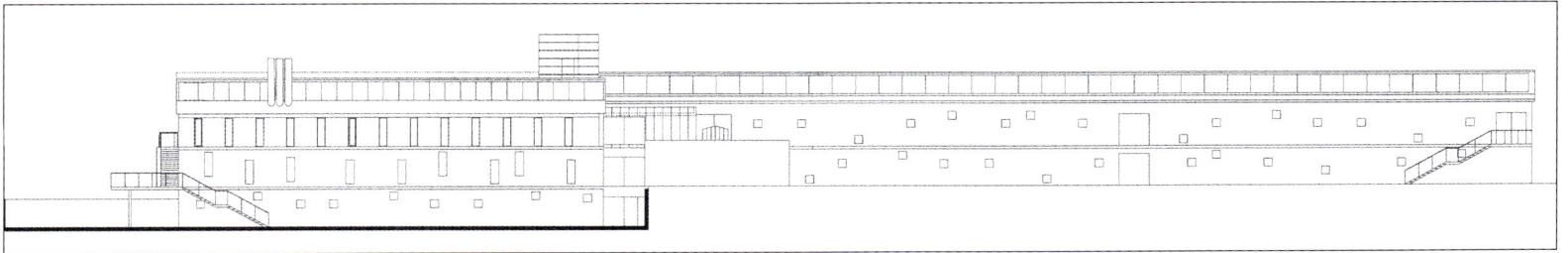

North elevation

Longitudinal section

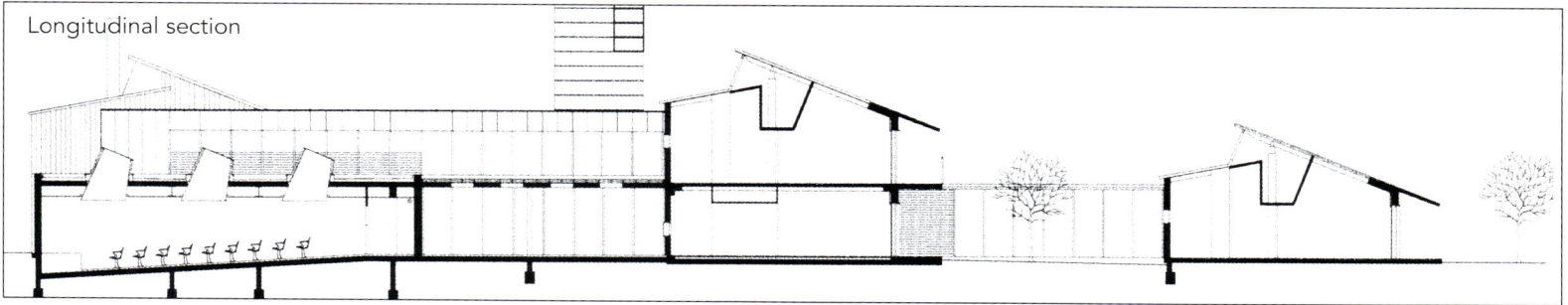

The construction responds to the site's unique weather conditions. It has been built with a reinforced concrete structure, with local stone cladding on the north facades, and wood insulation on the south facade. The roofs are sloped to handle snowfall and are clad in slate tiles.

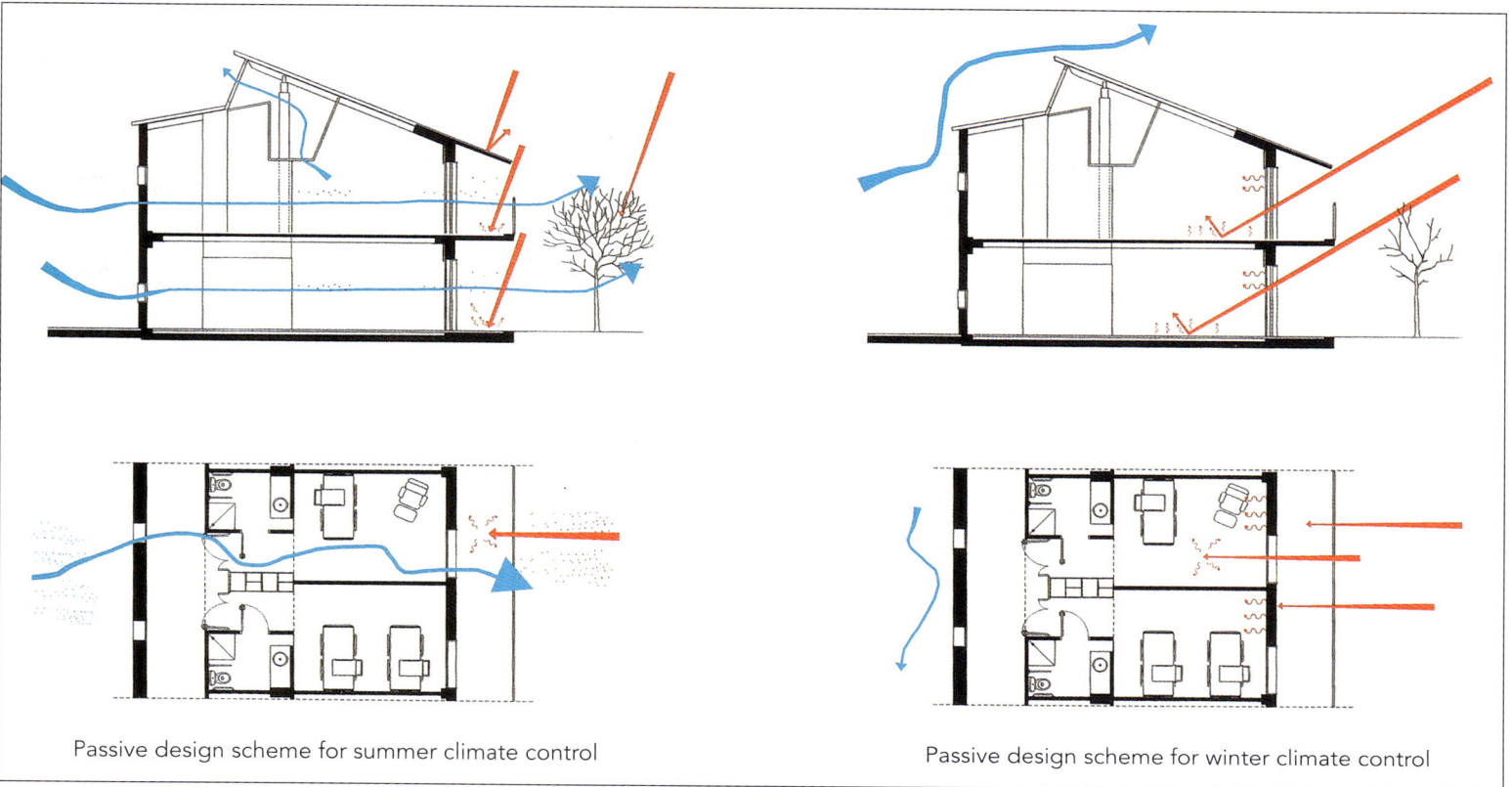

Passive design scheme for summer climate control

Passive design scheme for winter climate control

Alexandra Czerner

Multavitahof Bremen

Bremen, Germany

Photographs:
Klaus Frahm / Artur

Architect:
Alexandra Czerner

Multilava is Germany's largest women's shelter to date. Its goal is summarized in the creation of a safe, inhabitable multi-purpose space of high quality for women. In adapting the surroundings to their needs, residents are offered the opportunity to realize their full potential. This affects not only the residence, but it also adheres to the principle of mixing leisure activities with elderly accommodation. Thus, in addition to the dwelling units, there are places for work and entertainment as well as childcare facilities, all of which is especially important for mothers. According to the architect, "the concept of integration gives way to a dynamic architecture, creating an urban space with multiple spatial situations. The segments of the building are laid out in spiral form, establishing a dialogue amongst them. They include communal spaces, from public and semipublic to semiprivate: the inner courtyard, lobby, square and garden. The permeability of the building's elements joins the surroundings and the people in it. Thanks to the placement of the buildings, an inner courtyard, which is shielded from outside noise, has been created. The construction's south wall protects it from the noise of the day and night-time loading and unloading of products at the adjacent market".

The center was the winner of the prize awarded by the United Nations Centre of Human Settlement (UNCHS) for outstanding projects from around the world which bring improvements to the field of human urbanization. Only eight other projects in the world have been awarded this prize. The prize, a bronze plaque set on a 30x25cm mahogany base, surrounded by a laurel wreath, bears the inscription: "For improving shelter conditions, safety and quality of life of single women through innovative housing solutions".

Site plan

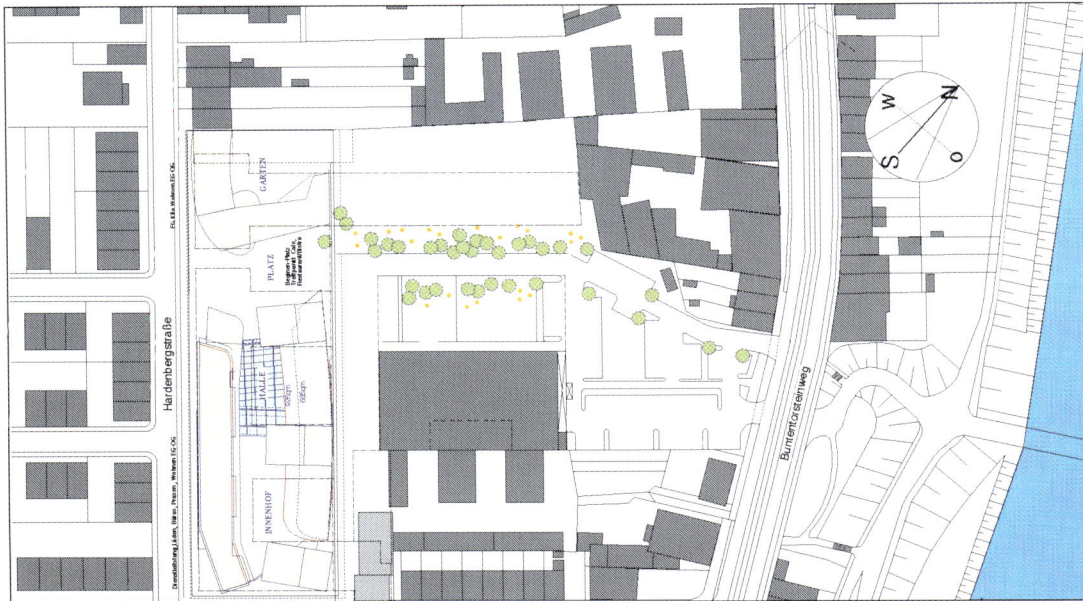

The center was designed as a small community, alternating private spaces with communal and gardened areas where inhabitants and visitors can socialize. Thus, for example, the placement of the building enables an inner courtyard which is shielded from outside noise.

Ground floor plan

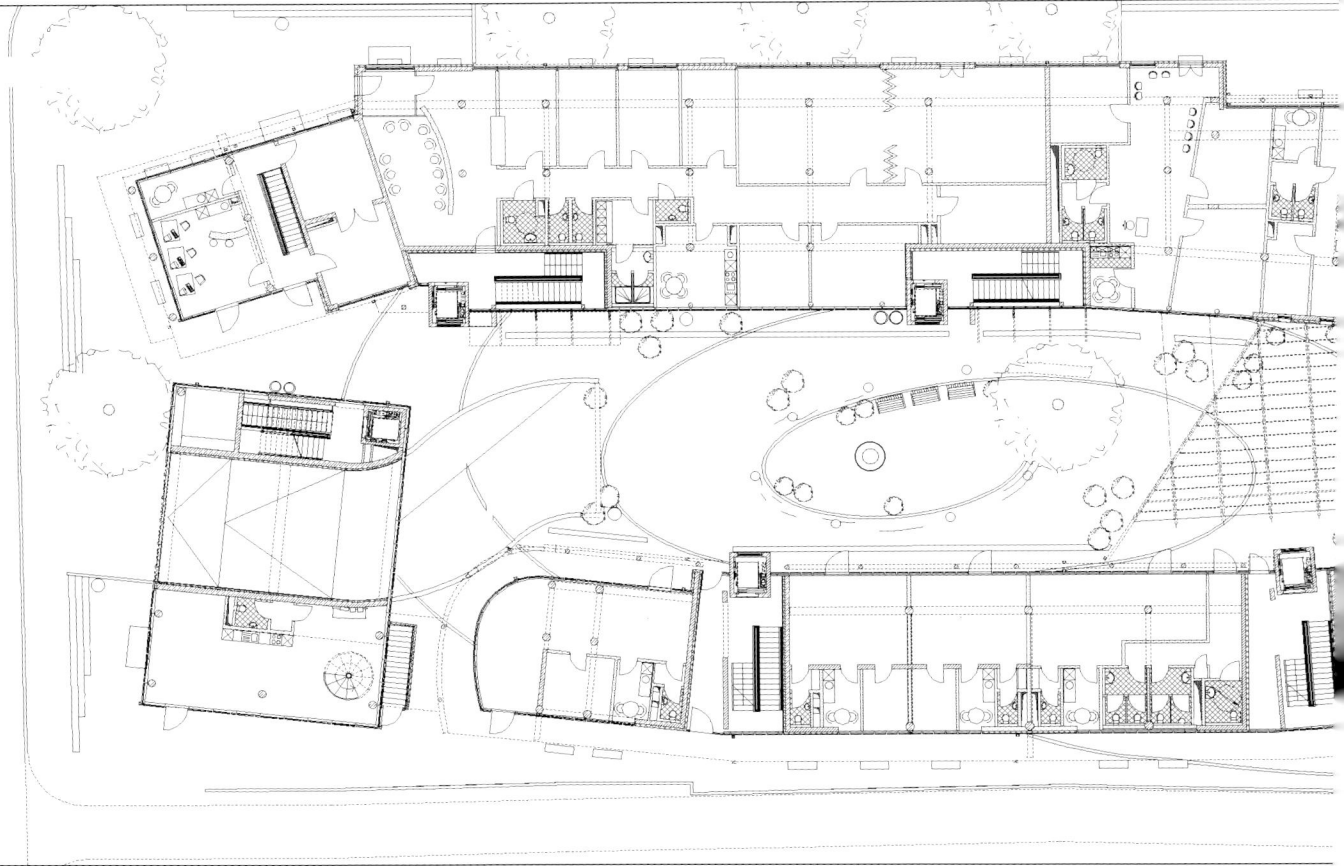

First floor plan

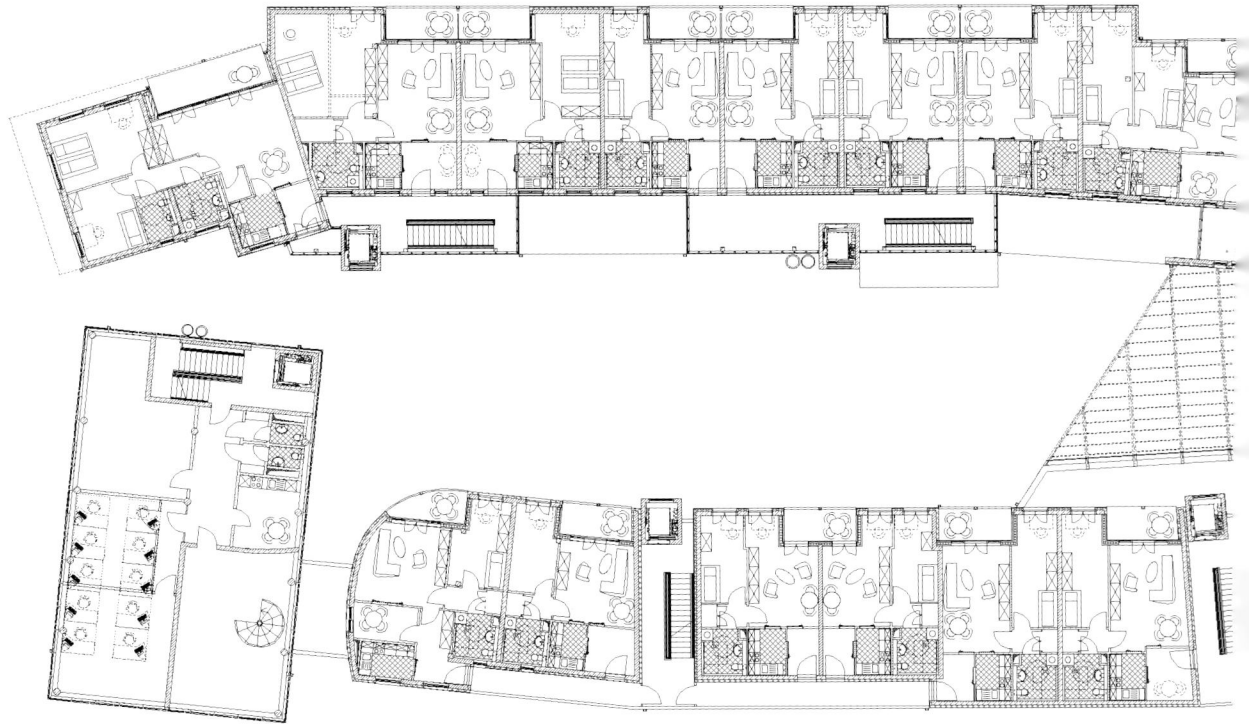

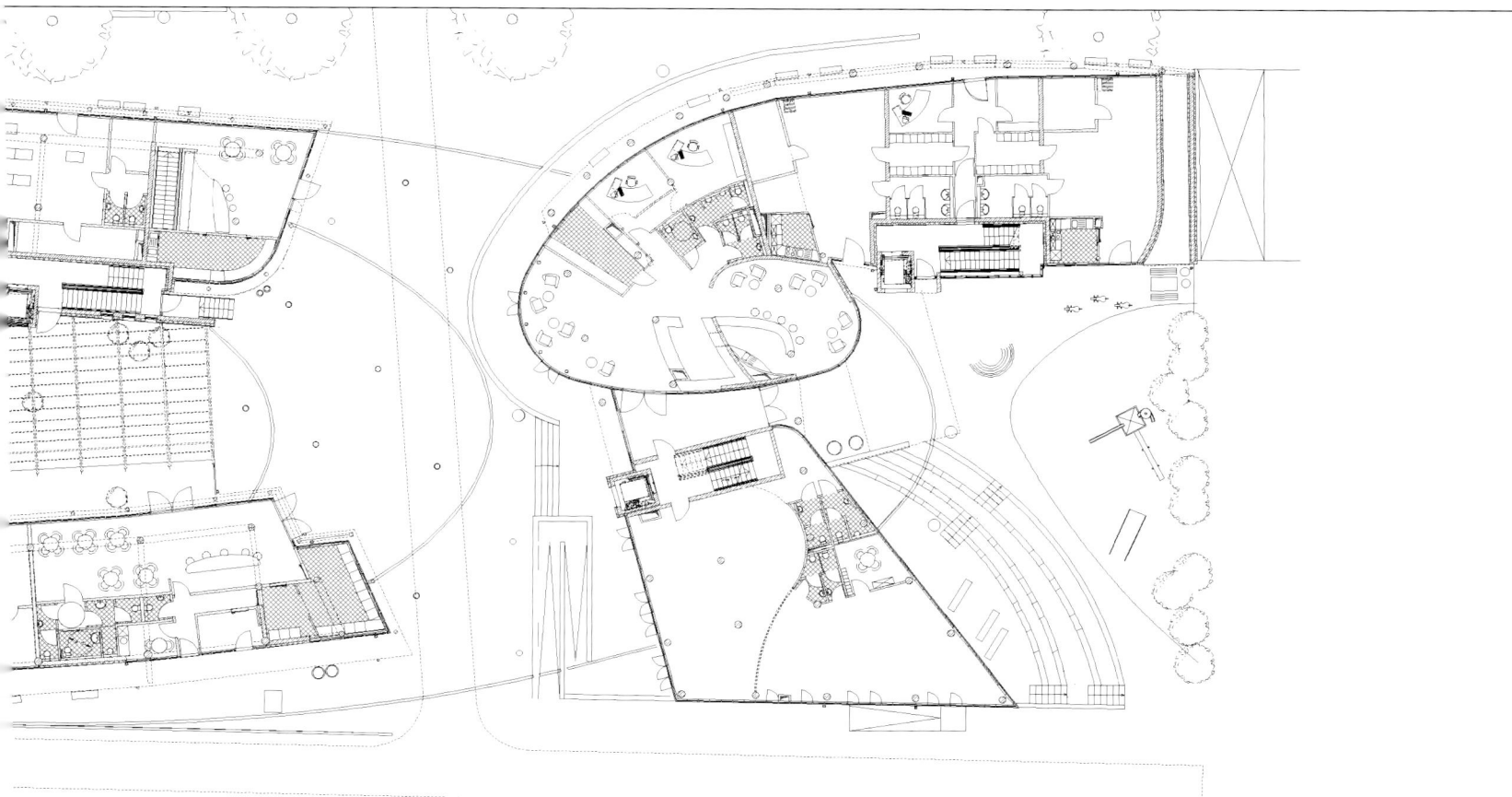

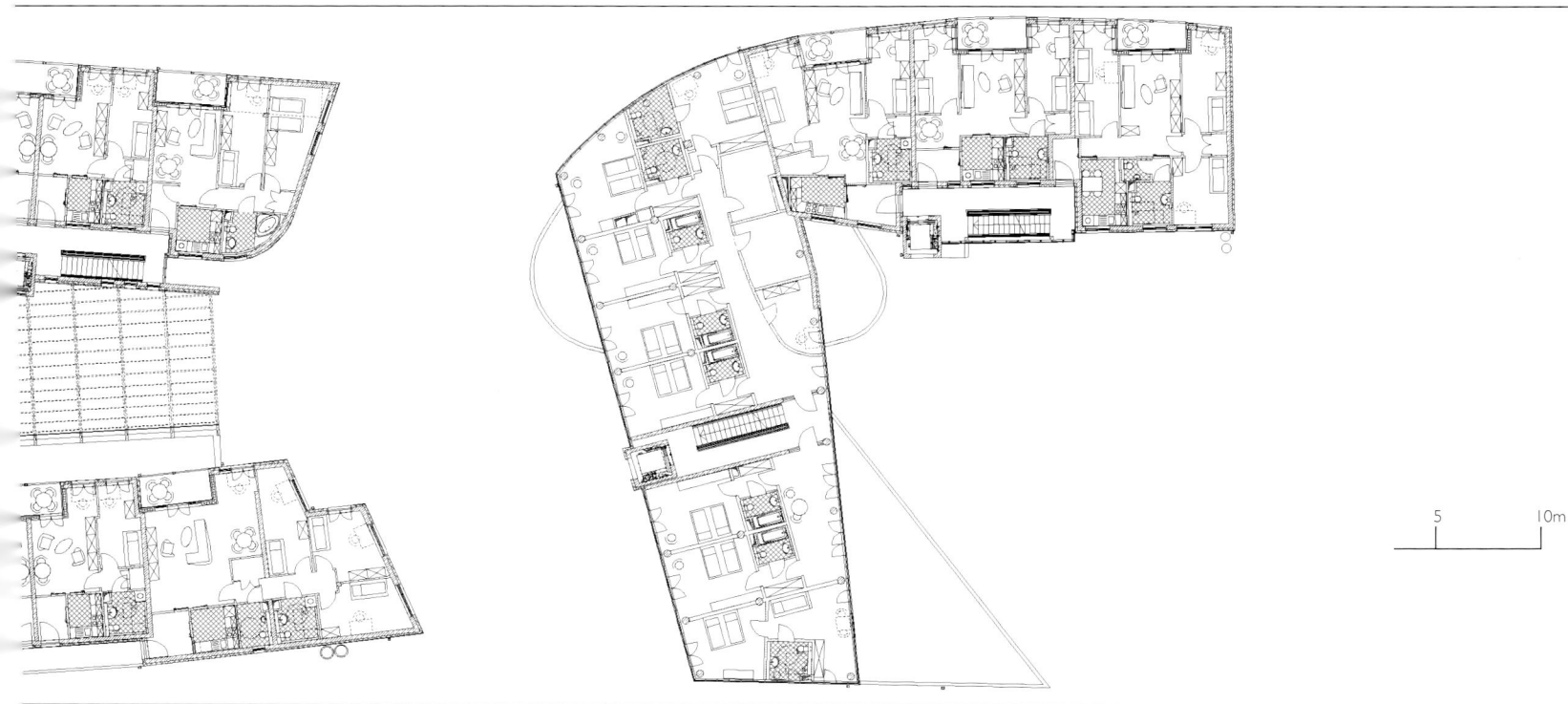

5   10m

The concept of integration has given way to a dynamic architecture, creating an urban space with multiple spatial situations. The segments of the buildings have been laid out in spiral form, establishing a dialogue amongst them.

Hardenbergstrasse elevation, house II

0   5   10m

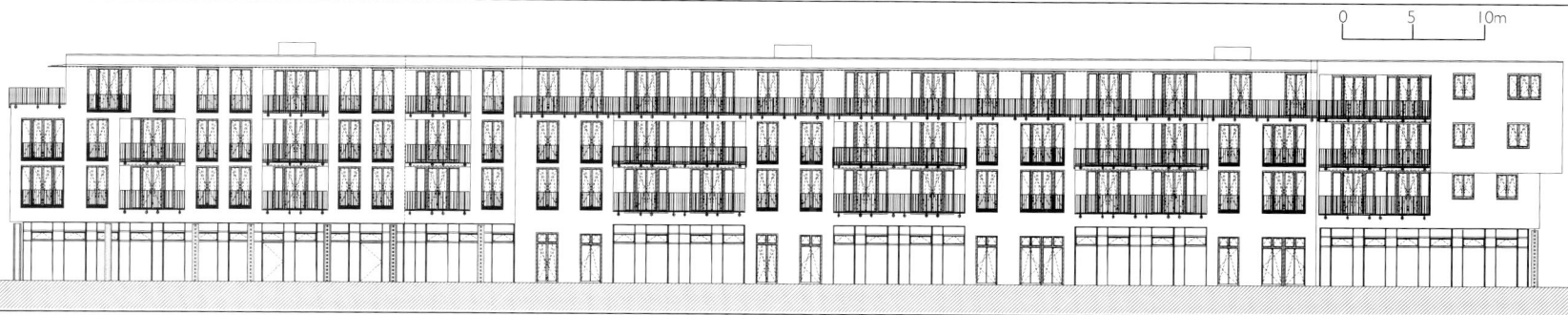

Hardenbergstrasse elevation, house I

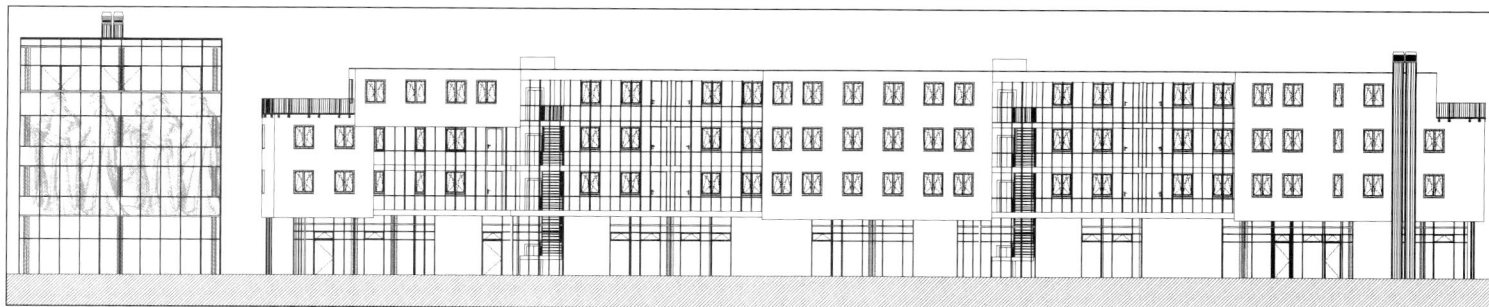

North-east elevation, house III

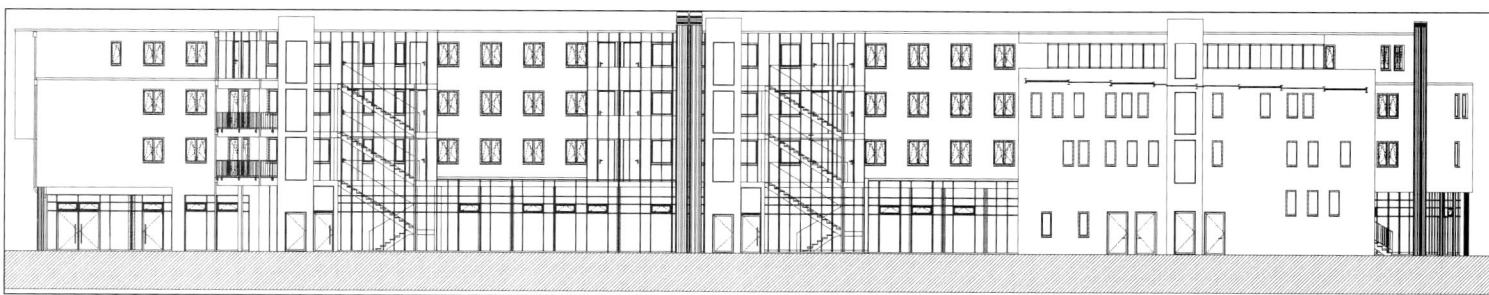

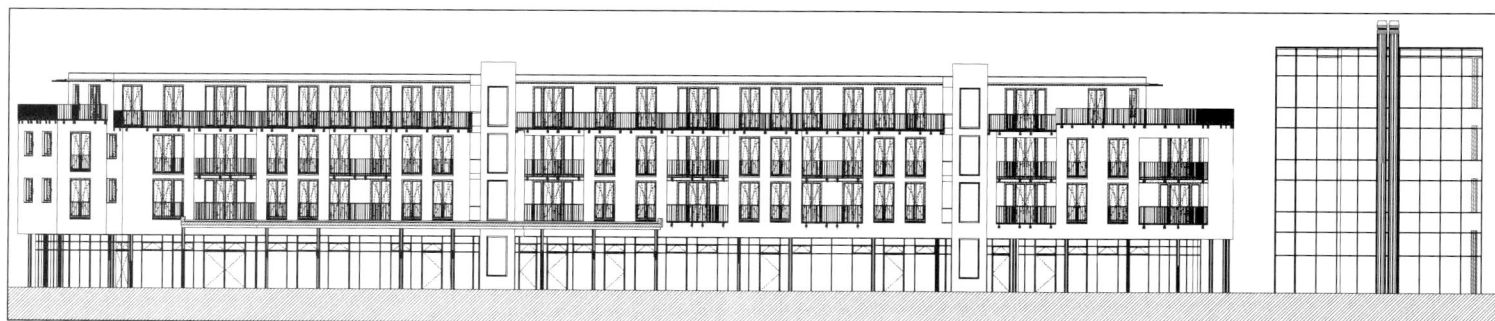

North-east elevation, house I

South-west elevation, house III

Elevation

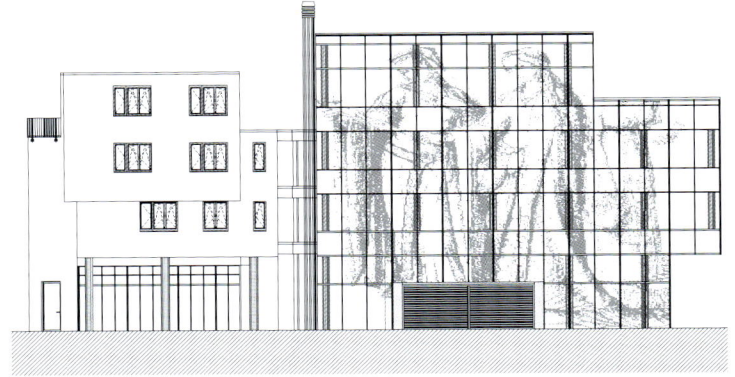

Section house II

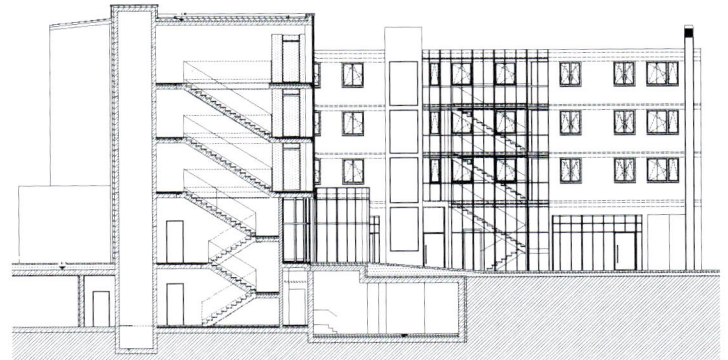

Section house I & III

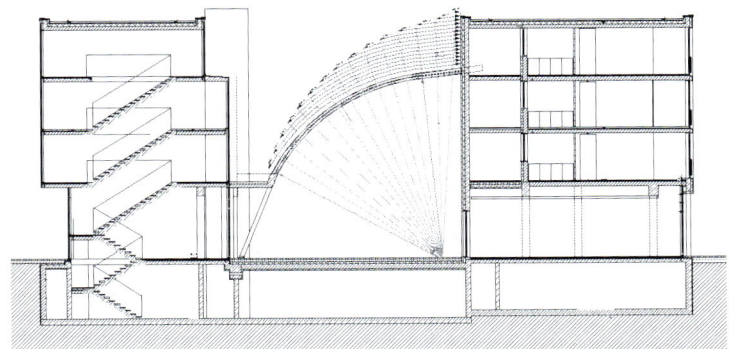

Feilden Clegg Bradley Architects

Beaufort House, Lillie Road

London, United Kingdom

Photographs:
courtesy of the architect

Architect:
Feilden Clegg Bradley Architects

As a model of modern affordable housing, this project epitomizes the government's housing agenda - high density with accommodation split between shared ownership and rental provision, with a range of unit sizes from one bedroom flats to large family houses.

Beaufort House demonstrates innovation in the construction methods: a prefabricated steel load-bearing system incorporating large-scale cold-rolled panels, large scale hot-rolled elements, and three-dimensional modular construction. It is the first social housing project in the UK to incorporate these three off-site fabrication approaches in one scheme.

The new scheme comprises three blocks arranged around a courtyard serving both the new development and the adjacent 1912 Peabody estate. This landscaped courtyard contains an all-weather sports pitch and, together with the new Tenants' Meeting room, provides amenity space for all residents, protected from the busy road.

The fabric of the building gives a high thermal and acoustic performance which will exceed current building regulations. The aim is to surpass current standards for energy efficiency and provide affordable warmth for the tenants. This is achieved by a combination of a thermally efficient envelope, a careful selection of materials, the orientation of the units to maximize daylighting and the use of green roof systems.

The scheme consists of 65 housing units on a restricted urban site, which was formerly occupied by a Victorian School that was demolished in 1998. It is located within an active area of residential, retail and commercial uses with a variety of properties, ranging from Georgian town houses to low-rise school buildings.

The design solution consists of three blocks forming edges to a protected enclosure on the north, south and east boundaries. The blocks are arranged around a raised landscaped courtyard that forms a focus for the site and sits above a semi-underground parking lot.

The three blocks are treated individually according to their locations on the site, type of accommodation and relationship to surrounding buildings and boundaries. The way in which the accommodation is distributed, with the majority of units contained in a six story block, permits the remainder of the site to be occupied by smaller-scale blocks and landscaping, thus maximizing the amenity space and giving the impression of lower density.

©The Forge Company

All apartments have private balconies, and the ground floor houses have private backyards evoking those of the neighbor's. The structural system allows large openings for windows and balconies. Except for the foundations, the building system is dry construction.

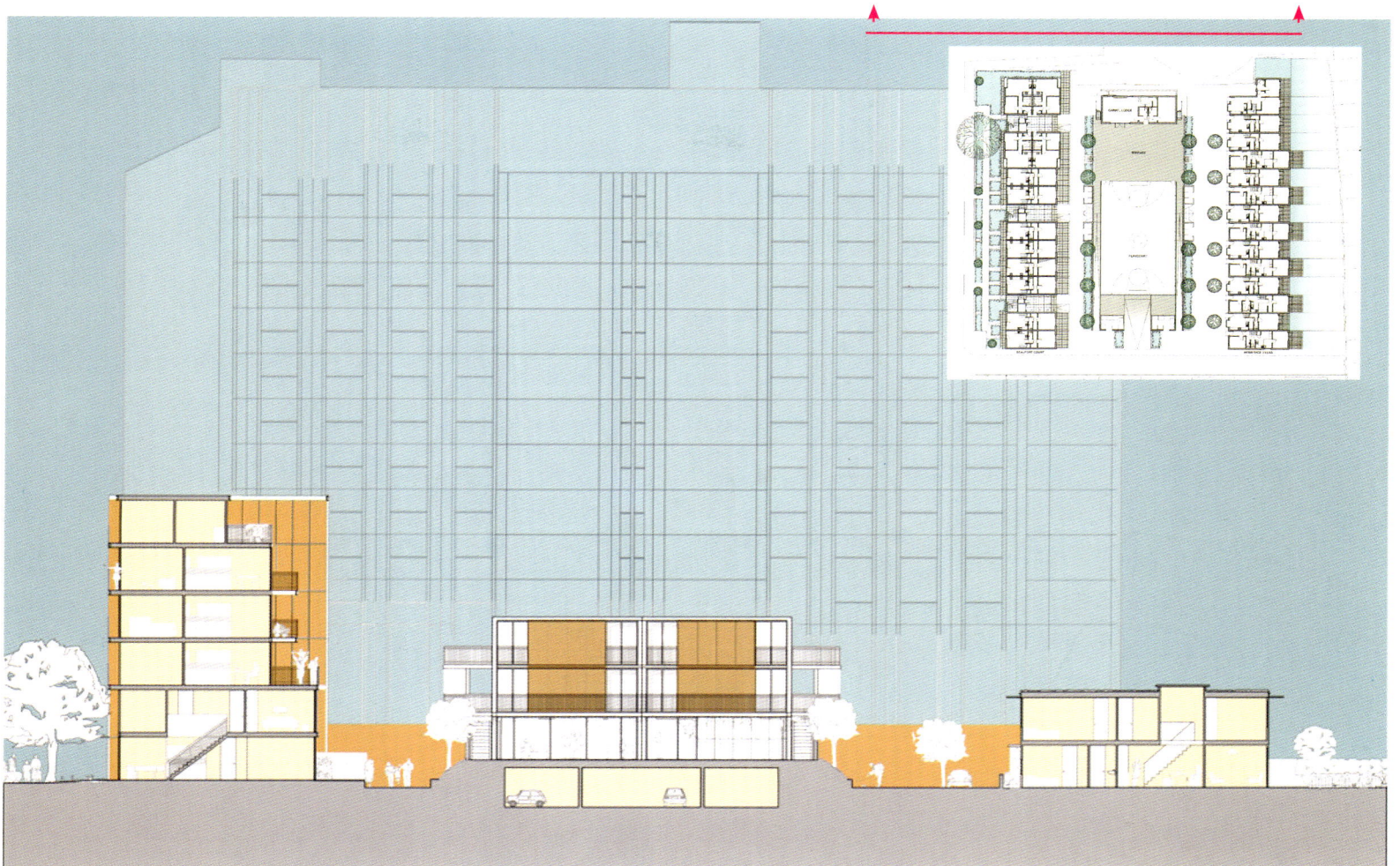

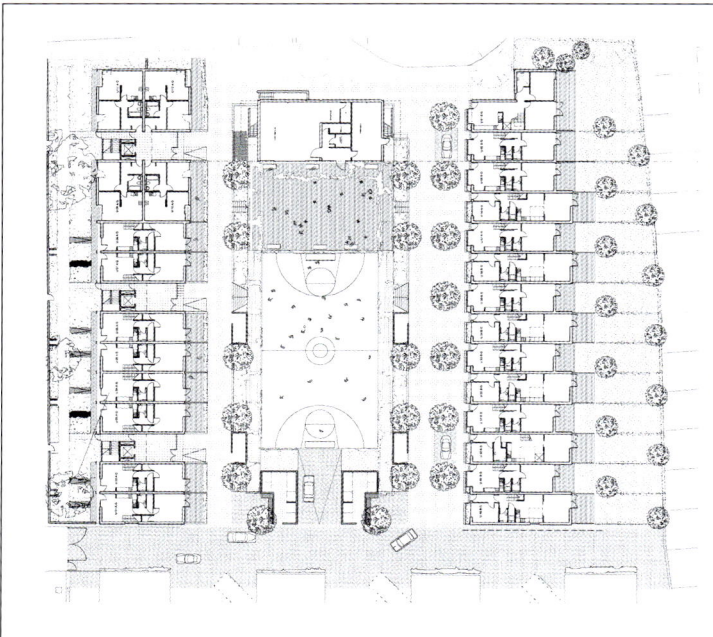

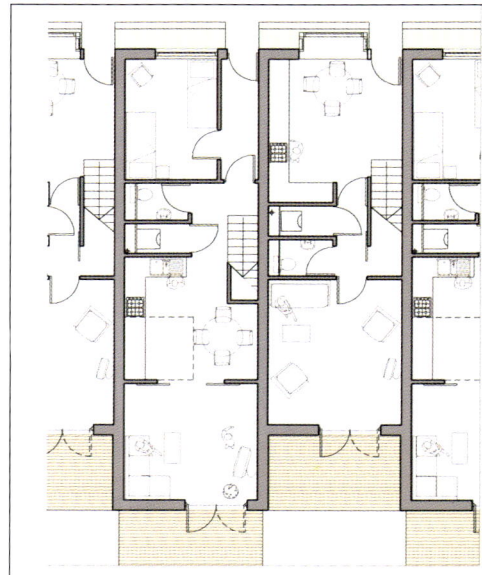

The blocks are arranged around an elevated patio, above the semiburied garage, which becomes the focal point of the site. The site has a surface of 0.53 hectares. The project develops 65 housing units with a total ground surface of 5785 sqm.

©Feilden Clegg Bradley Architects LLP

149

The central garden is a recreation and resting space for all the inhabitants and has been conceived to unite the two properties and host different activities.

The duplex has some semiprivate gardens in the front and private terraces at the back.

The loggias of the six-story building are glazed towards the south and ventilated naturally during the night to alleviate the effects of high summer temperatures.

The exterior elevation is composed of full-height glazing, terra cotta blocks with continuous head joint and grooved terra cotta rain screen.

The whole complex is illuminated through low consumption, high efficiency lamps. The housing units have been designed to take maximum advantage of the natural light. The building's fabric has been chosen for its high thermal insulation and a well insulated exterior structure that will proportion a greater thermal and acoustic insulation than the one required by building regulations.

Christian de Portzamparc

Residences on the Rue Nationale

Paris, France

Photographs:
contributed by the architect

Architect:
Christian de Portzamparc

A theme of the future: the "on-site" transformation of buildings, without moving the occupants, qualifying the neighbourhood, as much as the buildings themselves, with their lobbies, the facades and interiors. Here, in the 13th arrondisment, there is a hybrid urban configuration typical of Age III, with Age I streets and Age II building projects, perpendicularly arranged and perfectly indifferent to the streets. Portzamparc creates a clear demarcation between public spaces (streets and squares) and private spaces (hallways and gardens), by demolishing a small low-rise block and building two mewslike buildings that redefine the street aligments. In the gap between these two buildings he sets a new entrance overlooking a garden common to all the residences and new transparent lobbies linking several stairwells.

The structurally redundant vertical features of the large rectilinear blocks are removed and the windows replaced, the balconies on the west are doubled in sized and equipped with blinds, thus turning them into living areas.

The small low-rise building is completely transformed by the creation of loggias and new cladding.

On Place Nationale, a cubic, sculptural structure houses a neighborhood facility and artists studios. It gives new meaning to the square and new scale to the street, and marks an emphatic approach to the whole project.

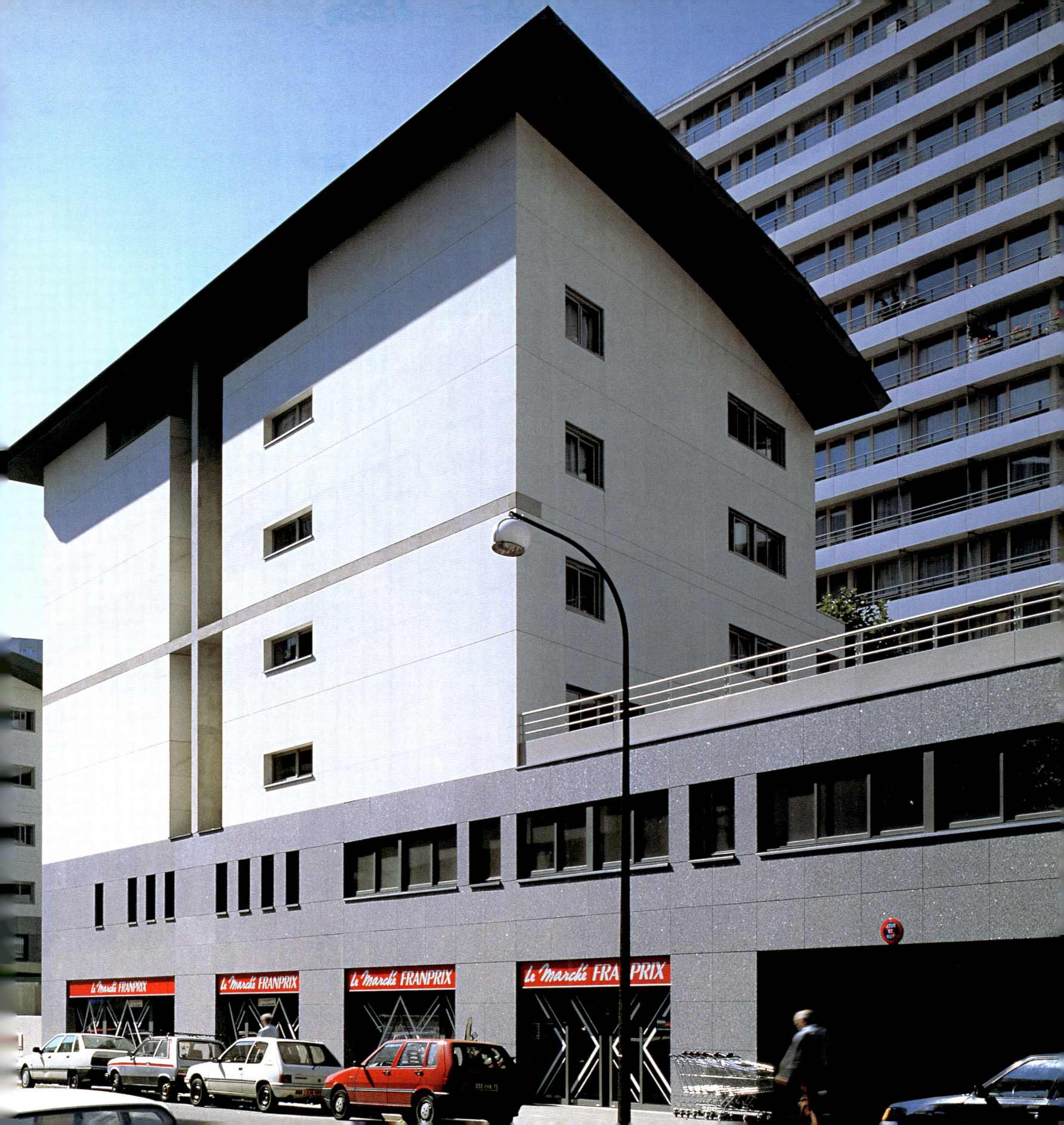

The programme of action for this project includes the restoration of several massive apartment blocks –over 500 dwellings– from the sixties (black and white photograph). Portzamparc's firm also designed and landscaped the common garden of the estate.

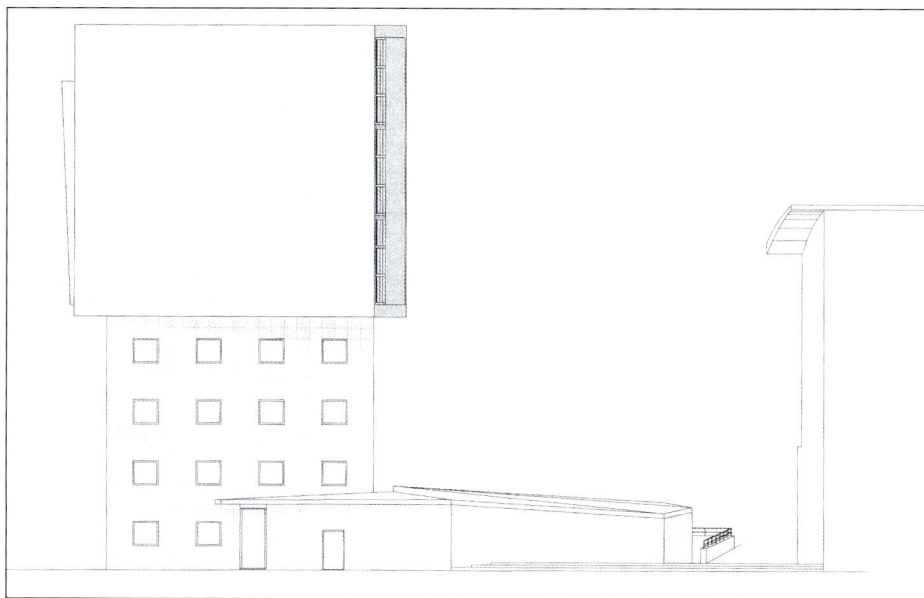

East elevation

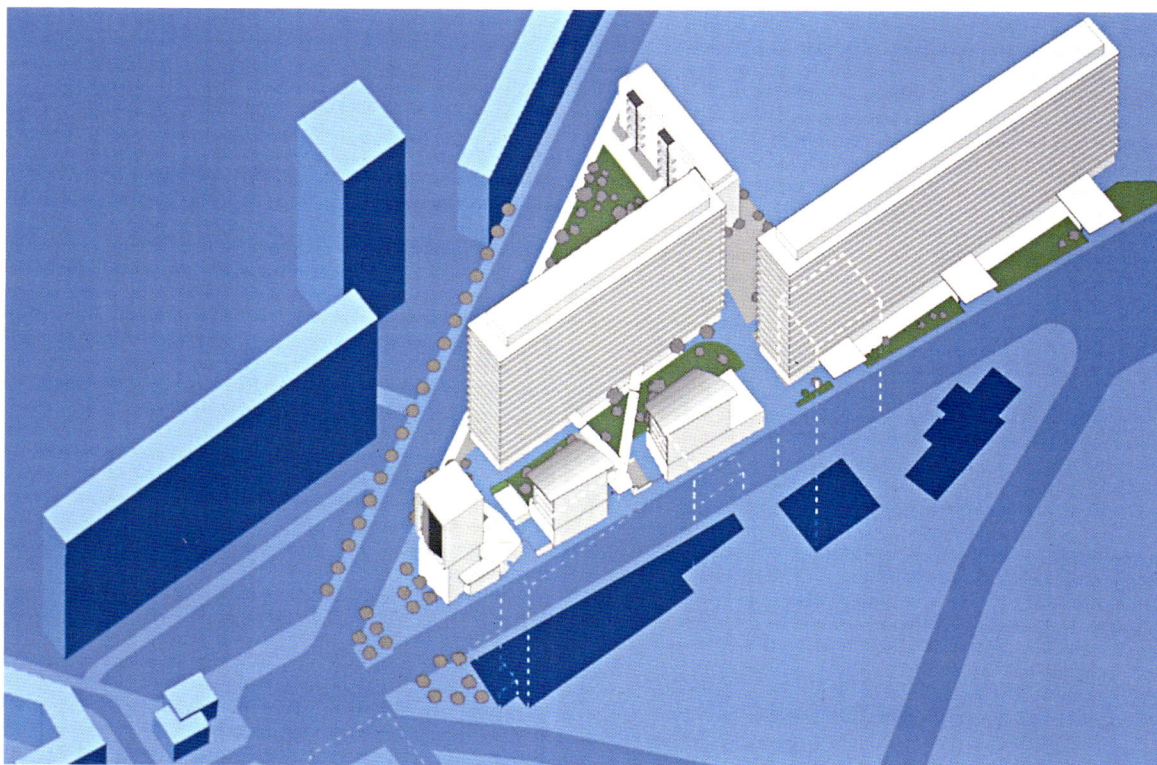

Above, Christian de Portzamparc's drawing which integrates one of the old volumes with the three new buildings that are included in the project.

The photographs show the apartment blocks before their restoration by Portzamparc. Built in 1963 in Rue National, Paris, they were designed by Rivet et Lassen.

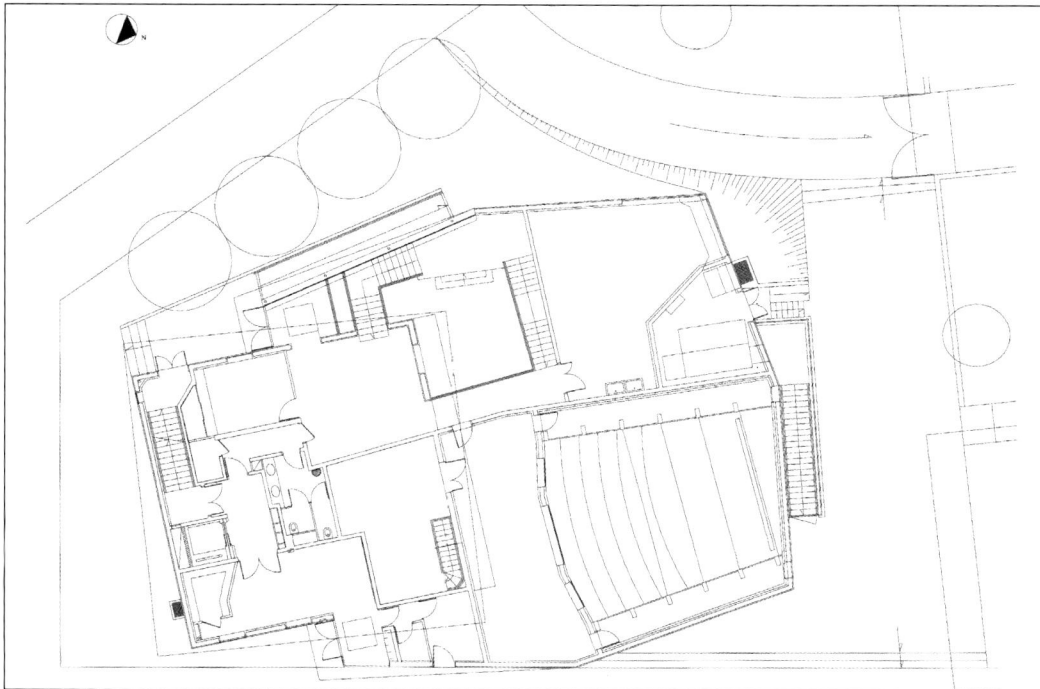

Ground floor plan

The new buildings house 19 apartments, two shops, a reception centre for the elderly and 181 parking spaces.

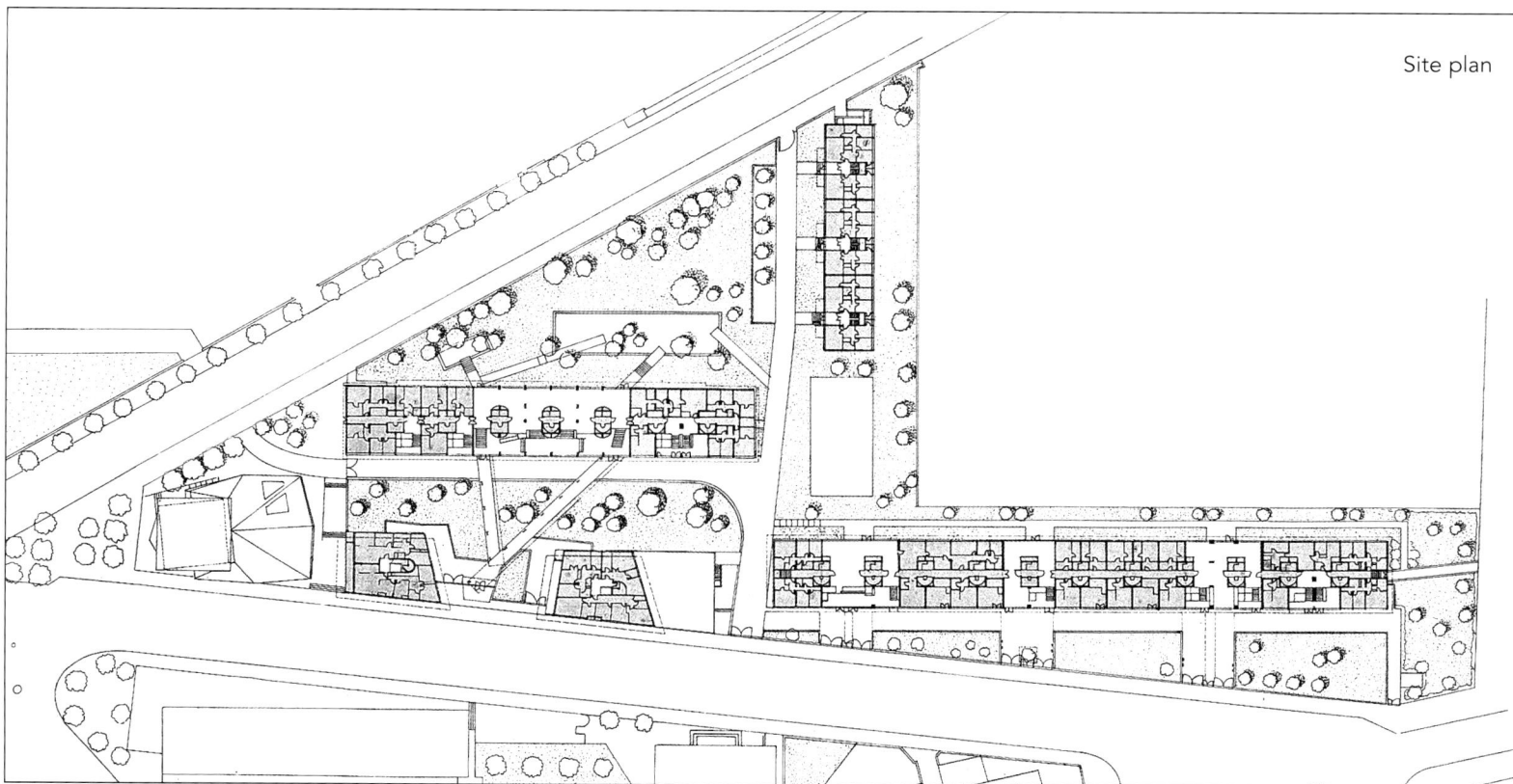

Site plan

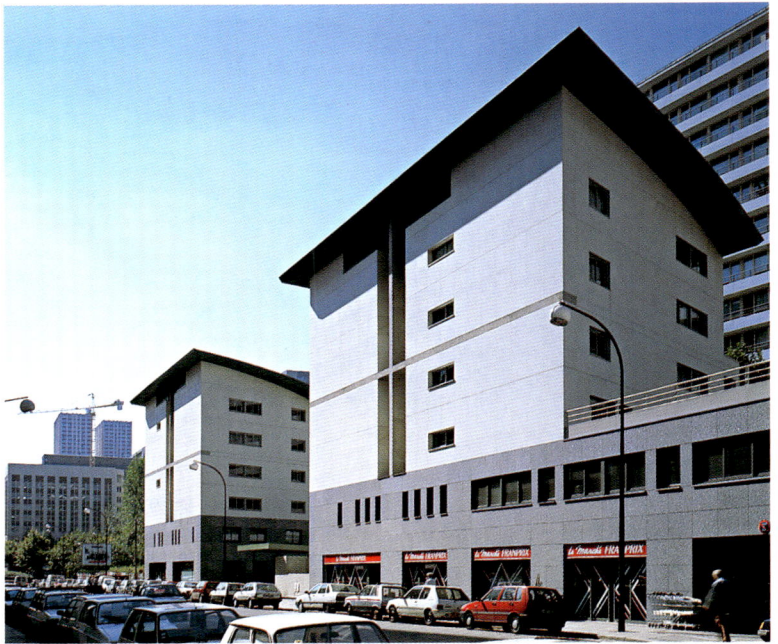

After the intervention, the markedly vertical elements of the large rectilinear blocks have been eliminated and the windows have been replaced; the width of the balconies toward the west has been doubled and awnings have been placed on all of them, giving the facade a more cheerful and cleaner image, as can be seen on this page.

North elevation

First floor plan

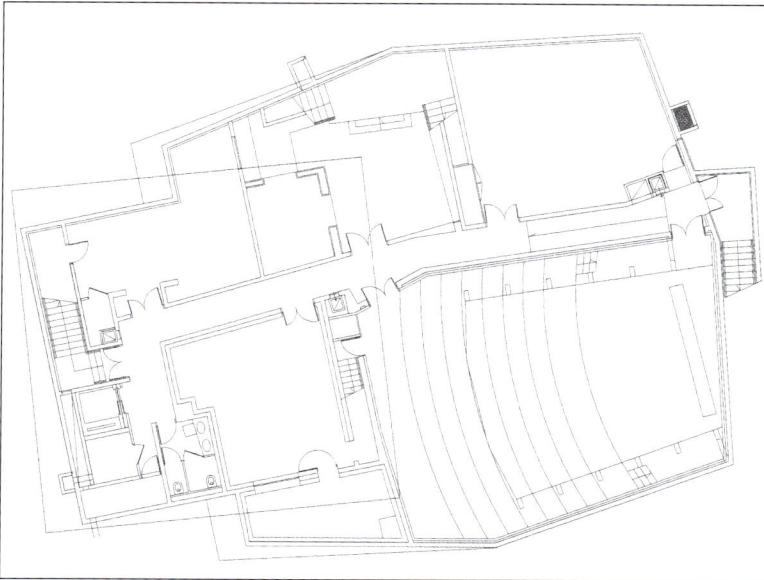

On Place Nationale the complex is crowned with a volume of marked geometry, an enormous urban sculpture that houses a series of workshops for artists and a floor of municipal offices for the community. The photographs on this and the following pages show several views of this construction.

South elevation

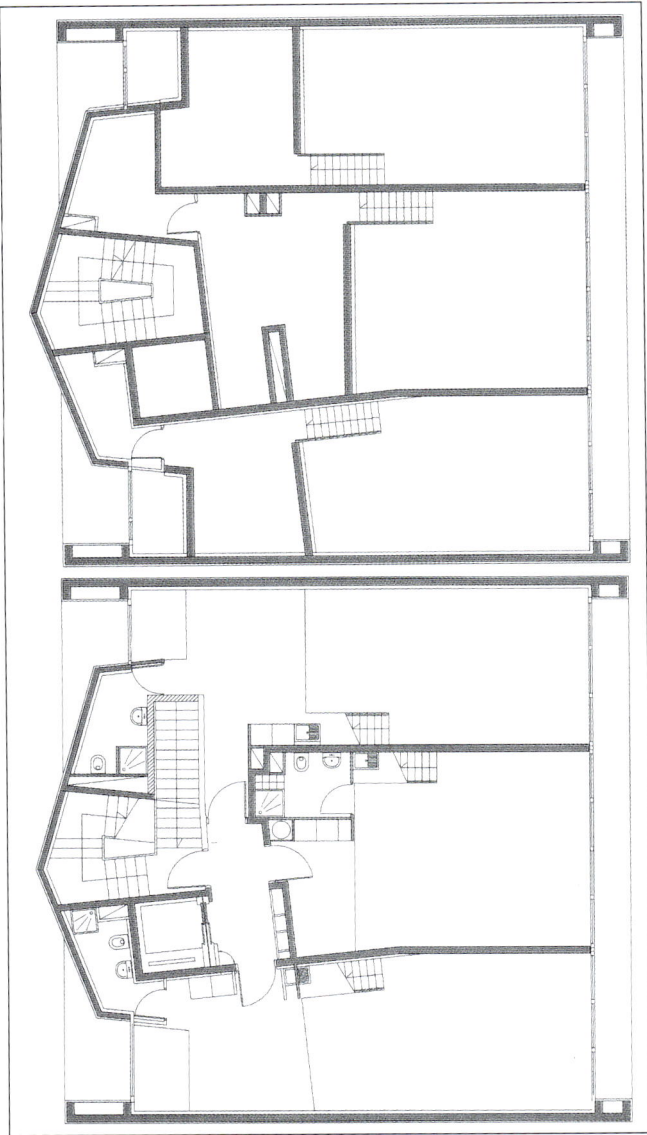

Fourth floor plan and mezzanine

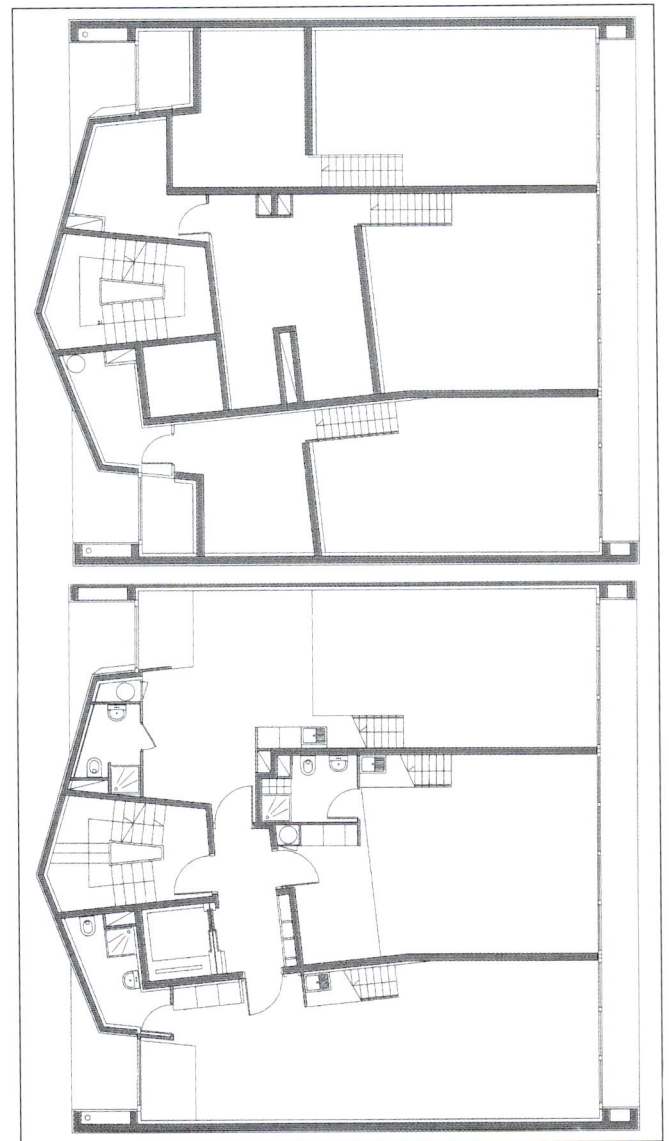

Fifth floor plan and mezzanine

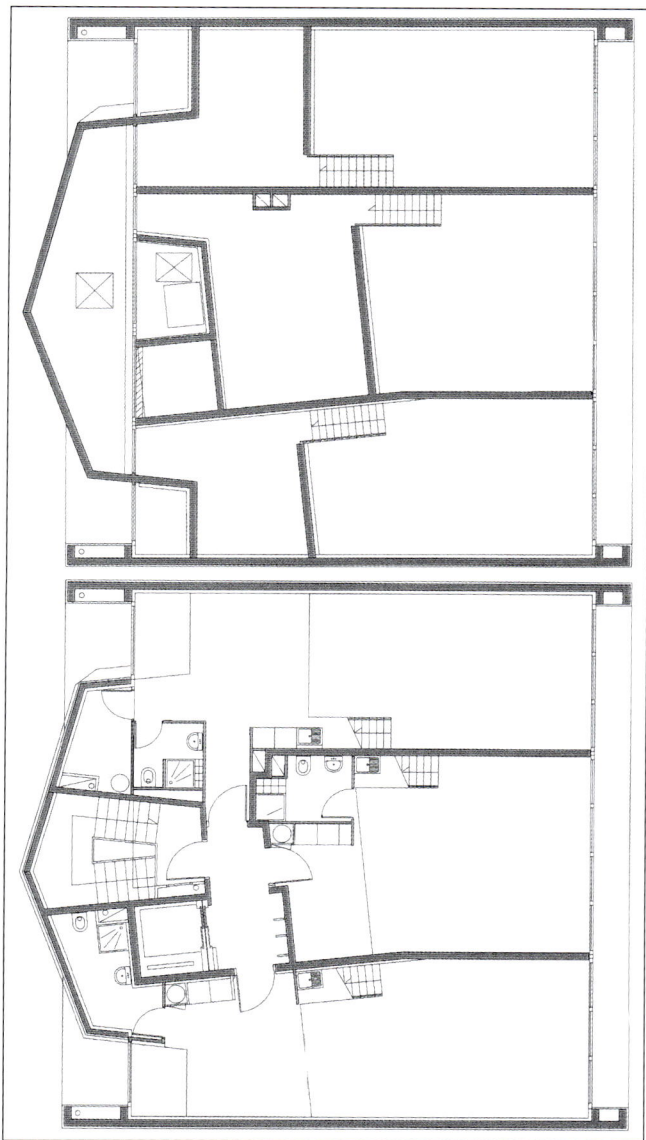

Sixth floor plan and mezzanine

Kauffmann Theilig + Partner

Residential Centre for Senior Citizens

Wernigerode, Germany

Photographs:
Roland Halbe / Artur

Architect:
Kauffmann Theilig + Partner

The project for the conversion, restructuring and extension of this senior citizens residence conserved the existing structure, and proposed the construction of a new section for senile dementia patients and a building with apartments for the elderly. The opportunity was taken to give a new identity to this environment, a quite dull area of gray lineal structures with prefabricated concrete elements.

The aim was to carry out tangible improvements in all areas of the project and to introduce a park in the center that could be enjoyed both by the residents and by the local people. This was designed as an open green carpet, with the new buildings distributed like pieces of furniture, drawing away from the uniformity of the environment's straight lines by means of more sophisticated geometric shapes and an apparently random layout.

The lineal building, a structure of prefabricated elements put up at the beginning of the 1970s, required important restructuring. The windows have been enlarged at much as possible to allow the maximum entrance of natural light into the rooms and corridors. The wooden surfaces create a warm, attractive and "tactile" environment that makes it look more like a hotel than a hospital. Some platforms in various colors in front of each room facilitate orientation, enlivening the rigid layout of corridors and generating a certain sense of individuality. On the south side, the rooms have large balconies with wooden handrails that eliminate the division between inside and outside, drawing in the garden. On the north side, galleries extend the rooms while providing them with some outstanding views.

The concept is complemented with "special" places to be discovered and to identify oneself with. Some proverbs and aphorisms lend humorous, sometimes profound, thoughts; they are come across on a window pane or when turning a corner. And there is more to be discovered: some cloth butterflies seem to go flying out of the window, two happy birds in the atrium add life to the space, ...

The building that houses the rooms of the residents requiring long-term attention is being extended, on the south side towards the garden, with a small tower that provides the shared spaces for eating, living, chatting, watching the television, etc.: a living room just like at home, a multipurpose space for social contact on every floor, which has even been thought of to invite the residents to take part in the household chores.

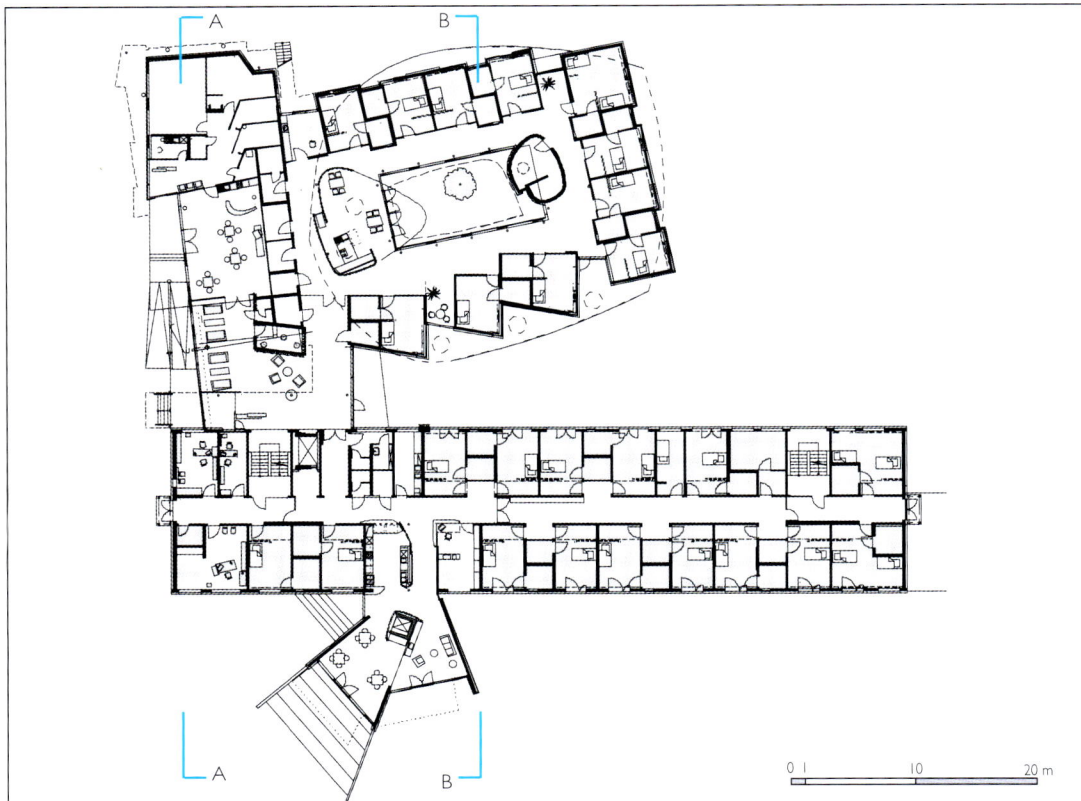

The complex is located in a park that not only integrates the different buildings but has converted into the real nerve center of the district: a privileged setting in which the residents can stroll and relax.

Ground floor plan

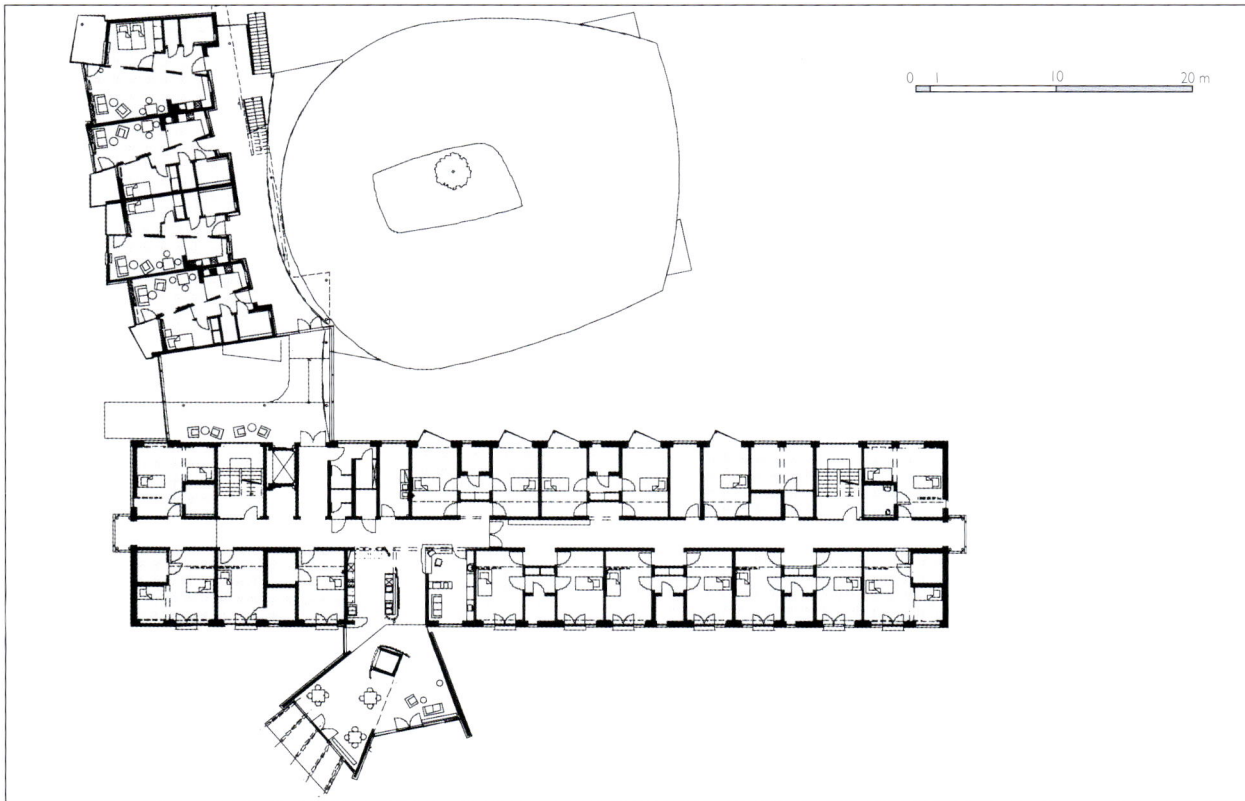

First floor plan

South elevation

West elevation

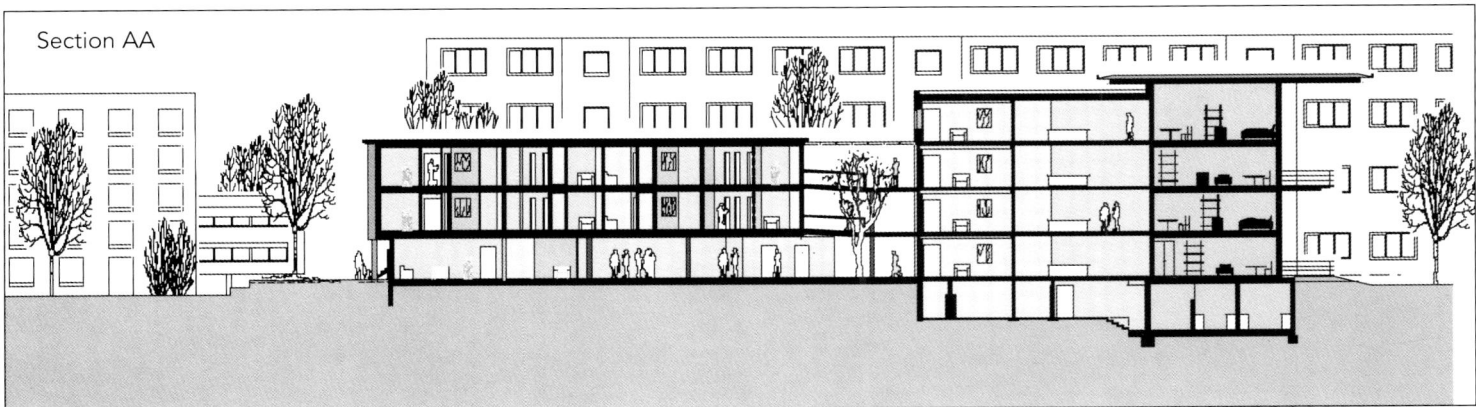

Section AA

Section BB

0   10   20 m

171

Jacques Schär & Christine Sjöstedt

Dwelling complex El Masr

Cologny, Switzerland

Photographs:
Jean Michel Landecy

Architect:
Jacques Schär & Christine Sjöstedt

This dwelling complex is located in Cologny, on the original land belonging to the El Masr castle, a Tudor-like building which dates from the end of the 19th century, and which is emblematic of the area.

In order to preserve the park linked to this residence, the building is located on the south-east border of the land, leaving room for views from the castle as well as from the apartments. The building follows the land's natural slope, and makes several successive level distinctions, bringing the building close to the scale of a private home or villa.

The notion of villa-building is equally present in the distribution of the apartments. Thus, on the ground floor, 4 large apartments open onto the private gardens towards the south-east. The 8 others are duplex style (on the first and second floors) with large terraces on two levels and fitting into the surrounding natural environment.

The base volume is a rectangle within which the architects have created terraces, double heights, and headers.

The work performed with this simple volume has been accentuated by the use of particular materials, such as Brazilian slate to surround the rectangular structure, and hemlock cladding for the retreating planes.

Although the building presents a non-repetitive facade for the 12 apartments, 8 of them have a different typology.

The living-rooms and libraries, located toward the south-east, have higher ceilings than the other rooms, and open onto the dining room and kitchen on the north-west, so that the "daytime" rooms can enjoy sunlight all day long.

The materials used for the interior are the same (Brazilian slate for the kitchen floors and bathrooms), or within the same color range (Oregon pine woodworks, parquet) as those used on the exterior, with the purpose of reinforcing the interior-exterior link.

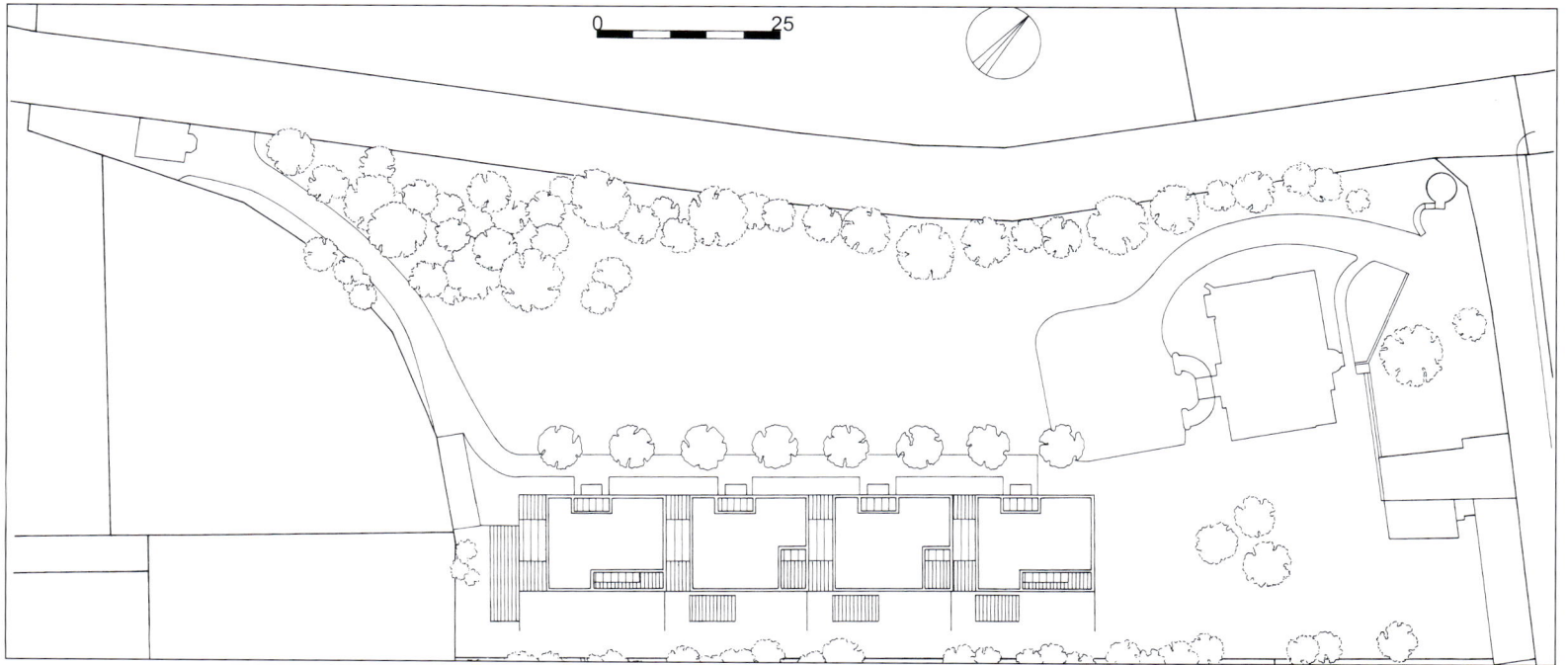

Site plan

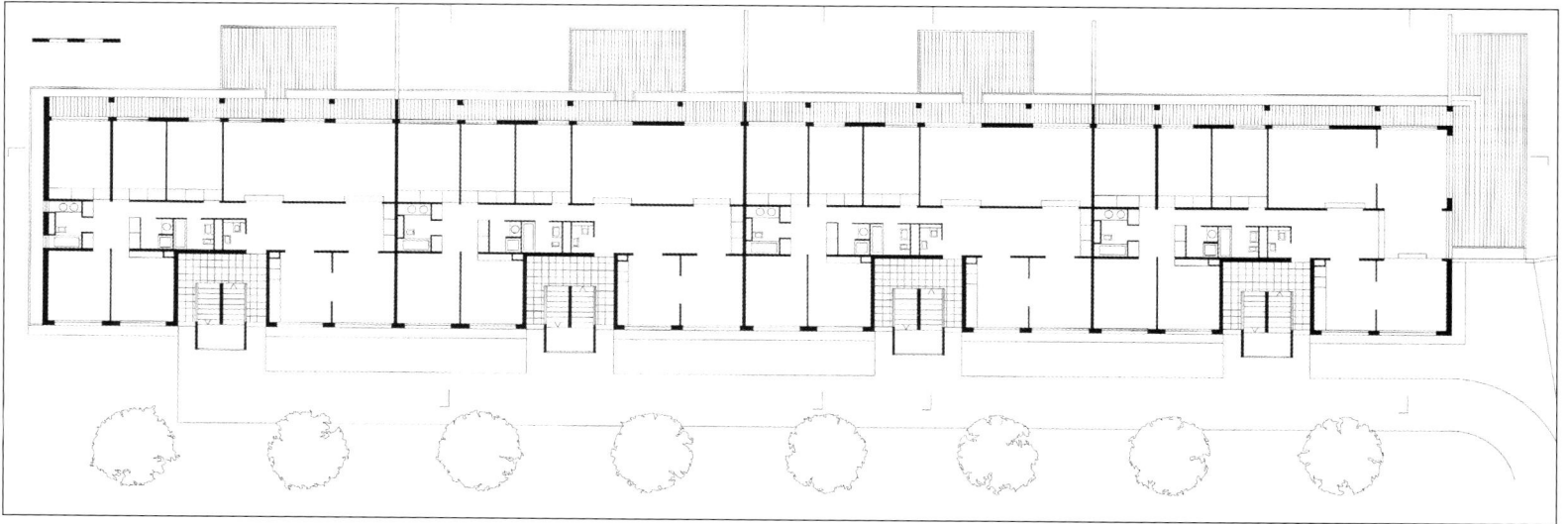

Ground floor plan

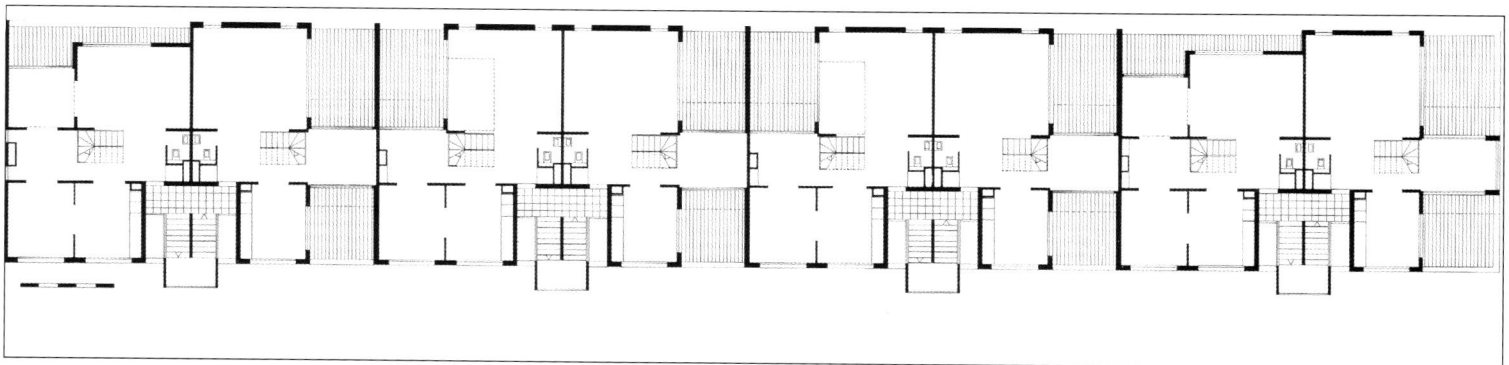

First floor plan

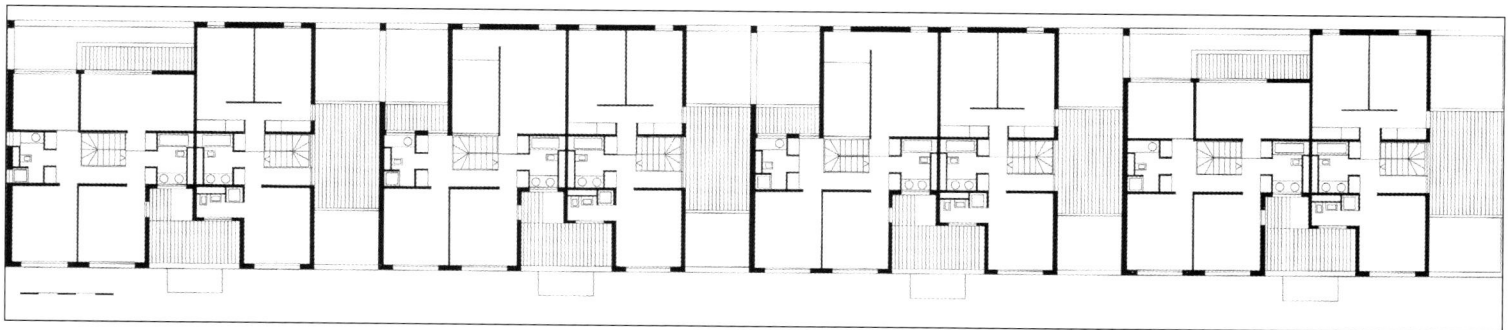

Second floor plan

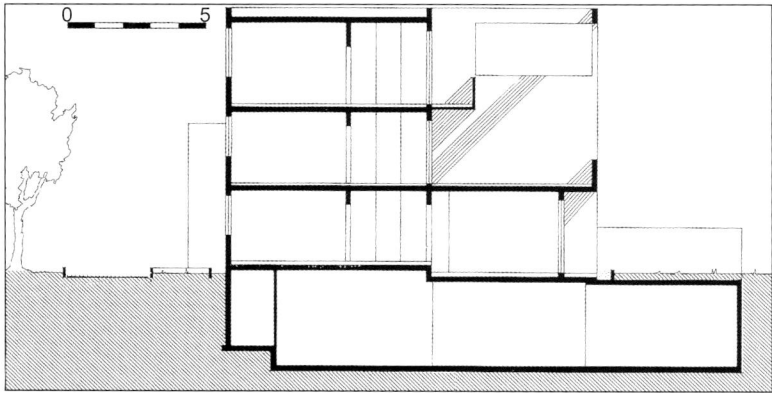

Section B-B

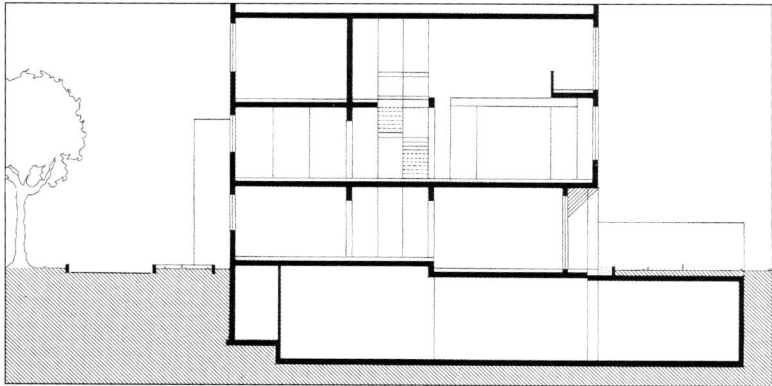

Section C-C

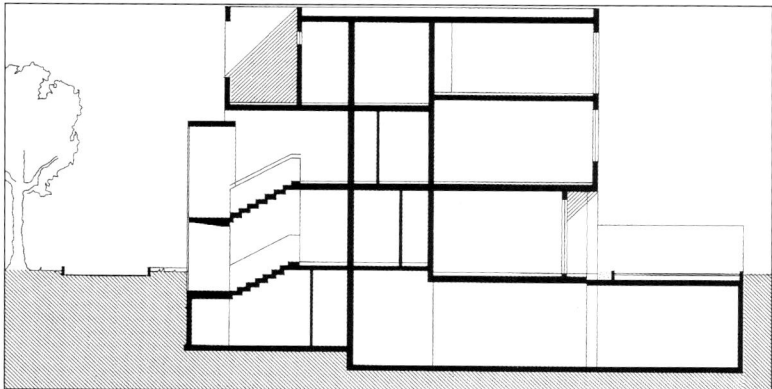

Section D-D

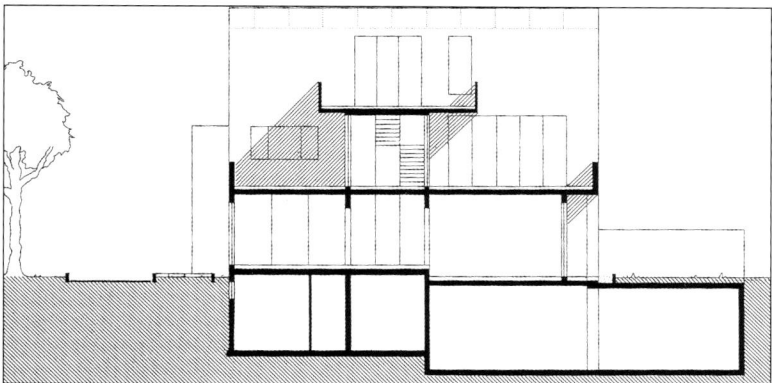

Section E-E

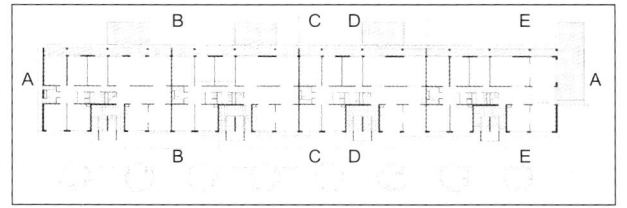

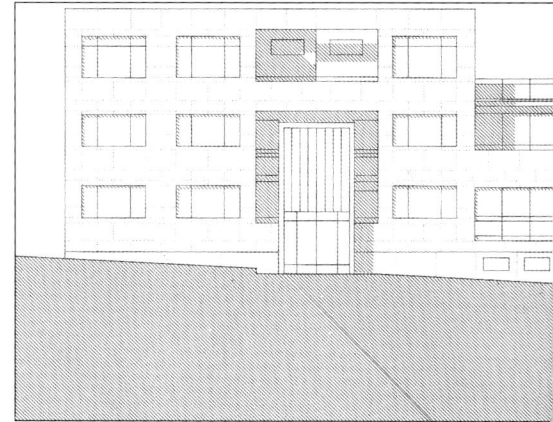

Section A-A

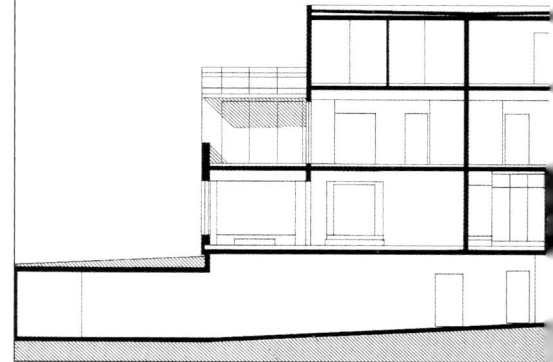

South-East elevation

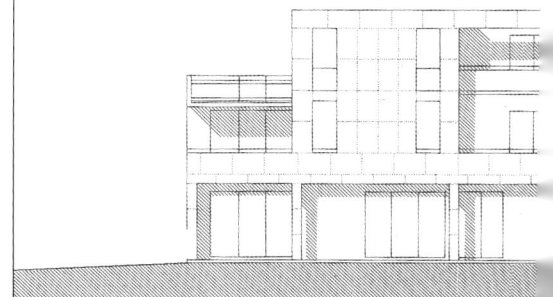

The building follows the natural slope of the terrain, giving it a scale in tune with the surroundings and respecting the views all around.

North-West elevation

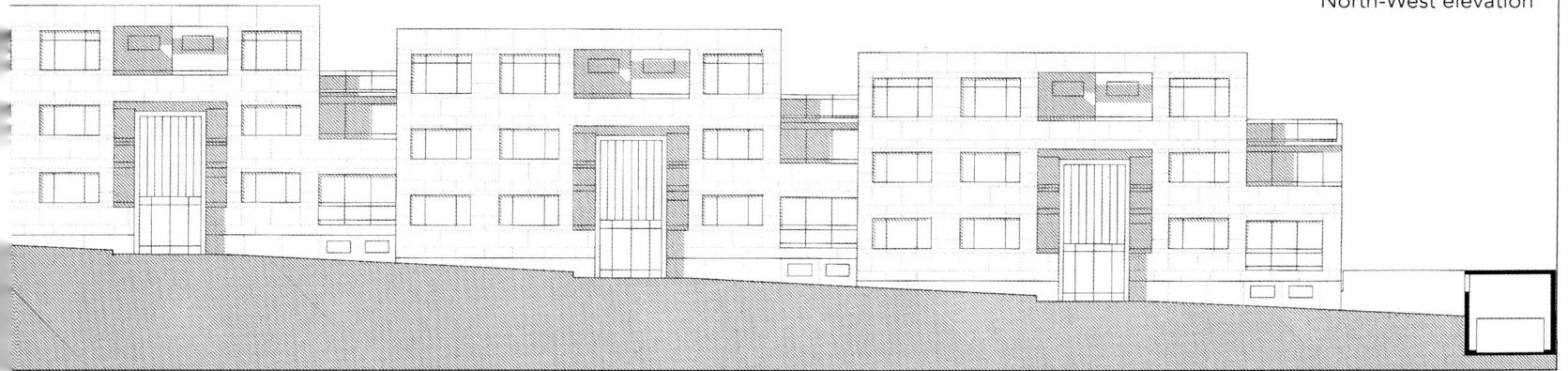

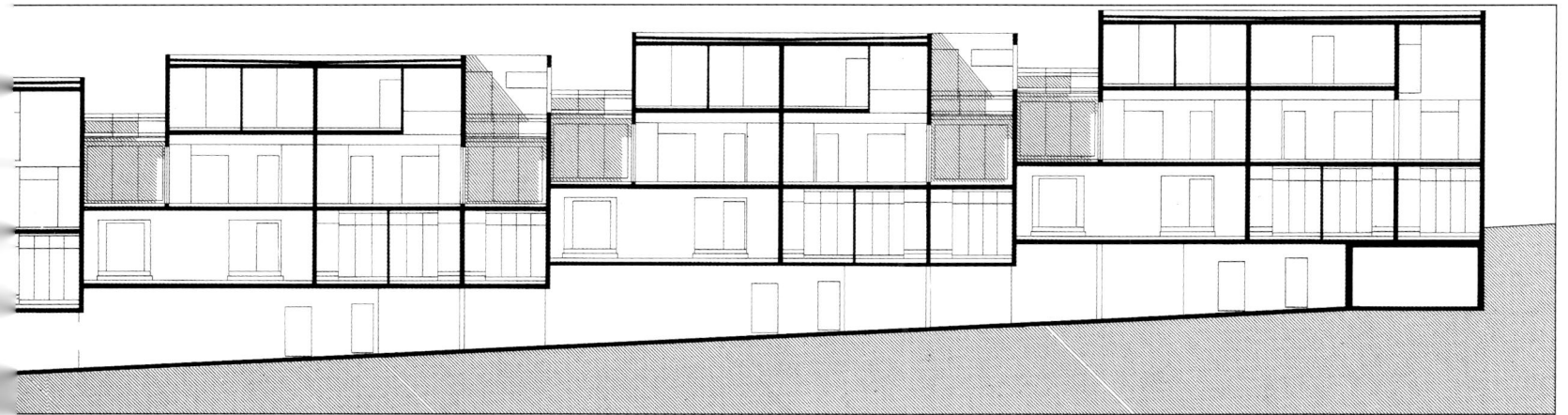

Philippe Gazeau

Postmen's flats

Paris, France

Photographs:
Jean-Marie Monthiers

Architect:
Phillippe Gazeau

"La Poste" commissioned the organisation in charge of building welfare homes for its employees PLA (prêt locatif aidé) flats for young postmen arriving to work in Paris. The Post Office wanted to give them the chance to live in flats in the city centre, their place of work, so they would not have to make long journeys on the underground.

Although most of the dwellers were single, special "studios" and two-room flats had to be built for the married couples. An additional area for temporarily accommodating children was provided for young couples.

The land allocated to Phillipe Gazeau was on rue de l'Ourcq in the 19th arrondissement, a working class district whose population density increased dramatically in the sixties and seventies. The district had no stylistic identity: It was almost entirely constructed this century.

Gazeau skillfully cut the building in two. This gave him two separate blocks to work with: one was 3.50 metres wide and 15 metres long, and was used for accommodating a "studio", the other was 7.50 metres wide. The building was therefore constructed around an empty space, a fault, defined by a large staircase, which does not overhang on the roadside but juts out at the back of the building.

The same attention to detail has been paid to both the interiors and exteriors, although more "precious" materials have been used for the exteriors to give the building the kind of dignity that is usually lacking in welfare buildings. Considerable attention has also been paid to the choice of materials: black brick, glass, aluminium and wood are skillfully combined. The facade overlooking the road is a composition of large glazed surfaces fitted with sliding aluminium panels to conceal the interior.

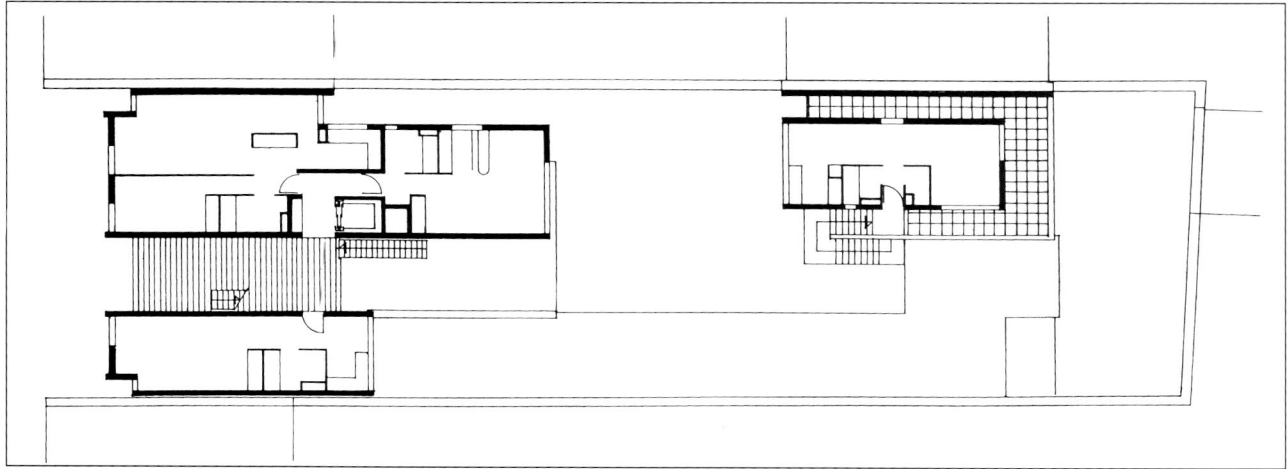

Second floor plan

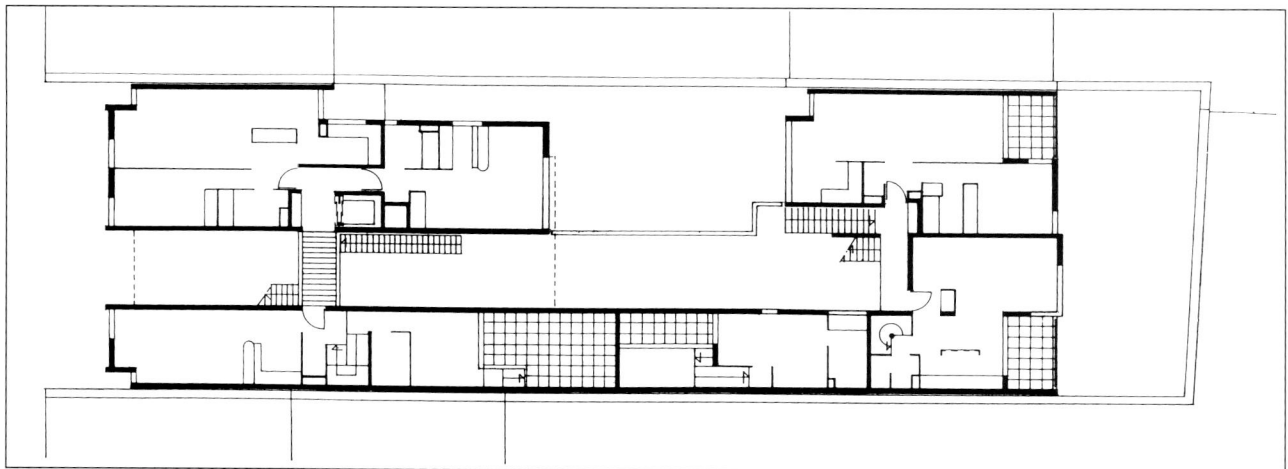

First floor plan

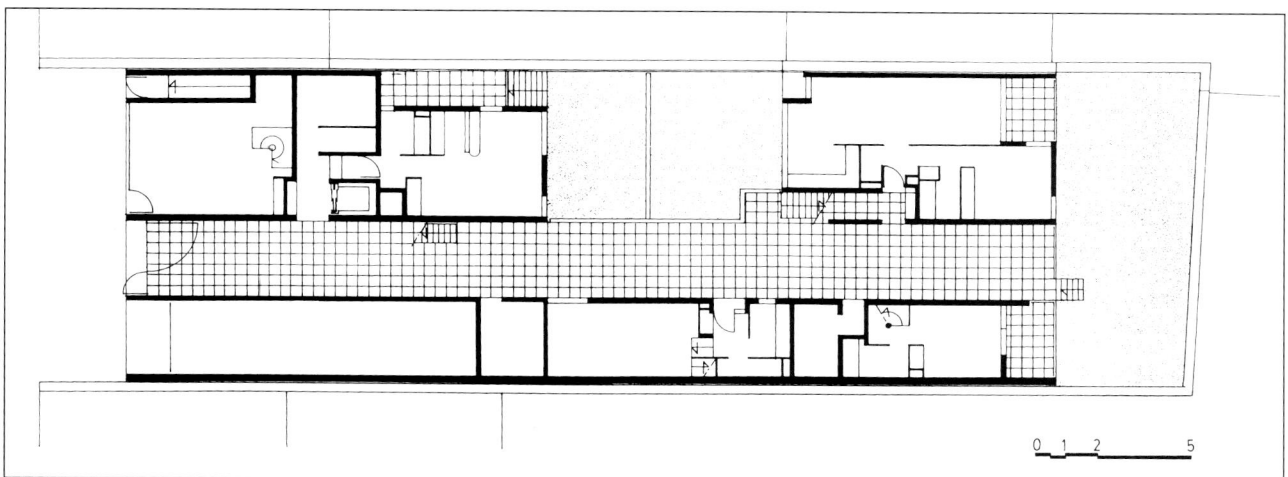

Ground floor plan

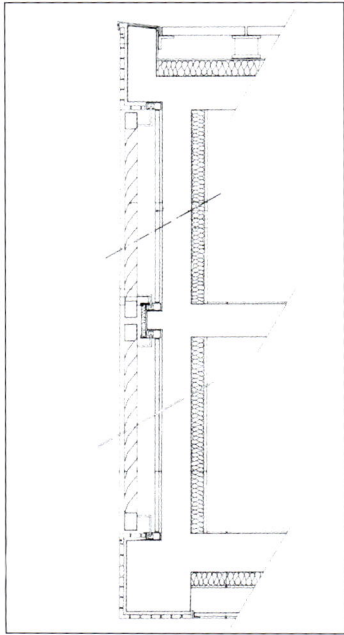

Constructive detail of the facade

This staircase leads into the buildings and constructs a shared space where people can congregate, exchange a few words or just stop and watch what is going on below. The same attention to deal has been paid to both the interiors and exteriors.

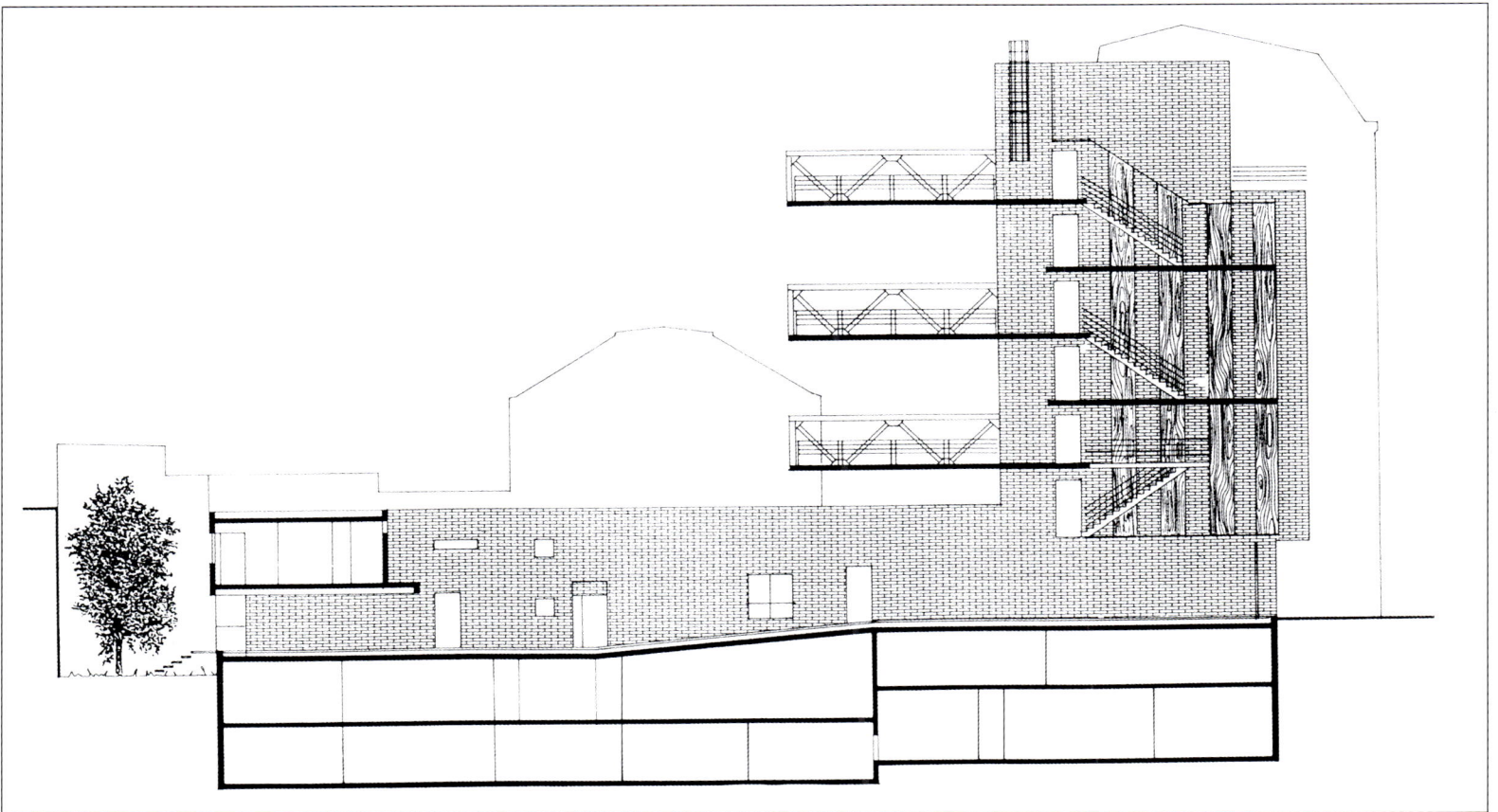

RUE DE L'OURCQ

RUE DE NANTES

Wilhelm Huber & Erich Kessler

Housing for the elderly

Eichstätt, Germany

Photographs:
Peter Bonfig

Architect:
Wilhelm Huber & Erich Kessler

The historic city outline shows a homogeneous structure on the western edge bordering on the Altmühl. The new development reflects the layout of a former abattoir on this site.

The long, straight roof line, on the other hand, stands in contrast to the roofscape of the old city centre.

A rupture in the building volume allows views of the Altmühl on one side and of the old town on the other side. The project included the rehabilitation of the adjoining historic Jura House to provide additional accommodation in the form of several old apartments after minor conversions.

Some of the features of the older building, such as the solid external wall construction punctured by window openings, were adopted in the new design. The loggias and living room windows facing the river can be darkened by closing perforated metal sliding screens. The side facing the town is distinguished by the timber stores in front of the flats, by the generous access balconies and by the broad roof projection at the top.

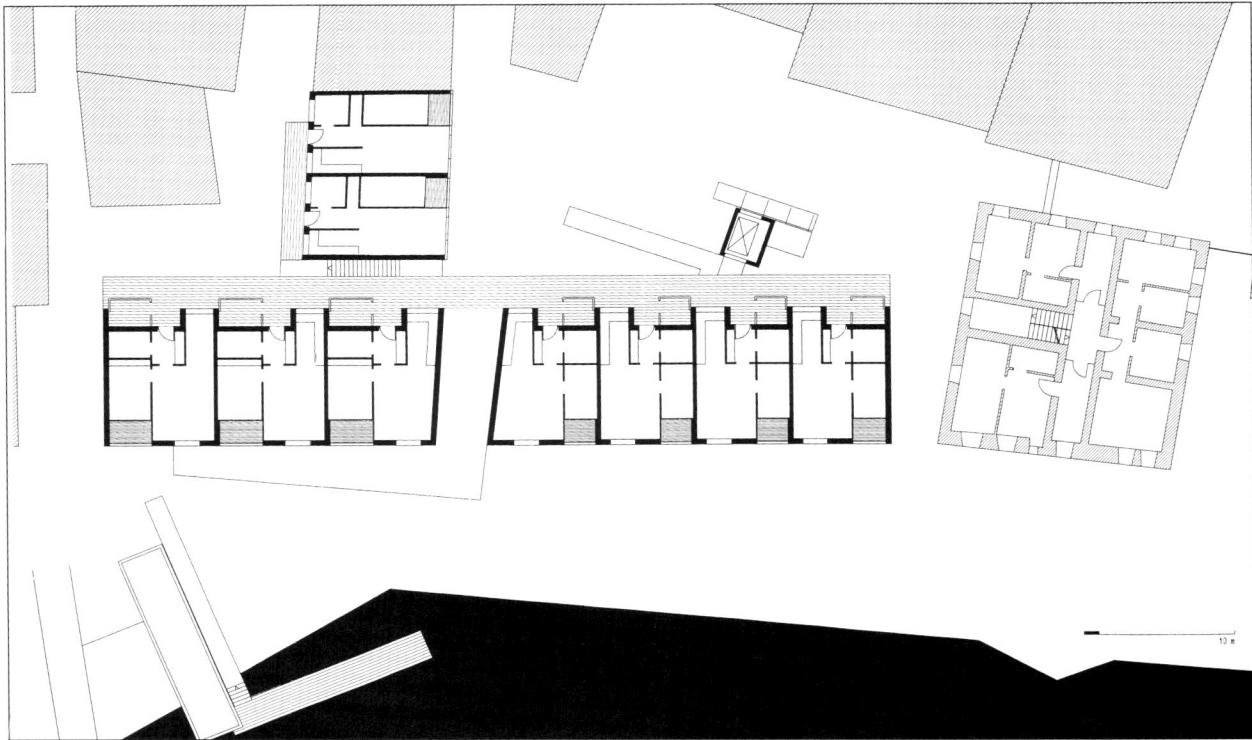

Typical floor plan

Ground floor plan

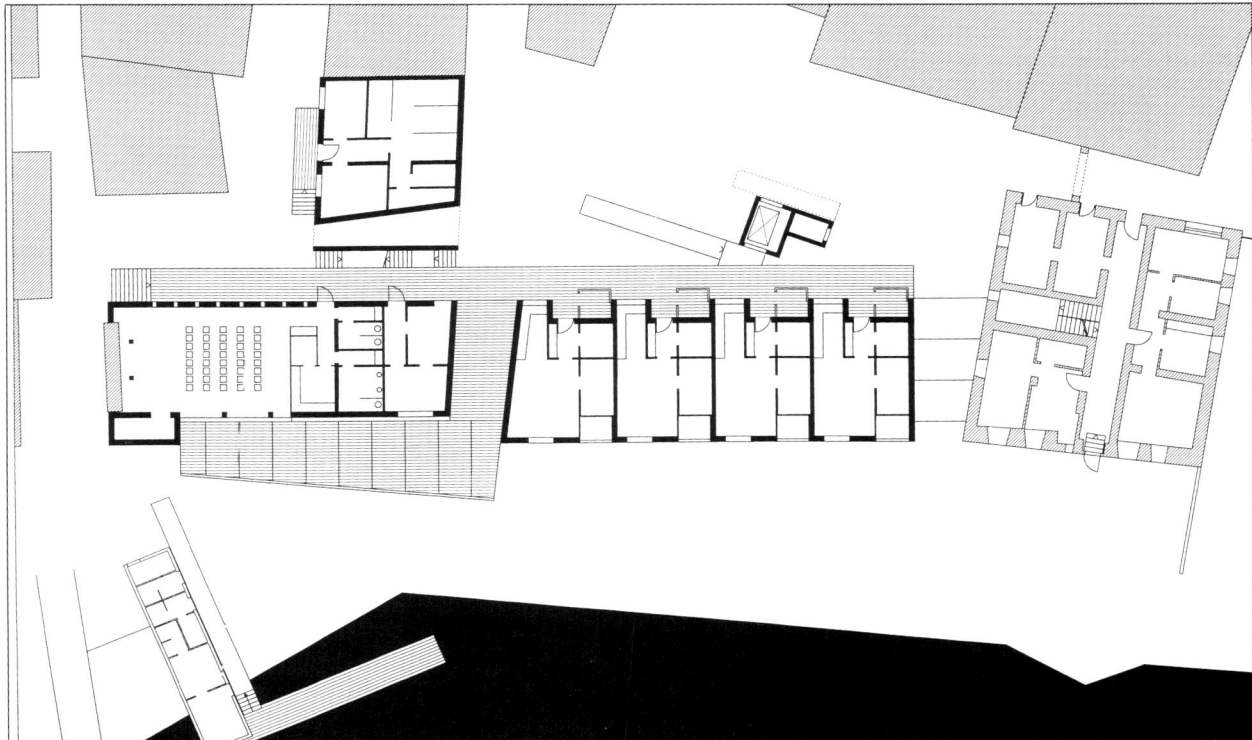

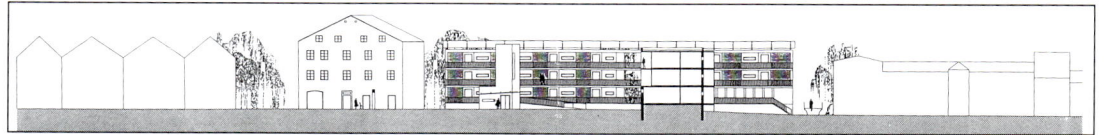
East elevation

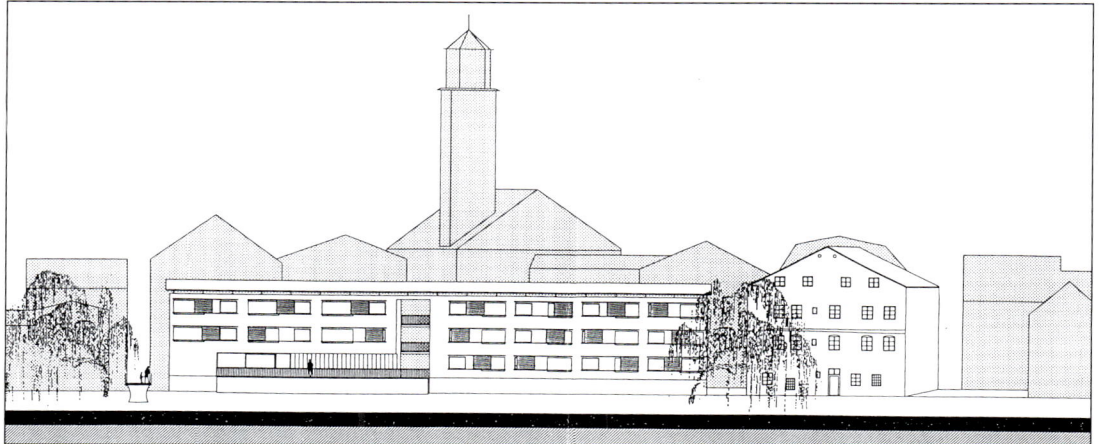
West elevation

Located at the edge of the historic city, the old people's residence faces the river Altmühl on the west side.

The linearity of the walkways that give access to the dwellings is interrupted by the placing of a series of small box rooms that are totally clad in wood.

On the side that opens up toward the town, the building is characterized by its wide access walkways to the dwellings and its generous, overhanging roof.

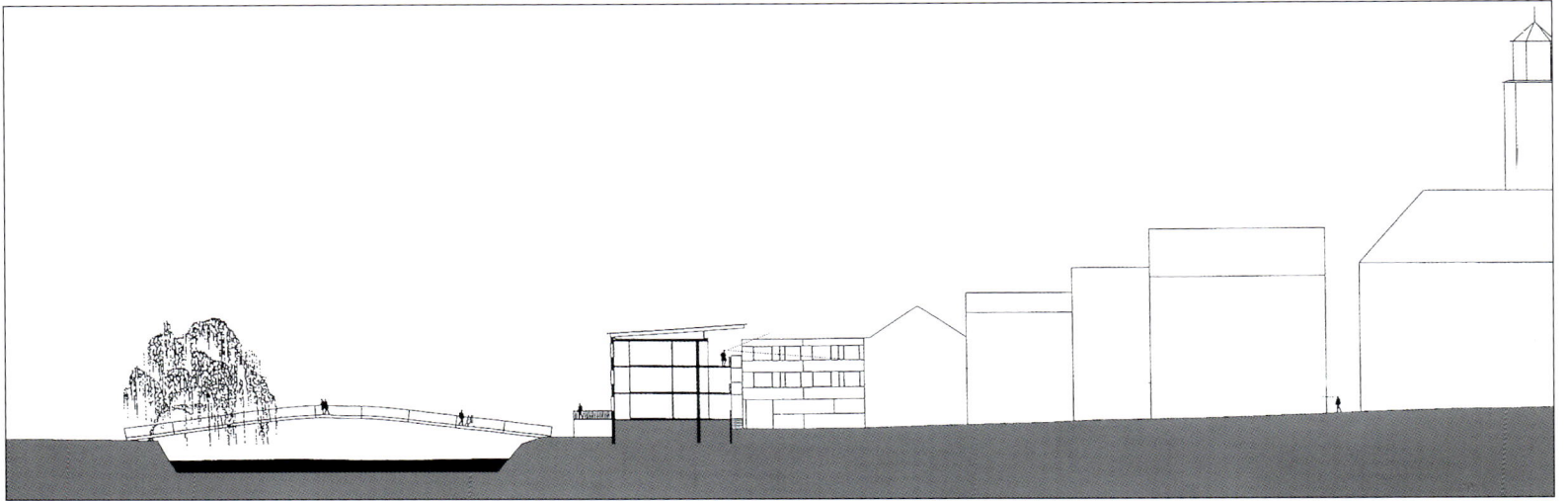

Cross section

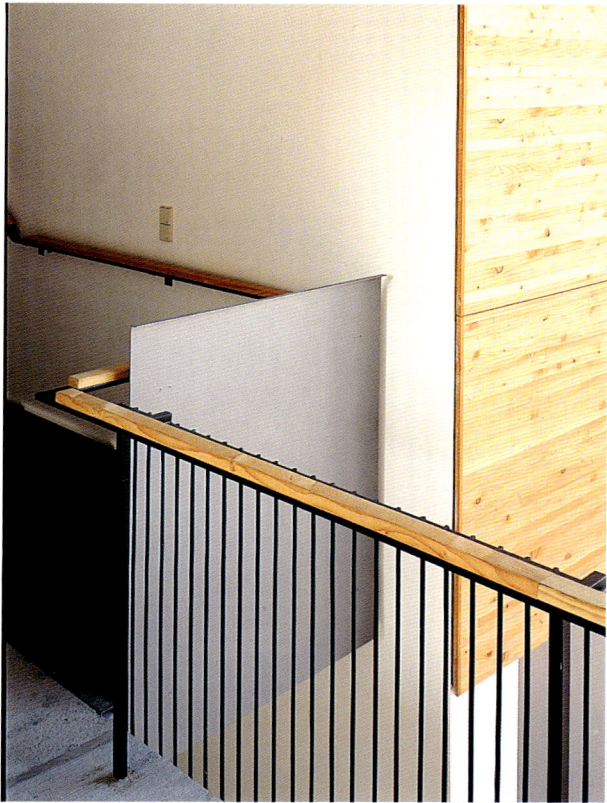

As can be seen in the photograph on the left, the west facade filters the incoming light by means of a system of sliding panels of perforated metal.

Construction detail of the west facade

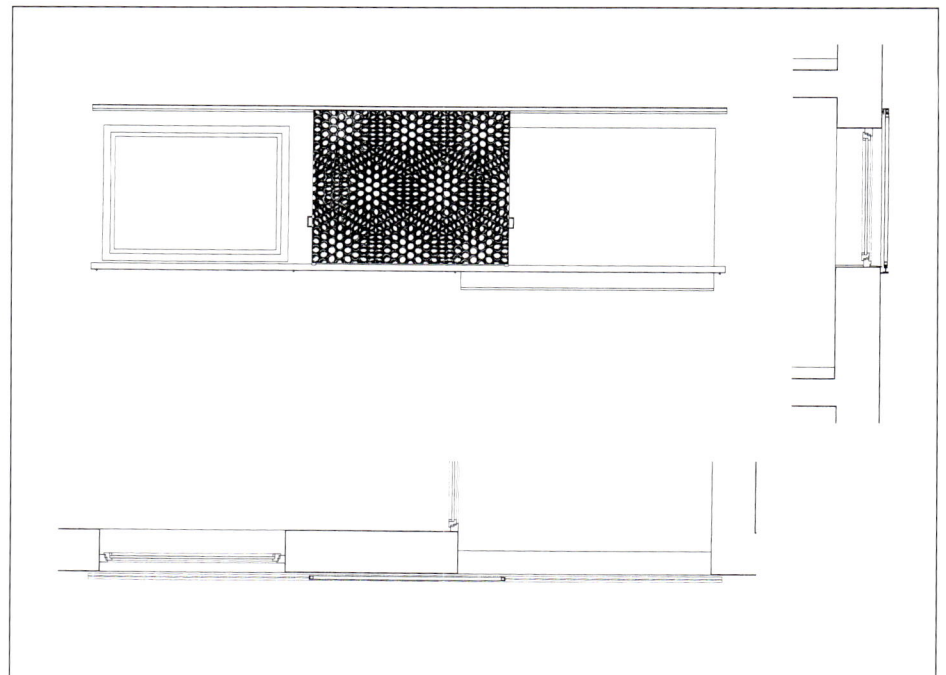

TEN Arquitectos

Parque España Residential Building

Mexico City, Mexico

Photographs:
Jaime Navarro

Architect:
TEN Arquitectos

This residential project is located on a corner, in a dense area in Mexico City, across This residential project is located in a densely developed area in Mexico City, on a corner across the street from Parque España. The site has a total of 2,200 sqm. The building contains 5 single-family apartments and a duplex penthouse on the top two floors; there is a contemporary art gallery on the ground floor and a parking facility occupies the basement, with space for 14 vehicles.

The building has a long façade on one street and a much shorter façade on the other. The two faces of the building display totally opposite personalities: although balconies exist on both, the delicate aluminum balconies of the long façade gain a measure of privacy and are shielded from the direct sunlight by translucent polycarbonate screens, which visually unify the whole surface; in contraposition to this, the short façade is characterized by wide cantilevered balconies that project far into space, opening up or revealing the building's inner structural distribution. The screens of the long façade are mobile and as the residents slide them into a variety of possible positions, they will randomly imprint a variable visual rhythm on that side of the volume. The sensitivity of this semi-transparent wrapper contrasts sharply with the plain concrete structural members of the building, lending it a feather-light and airy appearance.

The service areas have been collectively situated on the eastern side, in a continuous volume inside the building.

In the apartments, only the installations have been determined from the outset; the rest of the distribution has been left open, for the future residents to design and accommodate the spaces to their own needs and requirements.

At the top of the building, the residents share a roof garden with a lap pool and views over the park. The service stairs that connect all the floors, and the spiral staircase which leads up to the roof garden, are the items that characterize the rear façade. The apartments are connected to the stairs by little bridges that span the narrow gap.

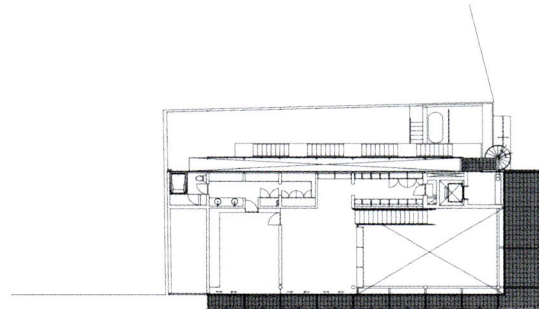

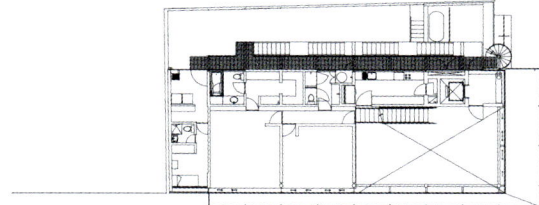

Penthouse-top floor

0   10

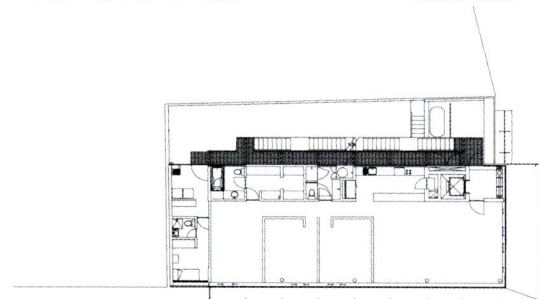

Penthouse-lower floor

0   10

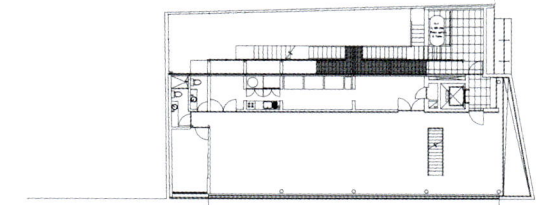

Typical floor

0   10

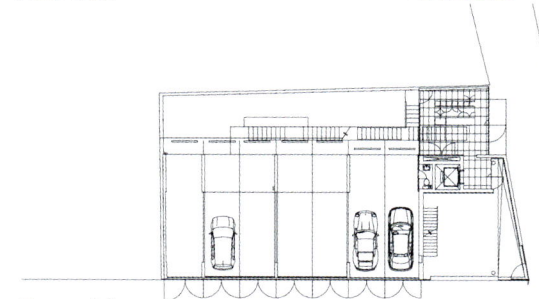

First floor

0   10

Ground floor

The two faces of the building display totally opposite personalities: although balconies exist on both, the delicate aluminum balconies of the long façade gain a measure of privacy and are shielded from the direct sunlight by translucent polycarbonate screens, which visually unify the whole surface; in contraposition to this, the short façade is characterized by wide cantilevered balconies that project far into space, opening up or revealing the building's inner structural distribution.

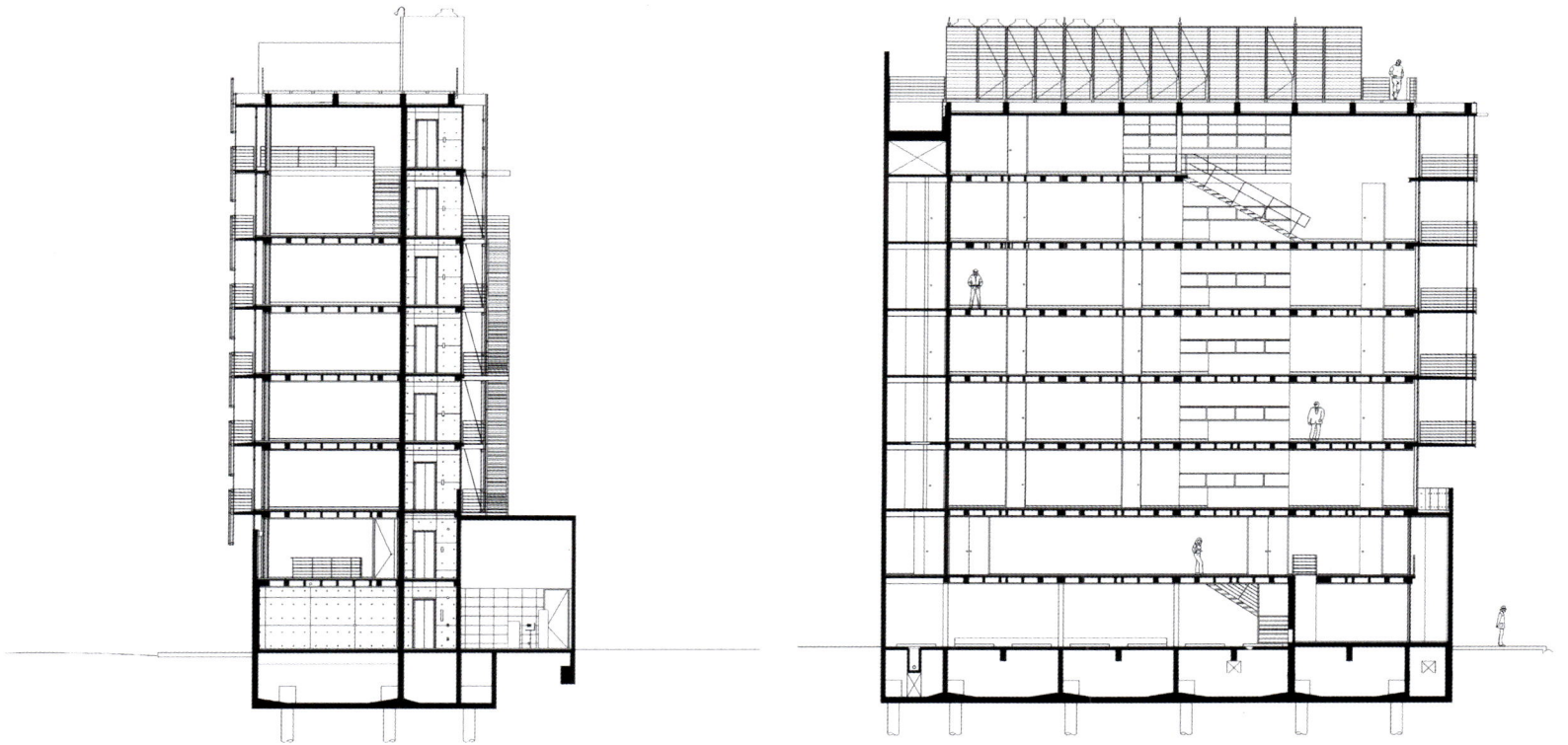

Marc Mimram

Apartment Block in Boulevard Barès

Paris, France

Photographs:
contributed by the architects

Architect:
Marc Mimram

The apartment block situated in Boulevard Barès is integrated into the continuity of the facades that give onto the street. Though homogeneous in width, the buildings of the boulevard are very heterogeneous: Hausmannian blocks, a low telephone exchange building and recent buildings that exceed the current permitted heights. The site, which does not receive a great deal of sunlight, was narrow (12-17 metres wide) and very deep, and had an east-west orientation. The layout of the apartments is essentially transversal, with the bedrooms towards the rear and the common rooms towards the street. However, the most attractive feature of the design lies in the composition of the facade, which is conceived as a medium that conceals the interior, and above all in the configuration of the openings. The curtain wall of the facade is composed of pre-fabricated modular elements, including sill-impost and vertical transom, all in fibre concrete. The cladding consists of panels of fine slats of marble-type stone with a film of fibreglass attached to a frame of metal sections. The extreme thinness of the marble slats allows the light to filter through. These panels are moved by means of a pulley and counterweight mechanism, and move up and down through slits in vertical transoms. During the night, the small panel of the upper part and the large panel of the lower part are joined to conceal the glazed part of the facade module. The independence of their movements permits a great variety of intermediate positions.

This composition is repeated on the rear facade. The plinth of the building is marked by transparency, thanks to the glazing of the commercial premises located on the lower level. Finally, the inner structure is built in moulded architectural concrete, whose texture is enriched by the light.

On this double page, details of the innovative system of openings in daylight. By means of a complex sliding system, it allows the light to be used according to the needs of each moment.

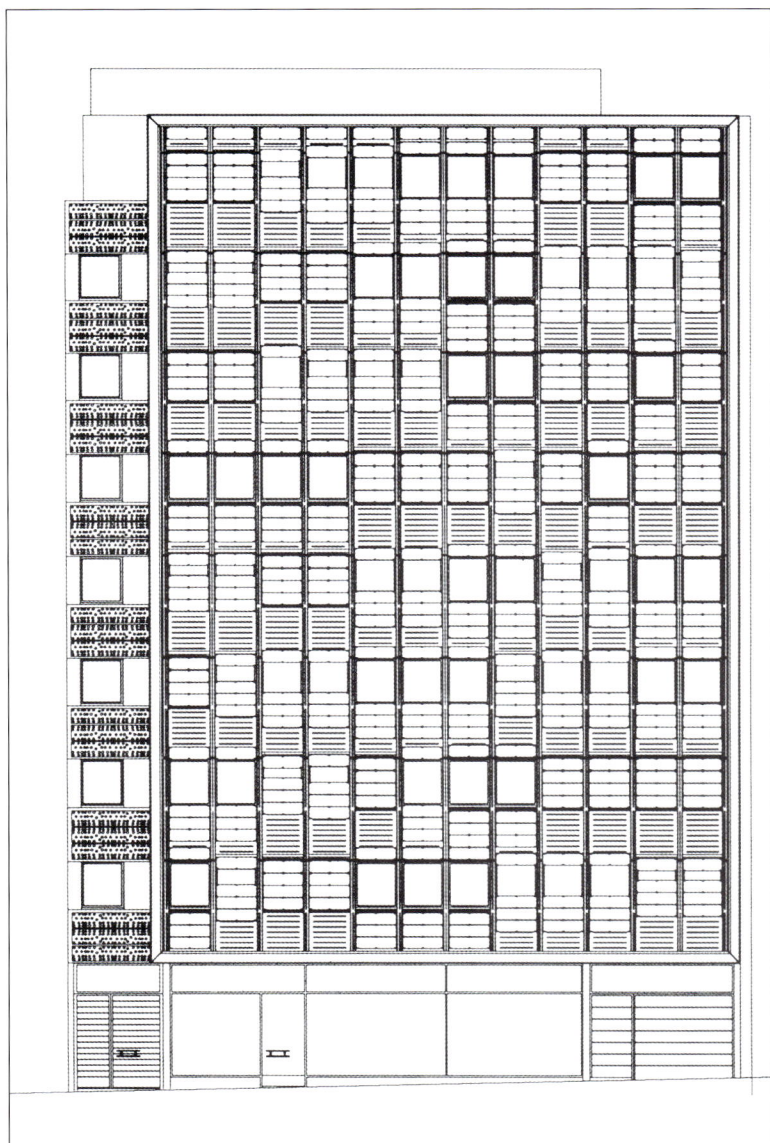

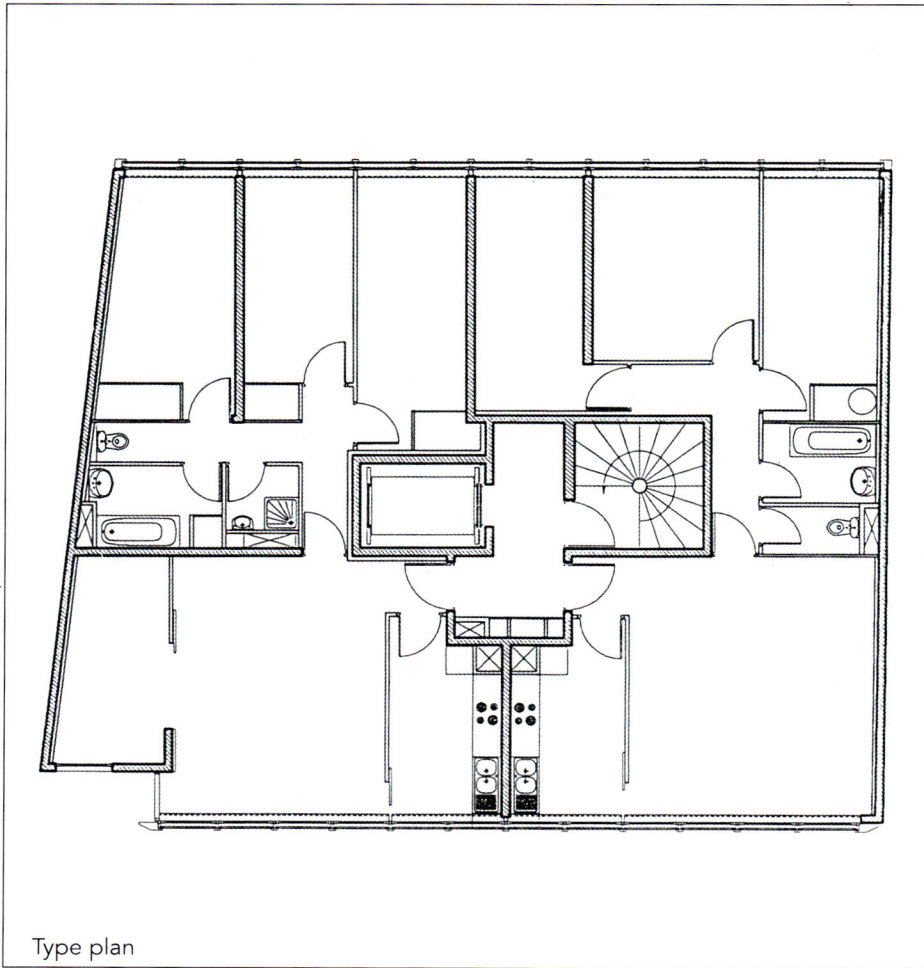
Type plan

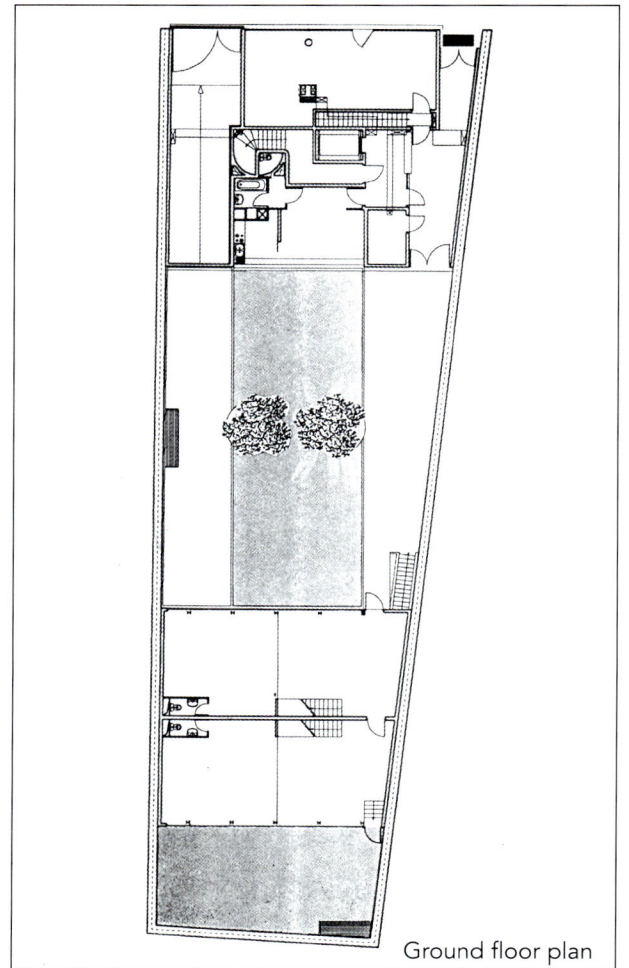
Ground floor plan

Functioning of the openings at night. The lower view shows the subtle grain of the very fine sheets of marble.

Herzog & de Meuron

Apartments on a long and narrow lot

Basel, Switzerland

Photographs:
Margherita Spiluttini

Architect:
Herzog & De Meuron

This commercial and apartment building was built on a parcel located within the city's medieval perimeters. Thus the long narrow measurements (23 by 6.3 metres) typical of medieval parcelling had to be accommodated. The architecture was strongly influenced by this parcel, which was utilised right to the back of the lot and exhibits a highly specific floor plan and section for life in a densely-built city. The apartments are grouped around a central courtyard aperture that opens on one side to the neighbouring parcel to the south. This side opening was not only intended to let light and sun reach the apartments but also to allow for the enjoyment of the branches of a large tree in the neighbour's yard. Like a periscope, the courtyard is recessed floor-by-floor to clearly separate the individual apartments.

The stairway has been separated from the elevator shaft to gain area for the central living space. The apartments are entered directly from the elevator. The stairs at the end of the parcel are an open construction, thus fulfilling the additional function of a small loggia.

On the ground floor, a two-story hallway leads from the street along the old parcel wall and allows access to the Swiss Fire Fighting Museum located in the back courtyard. The street facade is made completely of glass and is protected by a cast-iron curtain construction that can be folded back piece-by-piece at will. Wavy light slits lend the curtain construction a flowing textile-like feeling. While the construction hides the living space behind it, its heavy cast-iron material serves as a counterweight protecting against the noisy street side. In form and material, the facade components are related to sewer grates and to the protective grills placed around the trees.

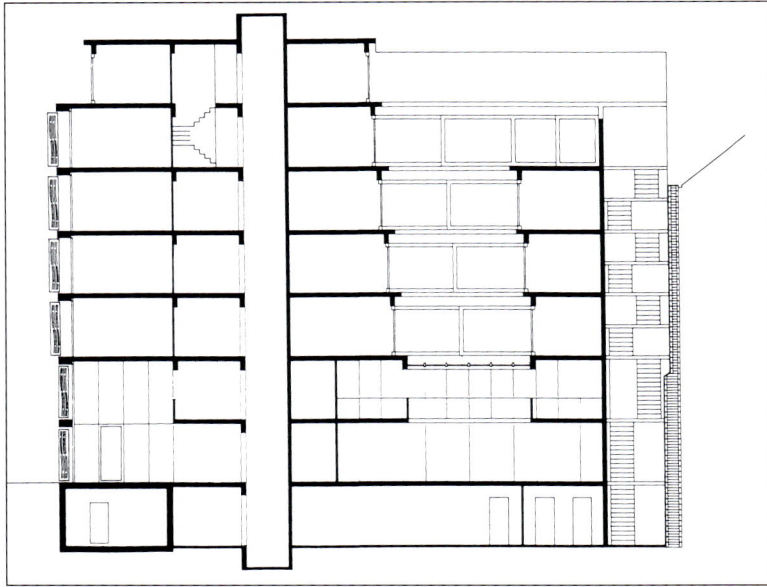
Cross-section

The apartments are grouped around a central courtyard, which is open to the south to take full advantage of natural light and the existence of a large tree standing nearby.

The apartments seen from the central courtyard. The outside walls are almost totally glazed, although here they are shown protected by wooden blinds.

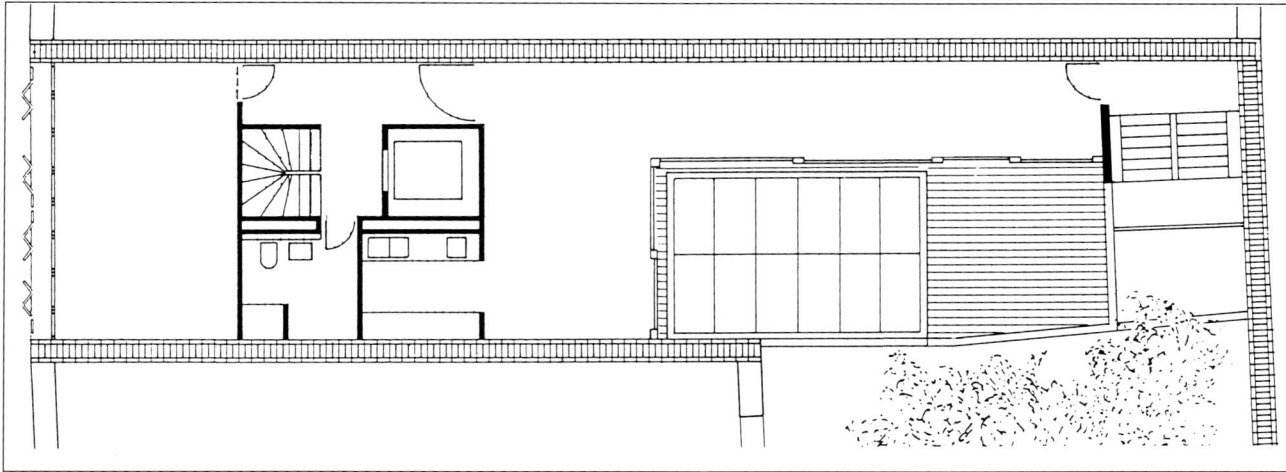

Fourth floor plan

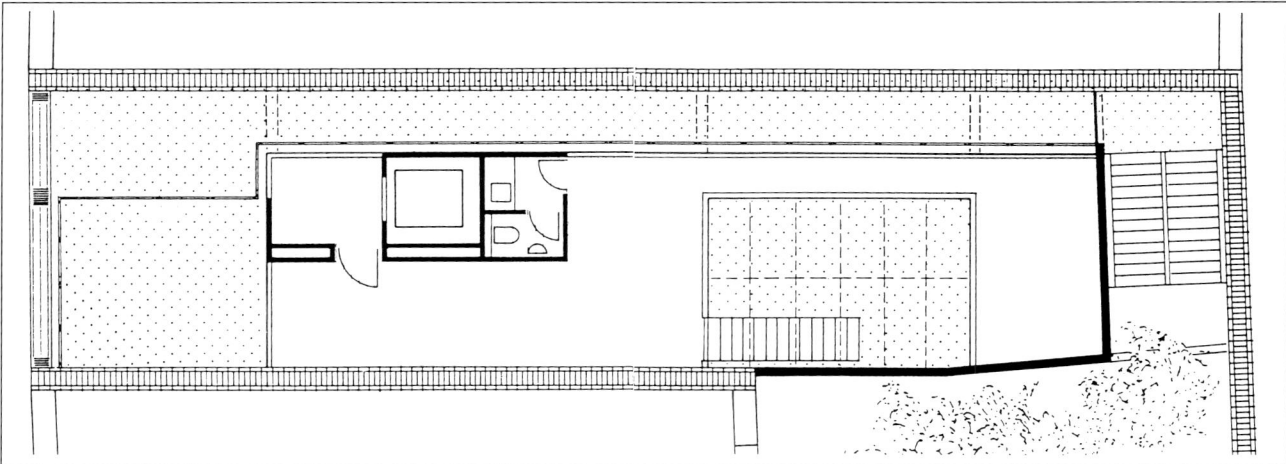

First floor plan

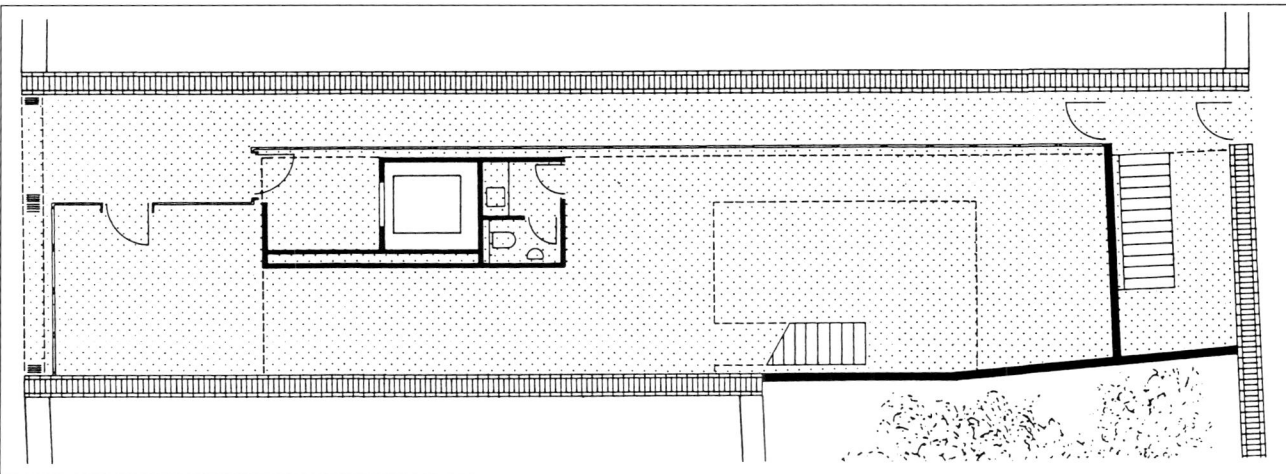

Ground floor plan

Two pictures showing the close relationship the interiors have with the exteriors: With the central courtyard (top) and with the street (bottom).

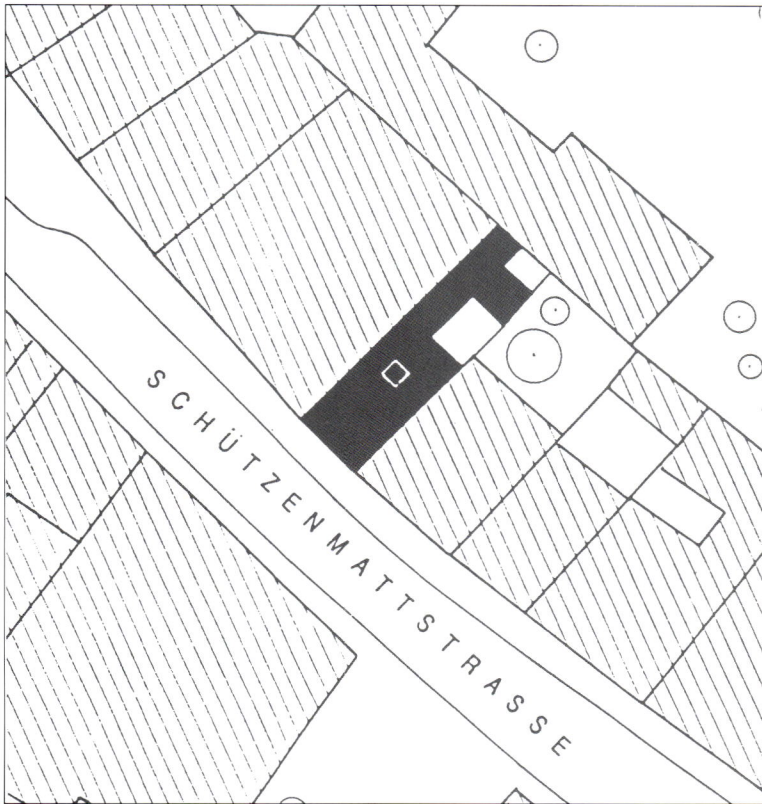

Front view of the main facade, characterised by the unusual cast iron curtain, which as it sways endows the whole scene with fluidity and dynamism. The detail below shows how the individual links of the curtain are joined together.

The photograph shows the total independence of the structure, as a result of which the residents can adapt it to their specific needs.

Ponsirenas-Puig

Torca Building

Badalona, Spain

Photographs:
Jordi Miralles

Architect:
Ponsirenas-Puig

The project consists of a detached building of 40 dwellings, commercial premises on the ground floor and a basement car park.

The building was designed with two wings, one facing east and the other facing south, accompanied on the ground floor by another detached building. The three buildings thus create inner pedestrian streets. Private access to the two wings is through a communications tower situated at the cross-roads of Calle Juan de Austria and Calle Ferrer Bassa. The tower can be accessed from the B-500 road through the private alley that links these two streets. From a formal point of view, the building relates to the buildings situated opposite it, both in the L-shape and in the use of materials.

Bearing in mind the new street layout that is planned, the building is located at a nerve centre of the city, thus justifying the form and the singular treatment of the facade and of the communications tower.

The horizontal composition of the building provides for interplay of the intercalated strips of stucco, the PVC strips and the aluminium panels. A large stone plinth (with marked horizontal joints) surrounds the whole building from the floor level of the first-floor apartments.

This stone plinth contains the openings corresponding to the commercial premises, composed according to the horizontal joints of the artificial stone.

The nucleus of vertical communications is formed by the same materials but with a vertical composition.

Other features are the greater height of the tower than the building, the anchoring of the building by means of free platforms and the combination of parallelepiped and curved forms that give the project character.

A stone plinth surrounds the whole building at ground level.

The building is organized through two wings facing east and south respectively.

Fernando Carrascal & Jose Mª Fernández de la Puente

Social Housing Vírgenes-Tromperos

Sevilla, Spain

Photographs:
Duccio Malagamba

Architect:
Fernando Carrascal
& Jose Mª Fernández de la Puente

For this project the heritage commission recommended the recognition of the different plots and the stitching of the construction to the party walls that determine solids and voids in the interior of the plots.

Having resisted the temptations of a new layout disregarding the perimeter, it seemed desirable for the project to be understood as unitary. This was helped by the application of the regulations that force the living room of the dwellings to ventilate to the adjacent plot. The party walls thus disappear, becoming authentic facades.

Special care is paid to the circulation, which leads to surprising dimensional illusions and like a labyrinth makes the perception of the spaces mutable and new. By means of a communication system of bridges, it has been possible to reduce the number of stairwells and to facilitate the circulation.

The changing typology marked by the subsidised housing developments is unified by the use of colour and the finishes, which include rendered and white-painted walls, and facades clad with glass reinforced concrete, also white. The GRC appears as a vibration of the facades in the cases of invasion of courtyards by adjacent constructions, to mark a change of height of some added element or in facades facing a different typological treatment. In those cases, metal slats with the same profile as the walls are used.

Day and night make the facade close and open with a multitude of eyes, like waking and sleeping.

The intention of the design was to distinguish the different plots and to stitch the building to the existing party walls, respecting and maintaining the marked perimeter and bearing in mind that the project had to be understood as a unitary group.

The fact that both the bedrooms and the kitchens can ventilate toward the adjacent plots transforms the party walls into authentic facades. Solar protection is provided by metal slats flush with the facade plane.

The raised walkways create the sensation of a labyrinth, facilitate communication and reduce the number of stairwells to a minimum. The large typological variety stems from the adaptation to the existing limits of the plot.

Dieter Jüngling + Andreas Hagmann

Refurbishment of Tivoli Housing

Chur, Switzerland

Photographs:
Ralph Feiner, Schenk+Campell

Architect:
Dieter Jüngling + Andreas Hagmann

This ensemble of residential blocks is located in an area of Chur that is very close to the Station Square. The buildings were originally built in 1943-1944 according to architect Karl Beer's design, which sought to combine modernity and tradition. The refurbishing concept of these buildings has involved a series of slight modifications to the building's external appearance.

The original layout, a discontinuous U shape, no longer satisfied current requirements. Nonetheless, the external composition of the ensemble, constructed in accordance with an open layout, allowed for an optimal use of the original building's openness.

The three existing blocks were refurbished, and new structures were inserted between them to create a protected internal landscaped courtyard, where a loggia extension was also added. These modifications not only increased the living area; they also created a buffer zone and made the insulation of the original facade easier.

In the new scheme, the living spaces have also been enlarged by relocating the internal staircases toward vertical communications units; the modified houses now have an area of 80 to 100 sqm. Along with the addition of external terraces, these communications units also modify the appearance of the ensemble, due particularly to the materials (steel and glass) used in their construction. Another important aesthetic modification was the relocation of the car park, which has been moved underground, freeing up space to plant birches in a series of shallow ditches. The main objective of the refurbishment was to improve heat efficiency on the facade, to provide adequate noise insulation in the houses, and to increase the amount of sunlight in external spaces.

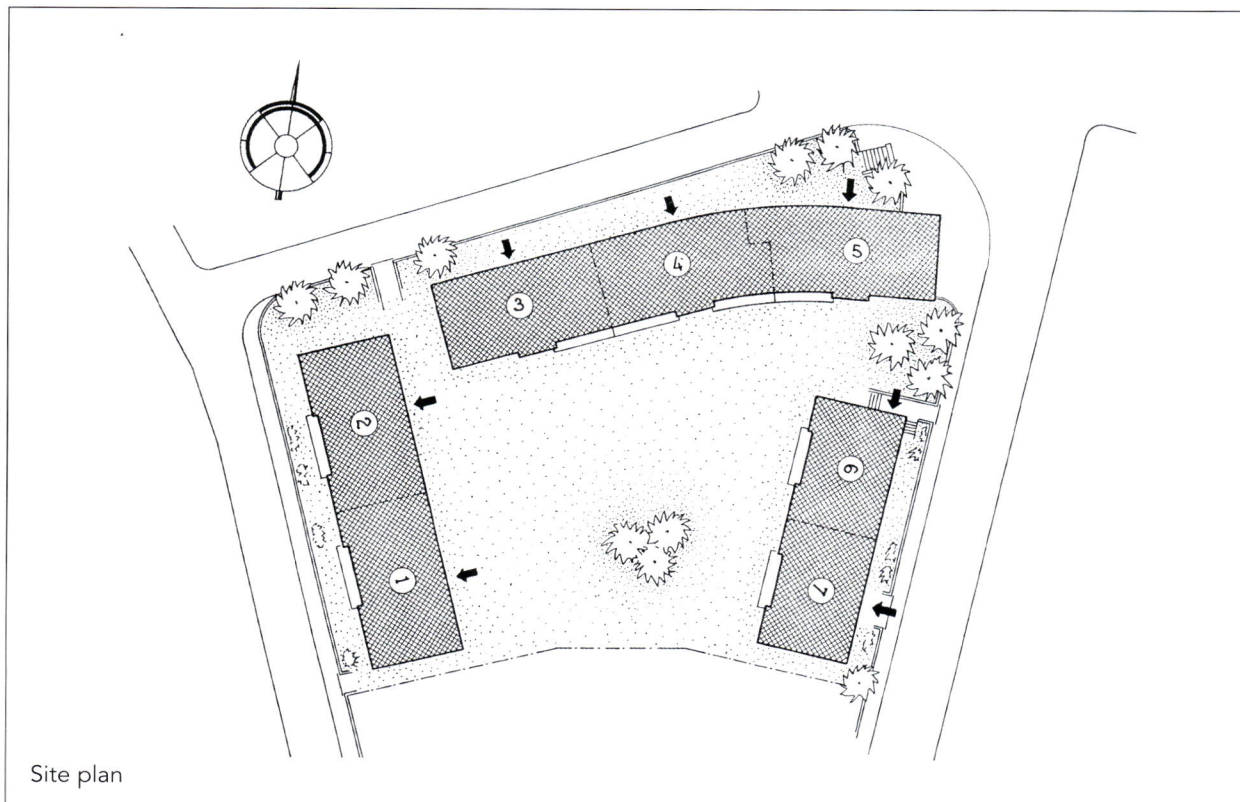

Site plan

Although the original buildings, built in 1943-1944, included empty spaces between the blocks, the refurbished set has filled these in with additional dwellings so that the complex forms a continuous U shape open towards the south.

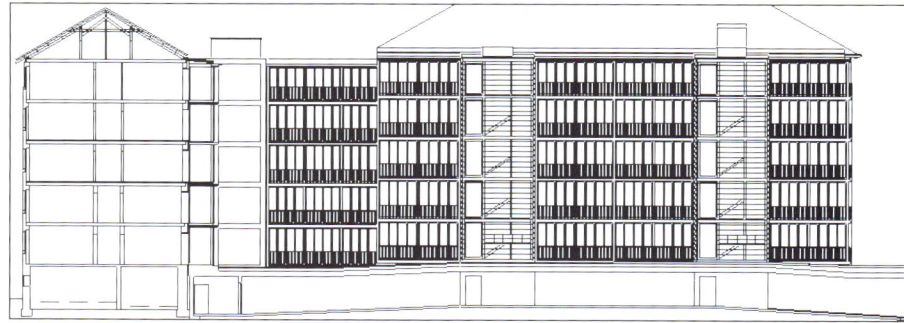

East West elevations

238

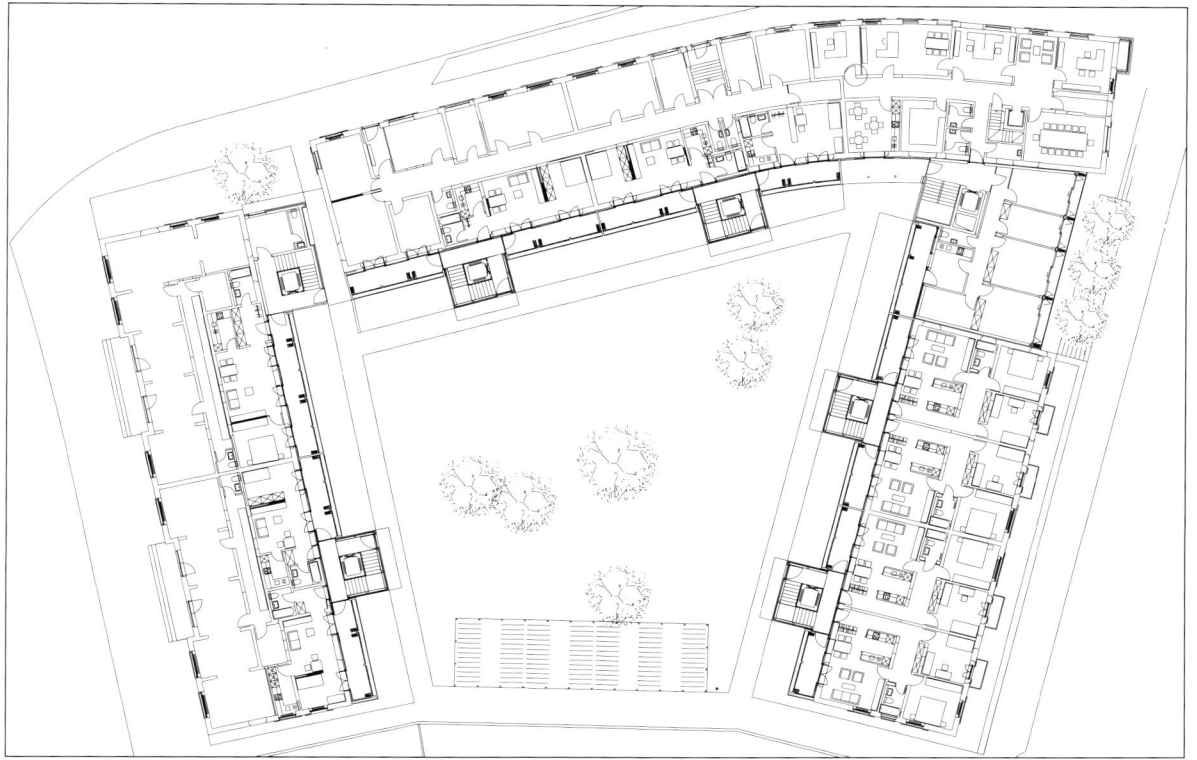

Ground floor plan

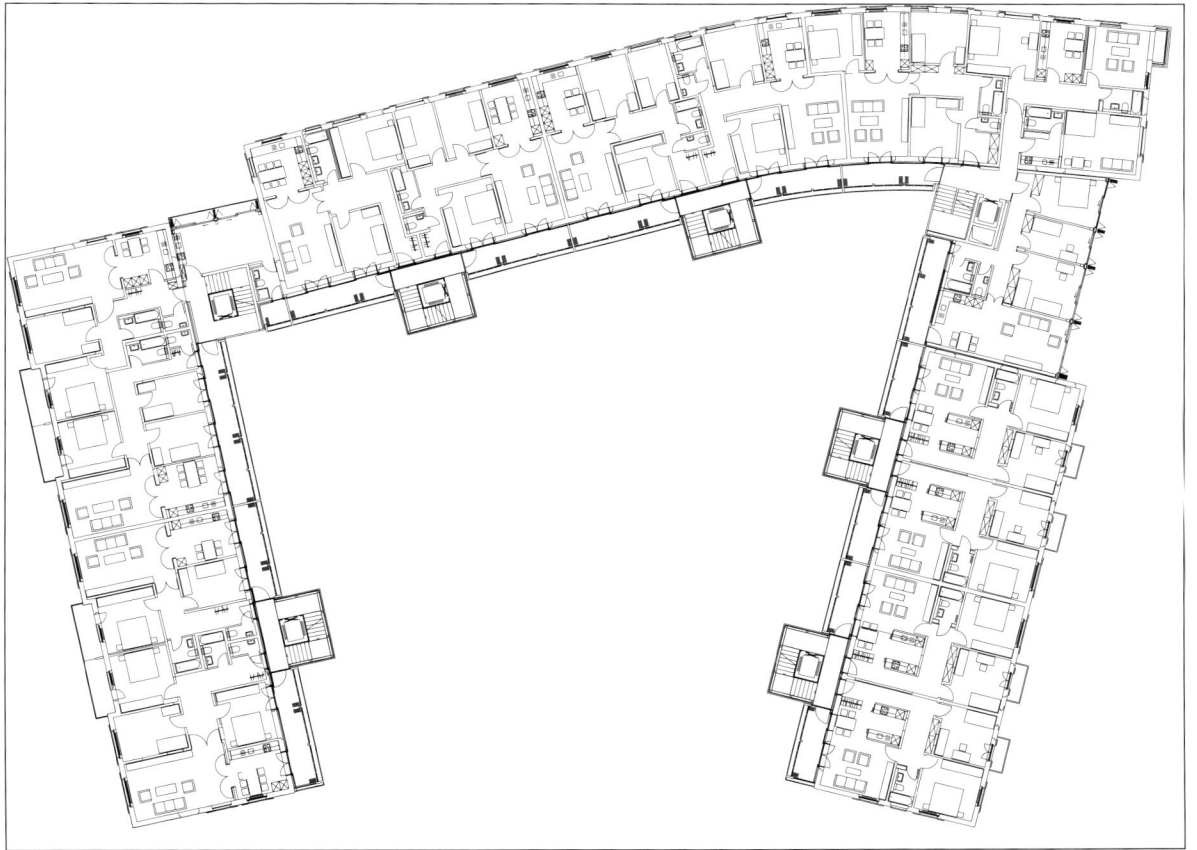

Upper floor plan